principles
of memory

ESSAYS IN COGNITIVE PSYCHOLOGY

North American Editors:
Henry L. Roediger, III, *Washington University in St. Louis*
James R. Pomerantz, *Rice University*

European Editors:
Alan D. Baddeley, *University of York*
Vicki Bruce, *University of Edinburgh*
Jonathan Grainger, *Université de Provence*

Essays in Cognition is designed to meet the need for rapid publication of brief volumes in cognitive psychology. Primary topics will include perception, movement and action, attention, memory, mental representation, language and problem solving. Furthermore, the series seeks to define cognitive psychology in its broadest sense, encompassing all topics either informed by, or informing, the study of mental processes. As such, it covers a wide range of subjects including computational approaches to cognition, cognitive neuroscience, social cognition, and cognitive development, as well as areas more traditionally defined as cognitive psychology. Each volume in the series will make a conceptual contribution to the topic by reviewing and synthesizing the existing research literature, by advancing theory in the area, or by some combination of these missions. The principal aim is that authors will provide an overview of their own highly successful research program in an area. It is also expected that volumes will, to some extent, include an assessment of current knowledge and identification of possible future trends in research. Each book will be a self-contained unit supplying the advanced reader with a well-structured review of the work described and evaluated.

FORTHCOMING
Mulligan: *Implicit Memory*
Brown: *Tip-of-the-tongue Phenomenon*
Lampinen, Neuschatz, & Cling: *Psychology of Eyewitness Identification*
Worthen & Hunt: *Mnemonics for the 21ˢᵗ Century*

PUBLISHED
Surprenant & Neath: *Principles of Memory*
Kensinger: *Emotional Memory Across the Lifespan*
Millar: *Space and Sense*
Evans: *Hypothetical Thinking*
Gallo: *Associative Illusions of Memory*
Cowan: *Working Memory Capacity*
McNamara: *Semantic Priming*
Brown: *The Déjà Vu Experience*
Coventry & Garrod: *Saying, Seeing and Acting*
Robertson: *Space, Objects, Minds and Brains*
Cornoldi & Vecchi: *Visuo-spatial Working Memory and Individual Differences*
Sternberg, et al.: *The Creativity Conundrum*
Poletiek: *Hypothesis-testing Behaviour*
Garnham: *Mental Models and the Interpretations of Anaphora*
Evans & Over: *Rationality and Reasoning*
Engelkamp: *Memory for Actions*

For updated information about published and forthcoming titles in the *Essays in Cognition* series, please visit: **www.psypress.com/essays**

principles
of memory

AIMÉE M. SURPRENANT AND IAN NEATH

Psychology Press
Taylor & Francis Group

New York   London

Psychology Press
Taylor & Francis Group
270 Madison Avenue
New York, NY 10016

Psychology Press
Taylor & Francis Group
27 Church Road
Hove, East Sussex BN3 2FA

Printed in the United States of America on acid-free paper
10 9 8 7 6 5 4 3 2 1

International Standard Book Number: 978-1-84169-422-1 (Hardback)

Library of Congress Cataloging-in-Publication Data

Surprenant, Aimée M.
   Principles of memory / Aimée M. Surprenant, Ian Neath.
     p. cm. -- (Essays in cognitive psychology)
   Includes bibliographical references and index.
   ISBN 978-1-84169-422-1 (hardcover : alk. paper)
   1. Memory. I. Neath, Ian, 1965- II. Title.

BF371.S885 2009
153.1'2--dc22

                                         2009013579

Visit the Taylor & Francis Web site at
http://www.taylorandfrancis.com

and the Psychology Press Web site at
http://www.psypress.com

CONTENTS

ACKNOWLEDGMENTS

Work on the ideas behind this book began while we were on sabbatical at the Memory Research Unit, Department of Psychology, City University, London. We thank colleagues at Bristol University, Cardiff University, City University London, the University of Essex, the University of Hertfordshire, the University of Reading, the University of Warwick, the University of York, and University College London for their hospitality and intellectual stimulation. Prior to our arrival in the UK, we were similarly well-treated by colleagues at Australian Catholic University, the University of Southern Queensland, and the University of Western Australia.

We started writing the book when we returned to Purdue University, and completed it at Memorial University of Newfoundland. Order of authorship was determined by a coin toss.

We thank our graduate students, Annie Jalbert and Brittany Faux, and the students in the Winter 2008 Special Topics in Memory course at Memorial University for their feedback on a draft of this book.

Preparation of this book was supported, in part, by the (US) National Institute on Aging Grant AG021071 and by the (Canadian) Natural Sciences and Engineering Research Council Discovery Grants to both authors.

Introduction

> [These] are my principles, and if you don't like them … well, I have others.
>
> —Groucho Marx

1.1 Principles of Memory

In 1976, Robert G. Crowder published a highly regarded book called *Principles of Learning and Memory*. Among the many reviews, critiques, and commentaries subsequently printed was one by Cohen (1985, p. 248), who noted that "Crowder's (1976) *Principles of Learning and Memory* lists no principles." Bob responded in his usual inimitable style: "I was once criticized for writing a book called *Principles of Learning and Memory* without ever really coming out and saying what those principles were. … Looking back, I must say Cohen had a point" (Crowder, 1993, p. 146).[1]

The purpose of this monograph is to propose seven principles of human memory that apply to all memory regardless of the type of information, type of processing, hypothetical system supporting memory, or time scale. Although these principles focus on the invariants and empirical regularities of memory, the reader should be forewarned that they are qualitative rather than quantitative, more like regularities in biology than principles of geometry.

---

[1] Crowder (1993) did propose four principles but concluded that "the more I think about them, though, the more I realise that these four principles are closely related to one another," namely, our encoding–retrieval principle (see Chapter 4).

1

1.2 Laws, Principles, and Effects

If the goal of any science is to identify invariants and regularities within a particular domain (Russell, 1931; Simon, 1990), one might ask, what are the laws and principles of human memory?

A first attempt at delineating the laws and principles of memory might involve a search of the literature. Teigen (2002) performed such a PsycLit search of journal abstracts for "law" citations and found a total of 3,093 between 1900 and 1999. The year with the most citations was 1927 (with 62). By 1999, there were so few mentions of the laws of psychology that one "must read around 1,000 journal abstracts before encountering a single law" (p. 109). None of the most commonly cited laws concern memory, and most of the laws were first proposed more than 50 years ago. In fact, the law that is cited most often (Weber's law, with 336 citations) was proposed in 1834. Very few new laws have been put forward, and of the few that have been suggested, almost all concern psychophysical phenomena of one kind or another (e.g., Shepard, 1987; Chater & Vitányi, 2003).

The few possible candidates for laws of memory that have been proposed have been proffered with great diffidence, if not outright reluctance. For example, Tulving and Wiseman (1975) describe a relationship between recall and recognition that suggests that the two measures are uncorrelated. Many papers refer to this description as the *Tulving–Wiseman law*, and indeed, it is the most cited memory law between 1990 and 1999 according to Teigen's (2002) search, with 10 citations. However, Tulving himself is ambivalent, sometimes referring to it as a function (Tulving & Flexser, 1992) and sometimes a law (Nilsson, Law, & Tulving, 1988). Similarly, the ratio rule (Glenberg, Bradley, Kraus, & Renzaglia, 1983; see also Bjork & Whitten, 1974) relates the size of the recency effect observed in free recall to the amount of time an item has to be remembered until recall and the amount of time that separates the items in the list. Despite its empirical regularity (e.g., Nairne, Neath, Serra, & Byun, 1997), it remains a rule, not a law.[2] As a third example, Watkins (2001, p. 195) discusses the gentle law of speech ascendancy, but he characterizes it as closer in spirit to "please keep off the grass" as opposed to "thou shalt not kill."

Cohen (1985) proposed four laws, but referred to them as "potential" rather than established laws. For Cohen, "a memory law should be a statement about some empirical relationship in memory, which has transsituational generality and which looks like it will be around for some time to come" (Cohen, 1985, p. 252). Briefly, these laws are as follows: (a) the better something is learned, the greater the likelihood it will be remembered;

---

[2] Wixted and McDowell (1989, p. 685) began a sentence, "One principle, termed the ratio rule ..."

(b) the longer something has to be retained in memory, the less the like-lihood that it will be remembered; (c) the likelihood of remembering something depends on the nature of the memory test, later reformulated as "the closer the match between encoding and retrieval conditions (the greater the overlap in episodic contexts) the better the memory perfor-mance)"; and (d) individuals differ reliably in their memory capacities. Nyberg (1995) refers to five laws of memory, adding the Tulving–Wiseman law to Cohen's four laws. [3]

We performed a search comparable to Teigen's (2002) for the term "principle."[4] The most commonly cited principle was the encoding speci-ficity principle (Tulving & Thomson, 1973) with 33 citations, but the next most frequently cited principle had only 2 citations (8 different principles were each cited twice). Between 1990 and 1999, only 22 abstracts contained named principles.

In contrast, a search for "effect" shows a different pattern. We found multiple citations to the acoustic confusion effect, the bizarre imagery effect, the changing distractor effect, the concreteness effect, the concur-rent articulation effect, the cue depreciation effect, the fan effect, the for-got-it-all-along effect, the generation effect, the Hebb effect, the irrelevant speech effect, the isolation (von Restorff) effect, the lag recency effect, the levels of processing effect, the list length effect, the list strength effect, the mirror effect, the modality effect, the part-set cuing effect, the picture superiority effect, the prefix effect, the primacy effect, the Ranschburg effect, the recency (and long-term recency) effect, the revelation effect, the serial position effect, the spacing effect, the stimulus suffix effect (and the context-dependent and preterminal suffix effects), the word frequency effect, the word length effect, and many, many others.

Thus, in over 100 years of scientific research on memory, and nearly 50 years after the so-called cognitive revolution, we have nothing that really constitutes a widely accepted and frequently cited law of memory, and perhaps only one generally accepted principle.[5] However, there are a plethora of effects, many of which have extensive literatures and hun-dreds of published empirical demonstrations.

One reason for the lack of general laws and principles of memory might be that none exists. Tulving (1985a, p. 385), for example, has argued that

---

[3] We discuss these laws and compare them to our principles in Chapter 10.

[4] This search required either "principle" or "principles" in the abstract, a publication year of 1900–1999 (inclusive), "memory" in the abstract, and "humans" as the population. It yielded 889 articles. This pool was then restricted to those articles that named a specific principle, as opposed to those that used generic phrases such as "memory principles" or "mnemonic principles."

[5] One exception is the proposed set of seven principles of memory by Kihlstrom (1994; Kihlstrom & Barnhardt, 1993). Jonides et al. (2008) propose a set of principles for short-term memory. We postpone discussion of these until Chapter 10.

"no profound generalizations can be made about memory as a whole," because memory comprises many different systems and each system operates according to different principles. One can make "general statements about particular kinds of memory," but one cannot make statements that would apply to all types of memory. One reason we have reservations about the multiple systems approach to the study of human memory is this predisposition to dismiss the attempt to formulate general principles (see Chapter 2 for an overview of the systems view). We consider our ability to formulate seven generalizations about memory as a whole as further evidence against such a view.[6]

Roediger (2008) also argues that no general principles of memory exist, but his reasoning and arguments are quite different. He reintroduces Jenkins' (1979) tetrahedral model of memory, which views all memory experiments as comprising four factors: encoding conditions, retrieval conditions, subject variables, and events (materials and tasks). Using the tetrahedral model as a starting point, Roediger convincingly demonstrates that all of these variables can affect memory performance in different ways and that such complexity does not easily lend itself to a description using general principles. Because of the complexity of the interactions among these variables, Roediger suggests that "the most fundamental principle of learning and memory, perhaps its only sort of general law, is that in making any generalization about memory one must add that 'it depends'" (p. 247). We fully agree with his arguments, up to a point: It is absolutely necessary to specify Jenkins' (1979) factors when applying and interpreting the principles. Where we differ is that we think it possible to produce general principles of memory that take into account these factors. For example, our encoding–retrieval principle explicitly takes into account the conditions at encoding and those at retrieval, several principles acknowledge the importance of materials and tasks, and although we do not have a principle specifically for subject variables, our specificity principle is at least a start.

Another reason for the lack of laws and principles may be that most of the regularities in memory are not unchanging enough to be given such a lofty status as law or principle. Given the complication that the human cognitive system must be dynamic in order to adapt to a changing world (Simon, 1990), laws and principles might not be possible. Some evidence consistent with this view might be that where laws and principles are proposed, they tend to be psychophysical in nature (e.g., Laming, 1985; Shepard, 2004), but as one moves from psychophysical tasks to ones that allow greater flexibility in how people might process information, there seem fewer and fewer laws and principles.

---

[6] Of course, it is entirely possible that our proposed generalizations are not "profound."

A fourth reason for the lack of principles might have to do with the *Zeitgeist* in which experiments are designed and articles or books are published. For example, Teigen (2002, p. 116) noted that "the emergence of the standard experiment in psychological research, based on Fisherian principles for null hypothesis testing, coincides with a steep reduction in law citations." Designs that allow easy analysis with *t*-tests and ANOVAs tend to emphasize a search for significant effects rather than a search for functional relationships. In addition, the designs focus on the construction of binary oppositions, the results of which do not lead to general theories of cognition (Newell, 1973).

A fifth reason for the lack of principles might be that memory researchers, similar to investigators in many other areas of psychology, often become fixated on a particular procedure (see, e.g., the discussion of this problem by Craik, 1985). Rather than trying to discover how memory works, they focus on explaining a particular task. The concentration on just one task (e.g., immediate serial recall) yields enormous amounts of information and understanding of the task, but may not offer any real connections to memory in particular or scientific psychology in general.

We disagree with views that suggest that "the most fruitful way to extend our understanding of human memory is not to search for broader generalizations and 'principles'" (Baddeley, 1978, p. 150). Rather, we answer Murdock's (1977, p. 332) question, "Have we not reached the point (at least in some areas) at which specific experiments might yield general principles?" with an emphatic "Yes!"

We note, in particular, two advantages of searching for principles. First, it forces researchers and theorists to step back and look at the accomplishments of the field as a whole rather than concentrating on single theories, specific effects, or particular tasks. Second, as Greene (2007, p. 54) notes, "some of the most important contributions made by general principles have been those times when they spurred investigations into how they fail."

We take the position here that general memory principles can be found and that we can take disparate-looking tasks and results and "put them all together" (Newell, 1973, p. 291). We also believe that there exist invariants in human behavior, at least at an abstract and qualitative level (Simon, 1990). We think it is time to assess the accumulated knowledge on memory and how it works and organize it in a fashion that allows us to "tighten the inferential web that ties our experimental studies together" (Newell, 1973, p. 306).

1.3 What Is a Principle?

As used in this monograph, a principle differs from a law in that it is more tentative, closer to a working hypothesis than to an incontrovertible statement. Nonetheless, our principles share much in common with most definitions of psychological laws (e.g., Cohen, 1985, p. 252; Teigen, 2002, p. 105). They must be empirically true and must be universal. In addition, we also require that principles have at least one (and hopefully more than one) of the following three properties: (a) they should state an important empirical regularity, (b) they should be able to serve as an intermediate explanation, and (c) they should offer useful information on how memory works.

One important function for a principle is to state an empirical regularity. As Toth and Hunt (1999, p. 254) put it, "One might imagine an outside observer ... [inquiring] into the goal of our theoretical debates: 'What are the fundamental empirical regularities of memory?'" To answer this question, one would (hopefully) want to tell such an observer the most important and most certain empirical regularities first. Thus, a principle should be a well-established regularity that is independent of a particular task or paradigm or situation and independent or not reliant on a particular theory or theoretical orientation. Not all empirical regularities, then, will qualify as principles. For example, we do not include the ratio rule (mentioned earlier) among our principles because it applies only to free recall and has not yet been shown to apply to other ways of assessing memory. This emphasis on empirical regularities is not intended to mean that theoretical considerations are not important, but rather, that at this point in the history of memory research, we should be able to agree on general empirical regularities that are solidly established.

A second important function of a principle is to serve as an explanation. A principle is thus "a more abstract statement, and as such, it suggests links to other effects. ... What is important for present purposes is that each of these findings can be explained simply by referring it to a single general principle" (Watkins, 2001, p. 192). For example, a wide range of findings from numerous different paradigms can all be explained as being due to the principle of cue overload (see Chapter 4). Although the principle itself might not be explained—indeed, one would want a satisfactory theoretical account of cue overload itself—it nonetheless offers an explanation and provides a link between various different paradigms.

A third important function of a principle is to offer useful information on "what work is accomplished and what the conditions are under which it is achieved" (Angell, 1906, p. 65). Principles should lay the foundations for answering the question, "What is memory for?" (Nairne, 2005). In this respect, our proposed principles follow from a functionalist approach to memory, reminiscent of our intellectual ancestors such as Crowder, Melton, Robinson, Angell, James, and Dewey, as well as many others.

1.4 Seven Principles of Memory

Our principles, then, will be qualitative statements of empirical regularities that can serve as intermediary explanations, and which follow from viewing memory as a function. They are more tentative than laws, and indeed, some are quite speculative, but nonetheless, all are intended to be valid, universal statements. We intend the set of principles to be useful, not only in the functional sense already described, but also in "inspiring theories" (Willingham & Goedert, 2001, p. 262): The principles themselves will require theoretical explanation. Few, if any, of our principles are novel, and the list is by no means complete. We certainly do not think that there are only seven principles of memory nor, when more principles are proposed, do we think that all seven of our principles will be among the most important.[7]

One final caveat: Although we intend the set of principles to apply to all types of memory, there are many areas of memory research where there is simply not enough data to assess, yet, whether our principles do indeed apply. For example, there are relatively few studies examining cues in certain short-term memory tasks. We speculate that this is because the dominant view is that cues are not used in such tasks (see Chapter 3). Similarly, there are no studies that we could find that examine cue overload in procedural memory tasks. In such situations, our principles can be taken as strong predictions that when appropriate studies are done in those areas, the principles will be found to apply. If the principles are not supported by this new research, then it demonstrates that our framework is empirically testable.

We begin by critiquing both the systems view and the processing view (Chapter 2) before reviewing the evidence for each of the principles. For those readers who wish to go no further into the book, here are our seven principles (and some corollaries) of memory:

1. The cue-driven principle: In all situations, the act of remembering begins with a cue that initiates the retrieval process.
2. The encoding–retrieval principle: Memory depends on the relation between the conditions at encoding and the conditions at retrieval. Accepting this principle entails accepting four consequences:
   a. Items do not have intrinsic mnemonic properties.
   b. Processes do not have intrinsic mnemonic properties.
   c. Cues do not have intrinsic mnemonic properties.
   d. Forgetting is due to extrinsic factors.

---

[7] Nor do we think there is anything magical about the number seven.

3. The cue overload principle: Cues can become associated with more and more items at various encoding opportunities, thus reducing their effectiveness at the time of retrieval.
4. The reconstruction principle: Memory, similar to other cognitive processes, is inherently constructive. Information present at encoding, cues at retrieval, memories of previous recollections, indeed, any possibly useful information, are all exploited to construct a response to a cue.
5. The impurity principle: One consequence of the reconstruction principle is the realization that on any task, people recruit and use a wide variety of information and processes. Therefore, tasks are not pure and processes are not pure, and inferences based on the assumption that a task taps a particular memory system or requires only one particular process are likely to be misguided.
6. The relative distinctiveness principle: Items will be well remembered to the extent that they are more distinct than competing items at the time of retrieval.
7. The specificity principle: Those tasks that require specific information about the context in which memories were formed are more vulnerable to interference or forgetfulness than those that rely on more general information.

Systems or Process?

You can know the name of a bird in all the languages of the world, but when you're finished, you'll know absolutely nothing whatever about the bird. ... So let's look at the bird and see what it's doing—that's what counts. I learned very early the difference between knowing the name of something and knowing something.

—**Richard Feynman**

2.1 Systems or Process?

As evidenced by the contributions to the book edited by Foster and Jelicic (1999), the two most popular contemporary ways of looking at memory are the multiple systems view and the process (or procedural-ist) view.[1] Although these views are not always necessarily diametrically opposed (e.g., Calkins, 1906; Roediger, Buckner, & McDermott, 1999; Tulving, 2002), their respective research programs are focused on different questions and search for different answers. The fundamental difference between structural and processing accounts of memory is whether different rules apply as a function of the way information is acquired, the type of material learned, and the time scale, or whether these can be explained using a single set of principles. The following sections outline the major strengths and weaknesses of the systems and process views of memory.

---

[1] Some versions of the process view are indistinguishable from a functional view.

2.2 The Systems View

Historically, the systems approach grew out of the structuralist tradition in which the purpose of the science of psychology is to analyze and describe the basic elements of cognition and to discover how those elements work together (Titchener, 1898). Structuralism has sometimes been called *atomistic psychology* and explicitly or implicitly assumes that reductionism is possible, at least up to a point. Proponents of the systems view of memory suggest that memory is divided into multiple systems. Thus, their endeavor is focused on discovering and defining different systems and describing how they work. A "system" within this sort of framework is a structure that is anatomically and evolutionarily distinct from other memory systems and differs in its "methods of acquisition, representation and expression of knowledge" (Tulving, 1985b, p. 3). Different systems develop according to different schedules both evolutionarily and developmentally and, at the other end of the spectrum, are differentially affected by trauma and increasing age.

Although there are many descriptions of the systems approach that differ in their details (e.g., Sherry & Schacter, 1987; Squire 1994), the dominant explanation (i.e., the one cited most often by memory researchers) is the one developed by Tulving and colleagues (e.g., Schacter & Tulving, 1994; Tulving, 1983). Even though we focus here on this one framework, the criticisms should apply to the other proposed structural theories. For a more in-depth consideration of this topic, the interested reader is referred to various chapters in Tulving and Craik (2000), Foster and Jelicic (1999), and Schacter and Tulving (1994).

2.2.1 The Five Memory Systems

Using a variety of techniques, including neuropsychological and statistical methods, advocates of the multiple systems approach (e.g., Schacter & Tulving, 1994; Schacter, Wagner, & Buckner, 2000) have identified five major memory systems: procedural memory, the perceptual representation system (PRS), semantic memory, primary or working memory, and episodic memory. Each of these systems follows its own rules or principles, and although they overlap with the other systems, each is functionally and physically dissociable.

2.2.1.1 Procedural Memory

In Tulving's version of the systems view (Tulving, 1983, 1985a), procedural memory is considered to be the oldest memory system from an evolutionary point of view and is identified as the system responsible for basic associations, motor learning, and simple cognitive skills. It is differentiated from the other memory systems (except the PRS) in that it is nondeclarative, meaning that the knowledge represented in this system is not consciously known and cannot be transferred from one person to another. Procedural memory is concerned with knowing "how" rather than with knowing "that." For example, if you know *that* two plus two equals four, the information is said to be in declarative memory. In contrast, if you know *how* to ride a bicycle, that information is said to be in procedural memory. In order to learn a procedure, one must perform the action itself—simply watching or listening ("keep your balance, peddle, and steer") will not suffice. Learning is also incremental and gradually accumulates over practice episodes. Forgetting in this system occurs through lack of practice or through interference due to learning an incompatible procedure. Tests of procedural memory are indirect (they do not refer back to the original learning episode) and often involve how long it takes to relearn a skill or facility in carrying out a task that increases with practice.

2.2.1.2 Perceptual Representation System

The second memory system, the PRS, is also nondeclarative and consists of a collection of domain-specific modules that operate on perceptual information about the form and structure of words and objects (Schacter et al., 2000). This information is stored in a very specific format based on the mode of presentation. Much of the data arguing for the existence of the PRS comes from studies of priming. Priming, as its name suggests, refers to the system's getting ready for a particular type of input. In the memory literature, it generally refers to the robust finding that responding to an item (or an item that is similar either in physical form or meaning) a second time is faster and more accurate than it was the first time. This occurs without an intention to learn, and the advantage can persist for a remarkably long period of time (see Schacter, 1990, for a review of the PRS). The effects of the PRS can also be seen in other indirect tasks such as word fragment completion and stem completion in which the subject is asked to fill in a response with the first word that comes to mind. In a sense, it is a bias in the system to process and respond to previously experienced sensory input. The variables shown to affect priming and word stem completion have been shown to be very different from those that affect other, declarative, memory systems. In addition, similar to procedural memory, the tasks used to access the PRS seem to be intact in individuals suffering from various forms of amnesia.

It is unclear how forgetting might occur in the PRS. Similar to procedural memory, the PRS is queried by indirect tests that do not necessarily refer back to the original learning episode. Recently, the PRS (or implicit memory, which might be PRS plus procedural memory) has been criticized as not actually having any coherent attributes (Willingham & Preuss, 1995). Schacter (1990) argues that this is because the PRS is a function of the "word form" and "structural description" areas that have been identified in the visual areas in the brain (and postulated similar areas for auditory priming) and thus are not driven by the same modules that drive other more conceptual or abstract implicit tasks.

2.2.1.3 Semantic Memory

Semantic memory is a declarative memory system and refers to memory for general knowledge and includes facts, concepts, and vocabulary (Tulving, 1983). A better term might be *generic memory* (Hintzman, 1984) because *semantic memory* implies storage of only semantic information, which is not the case. The distinguishing feature of this system is the combination of conscious knowledge about its contents but lack of conscious awareness of the learning episode. For example, people who are aware that they know the capital of France are often unaware of the episode in which they learned this information. This information is held in long-term memory and the store is generally thought to have an unlimited capacity. How information gets into semantic memory is not specified precisely, but it is clear that it does not require transfer from episodic memory (Tulving, Hayman, & MacDonald, 1991). Forgetting in this store is generally thought to be from lack of access due to interference, and therefore is more of a temporary inaccessibility than a permanent loss of information. Tests of semantic memory often involve general knowledge questions, asking people to decide which category an item belongs to, or similar sorts of tasks.

2.2.1.4 Working Memory

Working memory is a system for the temporary maintenance and storage of internal information and can be thought of as the place where cognitive work is performed. There are many different versions of working memory (see, e.g., the ten different models described in Miyake & Shah, 1999). Perhaps the most well known of these is Baddeley's (1986, 1994) version. According to this account, the central executive is a controlling attentional mechanism with two subsidiary slave systems, the phonological loop and the visuospatial sketch (or scratch) pad. The former handles verbal (or speech-like) stimuli, whereas the latter specializes in visuospatial information. Both of these are subdivided into a storage system (the phonological store and the visual cache) and an active mechanism (the articulatory control process and the inner scribe).

Although working memory has access to previously stored information, the basic structure is designed to keep information active for only a relatively short time period. The capacity of the store is strictly limited, and after a certain amount of time has passed (about 2 s), information that is not rehearsed decays from the store. The mechanism causing decay is generally not specified, but most proponents seem to assume that it occurs due to a passive fading of the information at a constant rate over time. Tests of working memory generally use very small numbers of items (around 6 or so) and immediately follow presentation of the material.

2.2.1.5 Episodic Memory

Episodic memory is the system that supports memories of personally experienced events or episodes and enables the individual to "travel back" mentally into his or her personal past (Tulving, 1998, 2002). Only episodic memory supplies contextual information, rendering information specific rather than general. Items are associated with a context within this store. Although its ultimate capabilities have rarely been tested, episodic memory is thought to have unlimited capacity (see the discussion in Capaldi & Neath, 1995) and forgetting is due to interference. Episodic memory is often thought to be synonymous with conscious awareness, and it is evolutionarily and ontologically the highest form of memory (Sherry & Schacter, 1987; Tulving, 2002). Thus, according to the systems view, it should develop according to a different time scale than other memory systems. In addition, this system can be destroyed without disturbing the other more primitive memory systems. Episodic memory is usually tested with recognition or recall of previously presented information.

2.2.2 Critique of the Systems View

There have been numerous critiques of the systems view on both empirical and logical grounds. In general, three criticisms are raised most often: The systems approach (a) has no criteria that produce exactly five different memory systems, (b) relies to a large extent on dissociations, and (c) has great difficulty accounting for the pattern of results observed at both ends of the life span.

2.2.2.1 Number of Memory Systems

The first major weakness of the systems approach is the lack of consensus on what the systems are and even on how a system should be defined. The most clearly specified and detailed criteria were proposed by Sherry and Schacter (1987), who suggested that four criteria need to be satisfied in order to argue that two systems are in fact separate:

1. Functional dissociations: An independent variable that has one effect on a task thought to tap System A must have either no effect or a different effect on a task thought to tap System B.
2. Different neural substrates: System A must depend on different brain regions than System B.
3. Stochastic independence: Performance on a task that taps System A should be uncorrelated with performance on a task that taps System B.
4. Functional incompatibility: A function carried out by System A cannot be performed by System B.

One problem with offering such a detailed and specific proposal is that it is readily testable. On the one hand, there are a large number of studies that illustrate how episodic and semantic memory meet all four criteria and therefore qualify as separate memory systems. On the other hand, the same criteria lead to suggestions of additional separate memory systems that are never proposed by multiple systems theorists.

As Roediger, Buckner, and McDermott (1999) noted, recall and recognition easily meet the first three of these criteria. A functional dissociation can be shown with the variable word frequency: High-frequency words are recalled better than low-frequency words, but low-frequency words are recognized better than high-frequency words (Gregg, 1976). Different neural substrates have been found for recall and recognition in amnesic subjects (Hirst, Johnson, Phelps, & Volpe, 1988). Stochastic independence is readily observable, as there are numerous studies that have found essentially no correlation between performance on the two types of test (Nilsson & Gardiner, 1993). The fourth of the criteria, functional incompatibility, is easily demonstrated: Memory for taste or odors is a function that is well supported by recognition but not very well supported by recall (Schab & Crowder, 1995). The problem, of course, is that no memory researcher proposes that recall and recognition are subserved by separate memory systems. The criteria of Sherry and Schacter (1987) might (or might not) very well define the five most popular candidates for the multiple memory systems, but they also allow for additional fractionation of systems that do not make sense.

A revised set of criteria has been proposed by Schacter and Tulving (1994, pp. 14–20). Essentially, they propose that memory systems should be defined in terms of their brain systems, the particular kind of information they process, and their principles of operation (but see the original for a detailed discussion). Nonetheless, this newer set of criteria still does not produce just the five systems mentioned earlier and still allows for additional systems that are not apparently wanted.

A further complication for the multiple-systems view is the difference between a system and a subsystem. Presumably, a system is a unitary entity, at least in terms of the construct. However, in many areas, this does not appear to be the case at either the system or subsystem level. For example, the working memory system is typically fractionated into three different parts (central executive, phonological loop, and visuospatial sketchpad), and these can be further broken down (e.g., the phonological loop is divided into the phonological store, articulatory control process). From a systems point of view, the construct "working memory" is not a unitary system, and there is no experimental evidence showing the existence of a general working memory module.

The constructs that make up working memory are similarly not unitary. For example, Parkin (1998) reviewed the neuropsychological evidence and argued (and used as the title of his paper) that the "central executive does not exist" as a unitary concept. He demonstrates that the experimental evidence for a single factor is weak and shows that there is no single neuropsychological locus for a central executive. Parkin describes several examples of neuropsychological data showing vastly different patterns of brain activity associated with tasks that have been argued to tap executive functioning. He concludes by stating that "there is quite clearly an extremely varied state of affairs with different executive tasks subsumed by different neural substrates" (p. 521).

Moreover, the whole idea of a working memory system seems to lack a contribution from memory at all. Tasks that theoretically tap the phonological loop activate areas long associated with language production and perception (e.g., Gabrieli, Poldrack, & Desmond, 1998) rather than areas related to memory. Similarly, visual–spatial memory tasks activate those areas of the brain that are responsible for visual–spatial processing (Slotnik, 2004) rather than those related to memory. At the very least, working memory is a combination of multiple different aspects of language, vision, and attention used in a coordinated fashion. These are processed all over the brain (i.e., it is hard to imagine one area that does both speech and spatial processing). From a functional point of view (what it does), working memory as a concept holds together quite nicely; from a systems point of view, it is a complete bust.

We use working memory as just one example of the lack of coherence in the proposed memory modules, but similar analyses can be made for the other systems, some of it by the proponents of the systems view themselves. For example, there has been substantial evidence that episodic encoding and retrieval may recruit different brain areas (e.g., Nyberg, Cabeza, & Tulving, 1996; Cabeza, Kapur, Craik, McIntosh, Houle, & Tulving, 1997; Tulving, Kapur, Craik, Moscovich, & Houle, 1994) and that different parts of semantic memory can be damaged while leaving other parts intact (Warrington & Shallice, 1984). Willingham and Preuss (1995) argue that constructs such as procedural memory are useful and make sense from a systems point of view only "if some attribute can be found that ties together motor skill learning, priming, conditioning, habituation, and so on." They conclude that "there is not an attribute that usefully does so."[2]

The multiple systems view, then, lacks a principled and consistent set of criteria for delineating memory systems. Given the current state of affairs, it is not unthinkable to postulate 5 or 10 or 20 or even more different memory systems (Roediger et al., 1999). Moreover, the specific memory systems that have been identified can be fractionated further, resulting in a situation in which the system is distributed in multiple brain locations, depending on the demands of the task at hand.

2.2.2.2 Dissociations

A second major problem with the multiple systems account is the reliance on dissociations. At its most simple, a dissociation is shown when one variable has different effects on two tasks. Although there exist numerous dissociations between episodic and semantic memory, for example, it has long been known that there also exist dissociations between two tasks thought to tap the semantic memory system (Balota & Neely, 1980) and between two tasks thought to tap the episodic memory system (Balota & Chumbley, 1984). Even some of the dissociations between episodic and semantic memory are questionable. As Parkin (1999) notes, many studies show that retrieval in episodic tasks involves right prefrontal activation, whereas retrieval of semantic information involves left prefrontal activation. This neuropsychological dissociation, however, reverses when the two tasks are equated for difficulty: Retrieval of semantic information produces larger amounts of right frontal activation than the episodic task. In one sense, then, semantic memory under one set of conditions has a different neural substrate than semantic memory under a second set of conditions.

Proponents of the multiple system view are well aware of the problem of single dissociations. For example, Schacter and Tulving (1994) suggest that convergent dissociations are necessary to support distinctions between systems. Convergent dissociations are simply multiple, single, or double dissociations that use a variety of tasks, materials, populations, and techniques. If a proposed memory system is indeed a memory system, then these multiple dissociations will all converge on the same conclusion. The problem, however, is that although there are multiple dissociations between episodic and semantic memory, there are also multiple dissociations within these systems. The question becomes, which dissociations count?

Another problem related to dissociations is the inability of the systems view to predict which way a particular dissociation will turn out

---

[2] They use the term *implicit memory*, but the tasks described are typically ascribed to PRS and procedural memory according to the five memory system view that we have outlined.

(Hintzman, 1984; McKoon, Ratcliff, & Dell, 1986). Thus, variables are found that have one effect on semantic memory and a different effect on episodic memory, but there is nothing in the systems view that predicts a priori which way round the dissociation should occur. Had the results come out exactly the reverse of what was seen, these completely opposite findings would still have been taken as evidence for the proposed distinction.

Weldon (1999) points a related methodological concern: In many types of neuropsychological studies, a subtractive method is used. That is, one image from one condition is subtracted from a second image from a second condition, removing anything in common in the two conditions. It is possible that these types of analyses might bias findings in favor of differences, given that the similarities are statistically removed.

It seems, therefore, that anatomical dissociations are not sufficient for anything but an anatomical level of description. An analogy from Willingham and Goedert (2001, p. 252) makes this point clearly:

> One could draw an analogy to a computer hard drive: If two Microsoft Word documents occupy different parts of a computer's hard drive, does that indicate that there is a fundamental difference between them? No, because the representation format and the processes (i.e., software) needed to interpret the two files are the same, despite their different "anatomic loci." By the same token, Microsoft Word and Microsoft Excel documents would be considered different, even if they occupied neighboring or even interleaved portions of the hard drive, because they use different formats and because different processes are required to interpret them. We could apply the same logic to memory. Anatomic separability is not enough. There must be a difference between the representations at a cognitive level of description to draw the conclusion that they are truly different and represent separate memory systems.

There are a large number of other published papers questioning the logic of dissociations and double dissociations as a way of identifying memory systems (Ryan & Cohen, 2002; Van Orden, Pennington, & Stone, 2001). Rather than immediately postulating multiple systems, our preference is to "grapple with the dissociated situations and show that each is a special case of a more general but much more complicated principle" (Crowder & Neath, 1991, p. 115). Indeed, there are numerous existence proofs showing that single-system quantitative models can easily account for neuropsychological and other dissociations (Brown & Lamberts, 2003; Kinder & Shanks, 2003; Neath & Brown, 2006; Nosofsky & Zaki, 1998; Zaki, Nosofski, Jessup, & Unverzagt, 2003).

2.2.2.3 Life Span Development

A third criticism of the multiple memory systems view comes from developmental data. The systems view, as articulated by Tulving (1985a), suggests that episodic memory is the "highest" form of memory and thus should be the last to develop and the first to decline: "Episodic memory is a recently evolved, late-developing, and early-deteriorating past-oriented memory system, more vulnerable than other memory systems to neuronal dysfunction, and probably unique to humans" (Tulving, 2002, p. 5).

However, Rovee-Collier (1999) argues that the same basic episodic memory processes are at work in both infants and adults. She shows that even very young infants can retain specific episodic-like memories for long periods of time (perhaps forever) if they are periodically reminded. She also has shown similar dissociations between implicit and explicit memory in young infants as have been found in adults. She concludes that both implicit and explicit memory are available and functional in infants, although at a lower level than in adults (Rovee-Collier, 1997). She argues that implicit and explicit memory follow the same "developmental timetable" and thus challenges the assumption that nondeclarative memory (PRS and procedural memory) develops before declarative memory and that episodic memory develops last of all.

At the other end of the development spectrum, Craik (1983, 1994) also argues that age-related differences in memory do not follow the pattern predicted by the systems view. Older adults generally perform worse than younger adults when performing tasks that require free recall, slightly worse with cued recall, and much the same when given recognition tasks. What matters is not so much the underlying system, episodic or semantic, but rather the type of test. This is not the pattern that would be predicted by the systems view. This interpretation will be elaborated in more detail in Chapter 9, as it supports one of our principles of memory, the specificity principle.

2.2.3 Summary of the Systems View

The most common multiple memory system account—the modal multiple memory model, if you will—posits five memory systems. Some researchers suggest the number is higher (adding, e.g., sensory memory), but others suggest it is lower. The fundamental problem is that there exist no generally accepted criteria that are detailed enough to produce exactly the five systems that are advocated. The reliance on dissociations is problematic, as any difference, no matter which way around the difference is, can be seen as evidence supporting a distinction. Moreover, while there exist numerous dissociations between proposed systems, there also exist numerous dissociations within proposed systems. Finally, the systems account, as typically formulated, has great difficulty accounting for data from infants as well as data from older adults.

The major strength of the systems view is usually taken to be its ability to account for data from amnesic patients (Gabrieli, 1999, Parkin, 1999). Those individuals seem to have specific deficits in episodic memory (recall and recognition) with very few, if any, deficits in semantic memory, procedural memory, or the PRS. As Tulving (2002) puts it, "it is difficult to imagine how, for instance, brain pathology could occur in which the patient loses all episodic memory functions while retaining those that rely on other systems unless there exists the potentiality for such a division in the healthy brain" (p. 12). As noted earlier, however, unitary accounts are increasingly able to address these data (e.g., Brown & Lamberts, 2003; Kinder & Shanks, 2003; Nosofsky & Zaki, 1998).

From our point of view, asking where memory is "located" in the brain is like asking where running is located in the body. There are certainly parts of the body that are more important (the legs) or less important (the little fingers) in performing the task of running but, in the end, it is an activity that requires complex coordination among a great many body parts and muscle groups. To extend the analogy, looking for differences between memory systems is like looking for differences between running and walking. There certainly are many differences, but the main difference is that running requires more coordination among the different body parts and can be disrupted by small things (such as a corn on the toe) that may not interfere with walking at all. Are we to conclude, then, that running is located in the corn on your toe?

Thus, although there is little doubt that more primitive functions such as low-level sensations can be organized in localized brain regions, it is likely that more complex cognitive functions, such as memory, are more accurately described by a dynamic coordination of distributed interconnected areas (Bressler & Kelso, 2001). This sort of approach implies that memory, per se, does not exist but, instead, "information … resides at the level of the large-scale network" (Bressler & Kelso, 2001, p. 33). According to this logic, different tasks (such as recognition and recall) and aspects of tasks (such as encoding and retrieval) recruit different coordinated activities among brain areas and result in different local brain activations. Any small failure of cortical coordination could likely have an impact upon the tasks requiring the most coordinated activity and the least effect on those tasks requiring less precise coordination.

It is always possible that as knowledge of underlying brain anatomy increases, researchers will specify an increasingly precise and principled set of criteria and will develop a consistent and useful taxonomy of systems (Willingham & Goedert, 2001). Until that time, however, many researchers have adopted a different approach, one that emphasizes processing and coordination rather than structure.

2.3 The Processing View

The processing view grew out of the proceduralist tradition (e.g., Bain, 1855; Bartlett, 1932; Kolers & Roediger, 1984) and emphasizes encoding and retrieval processes instead of the system or location in which the memory might be stored. Consider the following description (Wechsler, 1963, pp. 150–151):

> Memories are not like filed letters stored in cabinets or unhung paintings in the basement of a museum. Rather, they are like melodies realized by striking the keys on a piano. Memories are no more stored in the brain than melodies in the keys of the piano.

Rather than saying that performance on a memory test depends on the memory system that supports the information, processing theorists propose that what is important is the type of processing that the person uses. Processes, not structures, are what is fundamental. This view sees memory processing as quite similar to perceptual processing (e.g., Neisser, 1967): Remembering, similar to perceiving, is an active, constructive process that depends on the dynamic interplay of the cues in the environment (external or internal) and previously processed information.

2.3.1 Types of Processing

There are three major processing accounts: (a) levels of processing, (b) transfer-appropriate processing, and (c) components of processing. We briefly review each in turn.

2.3.1.1 Levels of Processing

Craik and Lockhart (1972) presented the first detailed modern account suggesting that processing might be more important than the presumed underlying memory store. They conceptualized memory as the result of a successive series of analyses, each at a deeper level than the previous one. Shallow processing typically focuses on perceptual features, such as how a word sounds, whereas deeper processing emphasizes meaning and semantic information. A key assumption is that the deeper the level of processing, the better the resulting memory. Rehearsal, then, will be beneficial only to the extent that it induces a deeper level of processing.

In order to control the type of processing, Craik and Lockhart suggested that experimenters not tell the subject that there would be a memory test. Instead, subjects should receive orienting instructions, such as being asked to rate words for pleasantness or indicate if two items rhyme. This allows the experimenter, not the subject, to control the type of process used in encoding the stimulus. Depth is the key variable, and intent to learn (Hyde & Jenkins, 1973), the number of rehearsals (Craik & Watkins, 1973), and the amount of time from initial processing (Craik & Tulving, 1975) are not particularly important variables.

The levels of processing framework suffered from two major problems. First, there is no objective, a priori way of assessing the depth of a particular type of processing. Although most reasonable researchers could agree that a rhyme judgment is more shallow and a meaning judgment is more deep, there are numerous tasks in which the exact depth of processing is unclear. Many suggestions for objectively and independently measuring depth have been tested, but none have proved successful (see, e.g., Craik & Tulving, 1975). Second, because of the assumption of a successive series of analyses, Craik and Lockhart (1972) emphasized the processing that occurs at encoding and did not really take into account the type of processing that might be done at test. Numerous studies demonstrated that a shallow level of processing at encoding could lead to better memory performance than a deep level of processing at encoding if one selected the right kind of test (Morris, Bransford, & Franks, 1977).

2.3.1.2 Transfer-Appropriate Processing

According to transfer-appropriate processing, a given type of processing at study will lead to better memory performance if it is appropriate for the particular test (see Morris, Bransford, & Franks, 1977; Tulving & Thomson, 1973). In other words, both the processing at encoding and the processing at retrieval are crucially important. We discuss transfer-appropriate processing in more detail in chapter 5; here, we illustrate one use of it to explain apparent differences between two different memory systems.

According to the systems view, indirect memory tasks in which no mention is made of the learning episode (such as word fragment completion) tap procedural memory or PRS, whereas direct memory tasks in which the subjects are asked to think back to a particular encoding phase (such as free or cued recall) tap declarative (specifically, episodic) memory. Blaxton (1989; Roediger & Blaxton, 1987) argued that most experiments using indirect and direct memory tasks have a built-in confound: The typical indirect memory task relies mainly on data-driven processing, whereas the typical direct task relies mainly on conceptually driven processing (see Jacoby, 1983, for a discussion of this distinction between processing types). Data-driven processing emphasizes more perceptual or low-level aspects of an item (e.g., whether a word is printed in upper- or lowercase, spoken by a male or female voice, or rhymes with ORANGE), whereas conceptually driven processing emphasizes more semantic or high-level aspects of an item (e.g., whether a word is an antonym or synonym of another item, or has pleasant or unpleasant associations).

Blaxton (1989) created tasks that varied data-driven and conceptually driven processing orthogonally with direct and indirect tasks. That is, she had a data-driven direct task as well as a data-driven indirect task; she also had a conceptually driven direct task as well as a conceptually driven indirect task. According to the multiple systems view, an independent variable (in this case, it happened to be whether the stimuli were seen or heard) should affect both indirect tasks in the same way, as both rely on the same underlying system, and be different from both direct tasks. According to a processing view, what matters is not whether the tasks tap the same underlying system, but rather what type of processing is being done. This view, then, predicts that an independent variable (e.g., presentation modality) should affect both data-driven tasks in the same way and be different from both conceptually driven tasks.

The results showed that both data-driven tasks were similar, regardless of the direct or indirect nature of the task: The presumed underlying memory system did not matter, but the type of processing did.

2.3.1.3 *Components of Processing*

Roediger, Buckner, and McDermott (1999) summarized a hybrid model based on ideas put forth by Moscovitch and his colleagues (Moscovitch, 1994; Moscovitch, Vriezen, & Goshen-Gottstein, 1993), which they called the *components of processing* framework. Within this framework, each task consists of a number of components that may or may not be the same as the components in another task. The job of the experimenter, then, is to identify which components pairs of tasks have in common and which components differ. The key assumption is that tasks which show dissociations must have at least one component process that is different (Hintzman, 1990). One might also be able to identify brain areas associated with components, rather than global systems, thus refocusing the neuropsychological efforts on the search for components of processing rather than entire memory systems.

The advantage of this approach is that it emphasizes both the search for differences across tasks as well as the search for similarities. Interestingly, this approach has much in common with task analysis in human factors, in which the components of each task are decomposed into a number of subtasks and the interaction among the components in how the task is completed is analyzed (Proctor & Van Zandt, 1994). It is perhaps still too early to assess how this approach has fared so far.

2.3.2 Critique of the Processing View

The major criticisms of the processing approaches parallel those that have been leveled at the systems view: (a) number of processes or components (instead of number of systems), (b) testability (instead of dissociations), and (c) issues with a special population (amnesia rather than life span development).

2.3.2.1 Proliferation of Processes

A persistent problem for the processing accounts is how to specify the particular kind of processing. There are no objective indices of depth of processing and no objective way of assessing whether two processes are in fact appropriate. One reason for this is that the depth of processing and transfer-appropriate processing theories lack formal specification. The distinction between data-driven and conceptually driven processing has been fruitful, but is only a first step. Similar to other characterizations of processing types, this distinction can break down. For example, most tasks likely require both types of processing, and it is difficult to assess the relative contribution of each.

Two attempts at making the processing views more specific are the process dissociation framework of Jacoby (1991)[3] and the episodic processing account of Whittlesea (1997; Whittlesea & Dorkin, 1993). Until a more complete account of the varieties of processing is provided, the processing view will remain vulnerable to the charge that it is vague in its predictions and certainly incomplete.

2.3.2.2 Testability

A related issue is the testability of the general processing accounts, especially transfer-appropriate processing. Any time a result comes out as predicted, clearly the subjects were using appropriate processing. If the results are unexpected, however, then perhaps some subset of the subjects were using different processing.

2.3.2.3 Amnesia

The major weakness of the processing view is the major strength of the systems view: patients diagnosed with amnesic syndrome. As mentioned above, it is difficult to account for data showing a complete abolishment of episodic memory with no apparent effect on

---

[3] See Chapter 7.

semantic memory, procedural memory, or the PRS without appealing to a separate memory store.

However, a number of specific counterarguments have been offered. One of them is that amnesiacs are unable to make use of contextual information and lack the ability to bind the memory of an event to its context (Chun & Phelps, 1999; Ryan & Cohen, 2003), and amnesics suffer from massive interference from other material (Warrington & Weiskrantz, 1970). Thus, the reason that there appears to be a difference between conscious memory for new information over the short and long term is that in the short term the context is relatively unchanging between study and test, whereas over longer time scales the context does change. This predicts that if we were somehow able to reduce interference and keep context the same over longer periods of time, we could show closer to normal memory performance even in the amnesic syndrome. If it could be shown that the amnesic syndrome could be explained without appealing to different structural systems in the brain, but instead a difficulty in a general process such as interference, this weakness in the procedural case could be nullified.

Della Sala, Cowan, Beschin, and Perini (2005; see also Cowan, Beschin, & Della Sala, 2004) performed an experiment showing that, under conditions of minimal interference, amnesic patients could exhibit close to normal episodic memory. They compared a condition in which amnesic patients with mild cognitive impairment were given a recall test of a story after a 1-hr delay spent either performing a variety of tasks or reclining in a quiet, dark room for an hour (some of the participants spent the time sleeping, as evidenced by their snoring). On average, both normal and amnesic participants benefited from the minimal interference condition, in one case improving from 0 to 38% correct. There were large individual differences, and some of the patients did not accrue a benefit from the low-interference condition. Nonetheless, it is an impressive demonstration of the power of interference in memory, not only for normal participants (Jenkins & Dellenbach, 1924) but also for individuals suffering from memory impairments. Certainly, this one experiment does not overcome the difficulties that procedural views have with amnesia, but it suggests a fruitful area of future experimentation.

2.3.3 Summary of the Processing View

Processing views of memory argue that what is most important is the type of processing rather than the underlying memory system. All three processing accounts described have difficulty identifying and specifying the exact processing that is done a priori, similar to how the systems view has difficulty defining a system. Unlike the systems view, the processing accounts typically ignore memory over the short term (but see Nairne, 2001). One intriguing difference is that, unlike multiple systems accounts, processing accounts are often invoked when offering guidance on how to improve memory.

2.4 Chapter Summary

How is our "principles" approach different from the preceding two approaches? We suggest that in the absence of a compelling reason to prefer the systems view over the processing view (or vice versa), it would be fruitful to consider memory from a functional perspective. We do not know how many memory systems there are or how to define what a memory system is. We do not know how many processes (or components of processing) there are or how to distinguish them. We do acknowledge that short-term memory and long-term memory seem to differ in some ways, as do episodic memory and semantic memory, but are they really fundamentally different? Both the systems approach and, to a lesser extent, the proceduralist approach emphasize differences. Our approach emphasizes similarities. We suggest that a search for general principles of memory, based on fundamental empirical regularities, can act as a spur to theory development and a reexamination of systems versus process theories of memory.

The Cue-Driven Principle

Suppose I am silent for a moment, and then say, in commanding accents: "Remember! Recollect!" Does your faculty of memory obey the order, and reproduce any definite image from your past? Certainly not. It stands staring into vacancy, and asking, "What kind of a thing do you wish me to remember?" It needs, in short, a cue.

—William James (1890, p. 117–118)

3.1 Principle 1: The Cue-Driven Principle

Our first principle states that all memory is cue driven; without a cue, there can be no memory (James, 1890; Jones, 1979; Tulving, 1974). By *cue* we mean a specific prompt or query, such as "Did you see this word on the previous list?" or "What word was paired with CHAIR?" or "Write down the words from the most recently presented list in any order you like" or "What were you doing on August 19, 2004?" or "Is STRINE a valid English word?" or "Where did I leave my keys?" or "Who was the only Nobel Prize winner to play first class cricket?"[1]

All of these examples use verbal cues, as those are often easier to demonstrate. However, cues can also be nonverbal, such as odors (e.g., Schab & Crowder, 1995), emotions (e.g., Uttl, Ohta, & Siegenthaler, 2006), nonverbal sounds (e.g., Mead & Ball, 2007), and images (e.g., Goddard, Pring, & Felmingham, 2005), to name only a few.

---

[1] Samuel Beckett (1906–1989) played first class cricket for Dublin University in 1925 and 1926 and was awarded the Nobel Prize for Literature in 1969.

Although in many situations the person is fully aware that the cue is part of a memory test, this need not be the case. For example, in indirect tests of memory, people are presented with a long list of items to rate for pleasantness (or some other dimension). A little while later, they are asked to complete word fragments, such as A_L_ _GY, with the first word that pops into their head. No reference is made to the study episode, and the person may truly have no awareness that the two events are, in fact, connected. The word fragment is also a cue. People who saw the word *ALLERGY* recently are more likely to complete the fragment correctly than people who did not.

The cues listed so far tap a variety of hypothetical memory systems, including episodic and semantic, short- and long-term, and implicit and explicit. Cues are also needed for tasks that tap what multiple memory system theorists would term *procedural memory*. For example, there are many studies that look at the cues used by fielders to catch baseballs and cricket balls (e.g., Dienes & McLeod, 1993; Marken, 2005) and the cues used by batters to hit the balls in the first place (e.g., Müller, Abernethy, & Farrow 2006). Kime, Lamb, and Wilson (1996) show how one can cue procedural memory, with both verbal and nonverbal cues, to help a patient with dense amnesia caused by trauma to function better. Perceptual-motor tasks such as touch typing and writing Chinese characters, which rely on procedural memory, also show not only sensitivity to cues, but also to the order in which the cues are experienced (e.g., Giovanni, 1994; Jordan, 1995).

Computer simulation models of memory acknowledge the importance of cues by building them into the system; indeed, computer simulation models will not work unless there is a cue. In general, some input is provided to these models, and then a response is provided. The so-called global models of memory, SAM, TODAM, and MINERVA2, are all cue driven. These models are called "global" as they account for performance in a wide range of paradigms, including recognition, free recall, serial recall, and cued recall. In SAM, a model of free recall and recognition, retrieval in a free recall task begins by assembling a cue that consists of the context in which the items were studied (Gillund & Shiffrin, 1984; Raaijmakers & Shiffrin, 1981). If an item is successfully retrieved, the next cue is the context plus the item just recovered. For recognition, the context is again used as a cue, but is accompanied by the test item. Similarly, TODAM begins with context as a specific cue to model serial recall (Lewandowsky & Murdock, 1989). MINERVA 2, designed to account for both episodic and semantic memory within a single system, similarly uses probes to obtain responses (Hintzman, 1987).

Models of immediate and working memory also use cues and are also cue driven. For example, in the Burgess and Hitch (1999) model, an instantiation of the phonological loop component of working memory (Baddeley, 1986), a slowly varying context-time signal is used to initiate the retrieval process. This type of cue is also used by OSCAR (Brown, Preece, & Hulme, 2000), a very different model that addresses many aspects of immediate serial recall. Yet another account of similar data is offered by the feature model (Nairne, 1990), which also requires cues. Connectionist models of memory are also cue driven (cf. Ratcliff, 1992). Humphreys, Bain, and Pike (1989) present a model that specifies the cues used not only in episodic and semantic tasks, but also those that tap procedural memory. In fact, it is hard to conceive of a computer model of memory that is not cue dependent, simply because the computer requires something to start the retrieval process.

3.2 Memory Without Cues

There is one area of memory research in which the opposite assumption is made, that is, memory does not require cues. For example, Kintsch, Healy, Hegarty, Pennington, and Salthouse (1999) summarized 10 different theoretical accounts of working memory, highlighting similarities and differences among the various conceptions. They explicitly noted that because of the common assumption that "information 'in' working memory is directly and effortlessly retrievable, ... retrieval from ST-WM is not cue dependent" (pp. 413–414).[2] Similarly, Wickens, Moody, and Dow (1981, p. 17) state that "the retrieval act is not required in the PM [primary memory] situation." More recently, Jonides et al. (2008, p. 202) note that "the central point of agreement" among current models of short-term memory is that "representations are directly accessible and available for cognitive action."

One particular version of working memory that posits cueless retrieval is called the *embedded processes model* (Cowan, 1995, 1999). Essentially, memory is divided into three parts (see Figure 3.1): Long-term store, activated memory, and the focus of attention. Together, the activated part of long-term memory as well as the contents in the focus of attention comprise working memory.

According to this view, an item becomes activated when it receives attention, and activated items can enter the focus of attention when they are the object of current processing. Thus, in terms of a typical memory experiment, retrieval means "entering the correct items into the focus of attention" (Cowan, 1999, p. 75). If an item is in the focus of attention, it does not have to be retrieved. The focus of attention is limited to approximately four unrelated items (Cowan, 2000); in addition to this item-based limit,

---

[2] It is interesting that when the various working memory theories are instantiated as a computer simulation (e.g., Burgess & Hitch, 1999), then a cue is required.

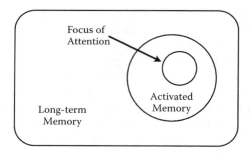

FIGURE 3.1 A schematic representation of the embedded-processes model of working memory. Working memory is made up of the activated portion of long-term memory (activated memory) and the focus of attention.

there is a time-based limit on the activation of an item in memory of approximately 10 to 20 s unless it is reactivated.

Many other researchers have proposed a similar conception (e.g., Ericsson & Kintsch, 1995; Garavan, 1998; Oberauer, 2002). Jonides et al. (2008) review much of the literature in this area, and note that, in their view, the data support this general notion of a "concentric" model of memory, in which working memory is simply activated long-term memory (as opposed to separate slave systems such as the phonological loop and visuospatial sketchpad seen in Baddeley's version), and the focus of attention consists of those small number of items that are currently being processed.

The focus of attention, then, bears many similarities to William James' (1890, p. 609) description of primary memory: "An object of primary memory is not thus brought back; it never was lost; its date was never cut off in consciousness from that of the immediately present moment. In fact, it comes to us as belonging to the rearward portion of the present space of time, and not to the genuine past." One difference, however, is that some items in the focus of attention have indeed been brought back from memory proper, via retrieval or rehearsal (Jonides et al., 2008).

Another example of memory retrieval that does not need a cue comes from a multinomial model proposed by Schweickert (1993). A multinomial model is a way of analyzing events (like remembering or forgetting) that can have multiple causes. One attraction of this kind of model is that it enables the researcher to estimate the contribution of each cause. Figure 3.2 shows Schweickert's model. The basic idea is that "subjects carry out immediate recall by first attempting direct readout and then guessing if that fails" (p. 70; see also Estes, 1991). "Direct readout" was not further explained, but the implication is that the information needed is still resident in consciousness and therefore does not need retrieving.

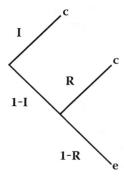

FIGURE 3.2   Schweickert's (1993) multinomial model. An item is either intact, *I*, which leads to a correct recall (*c*), or it is not intact, 1-I, and requires redintegration. Successful redintegration leads to a correct recall, whereas unsuccessful redintegration leads to an error (*e*).

At the time of the memory test, there is a probability *I* that the item is intact and can be directly read out, and a probability 1–*I* that the item is not intact. In the latter case, a process called *redintegration* is necessary, in which the degraded item is made interpretable, usually by comparing it to possible responses stored elsewhere in memory (see the following text for a discussion of redintegration). Correct recall is therefore the probability that an item will be directly read out of memory plus the probability of correctly redintegrating the item. In this type of account, the items that are not intact serve as cues that initiate a redintegrative process, but items that are intact are recalled without cues.

Note that Schweickert's (1993) model proposes, in essence, that sometimes memory is cue driven (i.e., redintegration is required because an item is not intact) and sometimes it is not cue driven (i.e., the item is intact and is read out directly). The other views (e.g., Cowan, 2000; Wickens et al., 1981) do not allow for any form of retrieval. The remainder of this chapter will focus, in some depth, on the rather narrow topic of whether these specialized forms of short-tem memory are indeed an exception and are not cue driven.

3.3 Evidence for Cues

Before reviewing the evidence for the use of cues in working memory and the focus of attention, it is necessary to consider two complex issues in assessing these effects: How can we be sure which memory system is responsible for an observed effect? How can we be sure a null result is a real null result?

Proponents of the view that one form of memory—working memory, primary memory, the focus of attention—is not cue driven are unanimous in distinguishing that form of memory from long-term memory. Given the involvement of multiple memory systems, the question arises, how can we be sure which memory system is responsible for a particular observed effect? We noted this problem in Chapter 2, but here we focus on its particular relevance to separating a short-term memory system from a long-term memory system.

There is a long history of trying to distinguish between those effects attributable to long-term memory and those attributable to a shorter-term store (e.g., Murdock, 1967; Raymond, 1969; Tulving & Colatla, 1970; Waugh & Norman, 1965). As Nairne (1996) points out, given the architecture of almost all models that make this distinction, there must always be contamination of one presumed store with the other. In what he refers to as the "standard" account, information coming into the system has to pass through working (or primary or short-term) memory on its way to long-term memory. When a stimulus is seen or heard, its identity has to be determined using long-term memory (where knowledge resides) before it can be converted into the code used by working memory. The fundamental problem is that any response from any task will reflect contributions from both stores, and therefore any measure of one memory system will reflect contamination from the other (see also the impurity principle in Chapter 7).

Because of this problem, we examine results from several different paradigms in which the role of one of the memory systems is minimized (but not completely eliminated) according to the logic of the multistore account. The goal is to determine whether the various studies show similar patterns of results. If they do, we can use this converging evidence (cf. Garner, Hake, & Ericksen, 1956) to draw a general conclusion because we are less concerned about problems with any one particular paradigm. If the cue-driven principle is reasonable, then effects related to cuing should be observable in a variety of tasks that are thought, by multiple memory theorists, to tap the hypothetical cue-immune system. On the other hand, if the various cue-immune theories are correct, then cueing effects should never be observed.

This brings us to the second complex issue: There are many examples of null results published, that is, studies in which it seems as if one kind of short-term memory does not demonstrate cuing effects. How can we assess whether these null results are real?

As we discuss in the following text, one type of evidence that indicates the involvement of a retrieval process is when information learned previously interferes with the learning of new information, called *proactive interference*, or PI. Although no theorists claim that long-term memory is immune to the effects of cues or is immune to proactive interference, it is trivially easy to construct an experiment in which these effects are absent. The absence of an effect of proactive interference is interpreted as being due to the subject's use of cues that preclude such interference from occurring. Our claim, substantiated later, is that instances of failing to find proactive interference (or other evidence of cuing) in short-term or working memory can be explained in a similar way. This point is somewhat easier to appreciate using an example from a different paradigm: implicit memory.

It was long thought that implicit memory was immune to interference, both retroactive (interference from more recent items) and proactive interference (interference from older items). Graf and Schacter (1987) reported an experiment that seemed to indicate immunity to PI.[3] In Phase I, subjects studied word pairs, such as SHIRT-WINDOW. These first pairs will be called *A-B pairs*. Subjects were asked to generate and read aloud a sentence that related the words in a meaningful manner, such as "The boy threw the shirt out of the window." This is incidental learning because the subjects were not asked to learn the word pairs. In Phase II, the subjects did the same processing with a second list of word pairs. In the control condition, this list contained all new words and so was called the *C-D list*. In the experimental condition, this list was designed to produce interference by reusing the first words from Phase I. These interference lists, then, are called *A-D lists*. Both groups of subjects were to be tested on the original A-B pairs, so this design should lead to retroactive interference: processing the A-D list can interfere with information already processed, the A-B list. Another set of subjects also received two learning sessions, but these were arranged so as to cause proactive interference. These subjects processed the A-D or C-D pairs in Phase I, and the A-B pairs in Phase II. They were then tested on the A-B pairs. This is proactive interference because information already processed (the A-D pairs) can interfere with new information (the A-B pairs). The design is sketched out in Table 3.1.

The direct test was cued recall; the subject was provided with the A word and the first few letters of the B word, and was asked to complete the stem with the originally studied word. This is a direct test because the subject is asked to refer back to a specific learning episode. The indirect test was word-fragment completion; the subject was provided with the A word and the first few letters of the B word, and was asked to complete the stem with the first word that came to mind. This is an indirect test because the task can be completed without reference to the learning episode. To minimize the chance that subjects became aware of the relationship between the word-fragment completion test and the study episode, only 12 A-B pairs were tested out of 44 other items. A third, separate group of

---

[3] This section is taken from Chapter 7 of Neath and Surprenant (2003) and is incorporated with permission of the copyright holder, Wadsworth.

TABLE 3.1 Schematic Representation of the Conditions
Tested by Graf and Schacter (1987)

	Phase I	Phase II	Tested On	Interference
Control	A-B	C-D	A-B	
Experimental	A-B	A-D	A-B	RI
Control	C-D	A-B	A-B	
Experimental	A-D	A-B	A-B	PI

TABLE 3.2 The Proportion of Stems Correctly Completed in a
Cued Recall Test (Direct) or Word-Fragment Completion Test
(Indirect) in Either a Retroactive or Proactive Interference Design

	Retroactive Interference		Proactive Interference	
Test Type	Control	Experimental	Control	Experimental
Direct	0.55	0.40	0.67	0.45
Indirect	0.34	0.32	0.32	0.35

Note: Based on data from Graf and Schacter (1987). *Journal of Experimental Psychology:
Learning, Memory, and Cognition, 13,* 45–53.

subjects received only Phase III; this group provides a baseline of how
many fragments would be completed when there was no opportunity to
learn. The subjects in the control and experimental conditions performed
more accurately than the baseline subjects did, confirming that memory
was indeed playing a role. The rest of the results are shown in Table 3.2.

First consider the retroactive interference manipulation. On the direct
test, the control subjects performed more accurately than the experimental
subjects did (0.55 versus 0.40), demonstrating the presence of RI. On the
indirect test, however, the control and experimental subjects performed at
about the same levels, indicating no interference. The pattern is the same
for the proactive interference condition: On the direct test, the control subjects outperformed the experimental subjects (0.67 versus 0.45), whereas
performance was equivalent on the indirect test. This represents a dissociation because the manipulation of both RI and PI affected performance
on one kind of test (direct) but had no effect on another test (indirect).

This and other results led to the not unreasonable conclusion that
implicit memory (or more specifically, indirectly tested memory of incidentally learned information) is immune to interference. However, it was
later pointed out (Lustig & Hasher, 2001a, 2001b) that such immunity is
most likely due to the cues that were used by the subjects in the task. In
Graf and Schacter's study, there were two cues, A and B. In the direct test,
the subject was given a cue such as *shirt-win-* and was asked to complete
the fragment using a word from the previously studied pair. Thus, *shirt*

is relevant because it was processed in relation to *window* and because it is provided at test as a useful cue. In the indirect test, the subjects were asked to complete the stem with the first word that came to mind. Only *win-* is relevant (it has to be processed so that a word can be generated). Although *shirt* was provided, it is not relevant and thus may not have an effect on performance.

Lustig and Hasher (2001b) tested this explanation using a word-fragment completion task similar to that used by Graf and Schacter. One group of subjects received only the word fragment completion task so that the researchers could determine the number of times a particular fragment was completed with a particular word without specific priming. The two experimental groups saw a list of words and, as a cover task, were asked to indicate the number of vowels that occurred in each word. This task induces processing of individual letters. After several additional tasks unrelated to the experiment, the key tests were presented. The difference between the interference and control groups was in the relation between the fragments shown at test and the words seen earlier. For example, both groups might receive the word fragment *a _ l _ _ g y*, and both groups would have seen the word *allergy* in the original list. If the fragment is completed to form the word *allergy* at levels greater than the baseline group, there is evidence for implicit memory. The key difference between the experimental groups is that the interference group saw the word *analogy* as well as *allergy*, whereas the control group did not see *analogy*. *Analogy* is sufficiently similar to *allergy* to interfere with it. Priming was above baseline for both groups, indicating implicit memory, but there was less priming in the interference condition than in the control condition. This is exactly what one would expect if implicit memory is subject to interference effects. In Lustig and Hasher's design, the interfering information is relevant at the time of test, given the processing that the subjects are asked to do; in the Graf and Schacter study, the interfering item is not relevant. When looking for the influence of cues in short-term memory tasks that multiple-memory systems theorists believe are not cue driven, it is critically important to ensure that the interfering material is relevant to the task.

Now we turn to an analysis of short-term or immediate memory. There are three kinds evidence that have been proposed to support the idea that some types of memory do not require cues: (a) the absence of redintegrative effects, (b) the absence of cueing effects, and (c) the absence of proactive interference. In examining the data from short-term memory, we expect to find a large number of studies in which the effects are absent. Our view (see also Humphreys & Tehan, 1999) attributes this to an experimental design in which the cues did not lead to the effect of interest rather than because the effect of interest cannot be obtained. The key claim concerns the studies that can be found that do show such effects when the experiments are designed to yield such results.

3.3.1 Redintegrative Effects

As used in the field of memory, the term *redintegration* (from the Latin word meaning "to make whole again") traces back to the Scottish psychologist Sir William Hamilton (1788–1856). Hamilton's theory, which he called the law of redintegration or totality, was a reaction against the dominant British associationism of the time. Hamilton argued that, far from any single idea triggering just one other idea, any one element can bring back the experience of the whole situation. Using just one aspect of the original, "the subject redintegrates in memory the original situation" (Murphy, 1929, p. 105; see also Hollingsworth, 1924). This key part of the definition is still current: As Groninger and Murray (2004, p. 360) put it, the "process of generating an image from a component of that image is called redintegration."

In terms of short-term memory, redintegration is the process used at retrieval to identify or interpret or complete a degraded item by comparing it to other, intact items, usually in long-term or semantic memory. For example, a person who has just seen a list of words and nonwords might have partial information about some of the items seen. Other things being equal, it should be easier to redintegrate the partial information about a word into the original word than it is to redintegrate the partial information about the nonword into the original nonword because there is no source of information, such as the lexicon, from which one can draw additional information about the nonword. If one can recall more words than nonwords, redintegration can be inferred.

Redintegration occurs only when retrieval occurs. If a system does not involve retrieval, then redintegrative effects should not be observed. Evidence of redintegration is also evidence that the to-be-remembered items were not simply "read out directly" as proposed by Schweickert's (1993) multinomial model or Cowan's (1999) embedded processes model.

First, consider memory span. Although this measure has a variety of definitions, the most common is the number of items that can be immediately recalled in their correct serial order. As Miller (1956) noted, this is often found to be around seven plus or minus two items and has long been taken as a measure of the capacity of short-term memory or working memory. However, if redintegrative effects are observed in measures of memory span, it suggests that retrieval is necessary and that cues are involved.[4]

Hulme, Maughan, and Brown (1991) compared memory span for words and nonwords. If redintegration occurs in memory span tasks, one would expect a higher span for words than nonwords. This is exactly what was found. In a second experiment, they compared span for English words and Italian words for people with no knowledge of Italian. Span was higher for

---

[4] It also suggests that long-term memory is involved, and that therefore, memory span is not a pure measure of short-term or working memory. We discuss this further in Chapter 7 as evidence supporting our impurity principle.

English than Italian words. Importantly, memory span for Italian words increased when the subjects were informed of the Italian words' meanings. From a redintegration perspective, the subjects now have more useful information to help them interpret an ambiguous or difficult-to-interpret cue. This type of result—an effect consistent with cue-driven retrieval and inconsistent with direct readout—has been replicated numerous times (e.g., Hulme, Roodenrys, Brown, & Mercer, 1995; Roodenrys, Hulme, Lethbridge, Hinton, & Nimmo, 2002; Watkins, 1977), so it does not depend on the particular stimuli used. These redintegrative effects are even found with lists as short as four items (Roodenrys & Hinton, 2002), the capacity of both Cowan's (2000) view and Baddeley's (2000) working memory, and well below the classic seven plus or minus two limit.

A second line of evidence showing results consistent with a general redintegration account pays attention to the serial position of the items. According to some accounts, items at some positions in the list are more likely to reflect long-term memory performance, whereas items at other positions in a list are more likely to reflect short-term or working or sensory memory (for a review, see Crowder, 1976). Rather than focusing on which particular position reflects which particular memory system under each particular theoretical account, we emphasize effects at all positions. That is, if one can observe redintegrative effects at all serial positions, one need not worry about exactly which positions reflect one type of memory or another. Instead, one can argue that if a theory posits that recall at a particular position is supported by a particular memory system, showing redintegrative effects at all positions means that redintegrative effects are observable in that system.

Just as Hulme et al. (1991) showed an effect of lexicality in memory span, Gathercole, Pickering, Hall, and Peaker (2001) observed a lexicality effect—better recall of words than nonwords—at all serial positions (see also Bourassa & Besner, 1994). Similarly, Roodenrys and Quinlan (2000) examined immediate serial recall of six-item lists of high- and low-frequency words and observed a word frequency effect at all serial positions (see also Hulme, Stuart, Brown, & Morin, 2003).

While some theories of memory do not ascribe performance at particular serial positions as indicative of a greater or lesser contribution from a particular store, many theories do. The repeated findings of redintegrative effects at all serial positions means that all memory systems that support recall of items at particular positions show redintegrative effects. This is what is expected if all memory is cue driven.

3.3.2 Cueing Effects

If all memory is cue driven, then we should be able to find evidence for cueing effects in short-term or working memory. There is comparatively little research that directly examines this question, particularly for items that are likely to be in the focus of attention. One reason for so few published studies might be that if a researcher assumes that a particular kind of memory is not cue driven (cf. Kintsch et al., 1999), why would she or he conduct an experiment to demonstrate that the cues used had no result? However, despite the relatively small number of studies, there are several experiments that show cueing effects in tasks that have been identified as tapping short-term or working memory as especially sensitive to the operation of those systems.

Tehan and Humphreys (1996, Experiment 2) used a task in which the subject was asked to remember only four items on any given trial. Two seconds after seeing the list, a cue was presented and the subjects were asked if one of the four words belonged to this category. For example, the cue might be *juice,* and one of the four words might be *carrot.* Note that the cue is directly relevant to the memory task. On half the trials, this was all that happened. However, on the remaining trials, subjects were presented with two sets of four items. The subjects were told that if a second list appeared, they should forget the first list and respond only on the basis of the four most recent items in the second list. The data of interest come from these trials.

On the control trials, there was no item that matched the cue in the first set of words. On same-category trials, a second instance of the category appeared in the first set of words (e.g., *orange*). On different-category trials, *orange* and *carrot* might still be in Lists 1 and 2, but the cue would be *vegetable* rather than *juice.* Performance in the control condition was 0.41 and was equivalent to performance in the different category trials, 0.39. Performance in the same category trials, though, was significantly less, 0.30. The reason that this result is important is because the stimuli shown at encoding were held constant. Therefore, the presence of interference in the same-category condition but not in the different-category condition indicates that the interference effects were cue specific.

Cueing effects are not limited to semantic cueing. Tehan and Humphreys (1996) also demonstrated another cueing effect, this time using rhyme as the basis. The category dominance effect refers to the finding that in cued recall tasks, the dominant items in a category are better recalled than are weaker instances. For example, a high dominant example would be seeing the items *glass cloud desk gun nose jazz* and then being cued with *Type Of Weapon.* A low dominant example would be seeing the items *glass cloud desk cannon nose jazz* and getting the same cue. *Gun* is more likely to be recalled than *cannon.*

Rather than using a semantic category, though, Tehan and Humphreys (1996, Experiment 5) used a rhyme category, with items being either dominant or weak rhymes. A six-item list was presented with one of the items being either a dominant or weak member of a rhyme category. Performance on an immediate cued-recall test showed better performance for the dominant item (0.88) than for the nondominant item (0.79). Tehan and Humphreys conclude that "short-term recall, like long-term recall, is cue dependent" (p. 719).

3.3.3 Proactive Interference

The third line of evidence used to support the idea that recall of items in the focus of attention is not cue driven typically concerns the claim that proactive interference is not found. Proactive interference, or PI, is inferred when the presence of an earlier item reduces performance when remembering a later item, relative to a control condition. However, some multiple systems theorists posit that "one can observe proactive interference (PI) in retrieval only if there are more than four items in a list to be retained. … This presumably occurs because four or fewer items are, in a sense, already retrieved; they reside in a limited-capacity store, eliminating the retrieval step in which PI arises" (Cowan, 2000, p. 103).

The key claim, then, is that when there are four or fewer items in memory, they can be retained in the focus of attention and are now immune to PI. In support of this claim, there are results from a variety of studies in which items in the focus of attention do indeed appear to be immune to proactive interference while items outside of the focus of attention are affected by PI.

The basic task (e.g., Halford et al., 1988, Experiment 1) is a variant of the Sternberg (1966) memory scanning procedure. The subjects saw a list of words presented all at once; there could be 4 or 10 words in the list. One second after the list disappeared, a probe appeared. The subject's task was to indicate if the probe was or was not in the list. Proactive interference was manipulated by using categorized lists. There were three consecutive test trials using words in one taxonomic category (i.e., trees), then three consecutive trials using another category (e.g., sports), then three consecutive trials using yet another category (e.g., spices), and so on. Trial 1 for a given category was designated as a low PI trial, as there were no trials preceding it on which the same type of items had occurred. Trial 3 for any one category was designated as a high PI trial, because it followed two trials that contained the same types of items. When there were 10 to-be-remembered items, subjects were faster and more accurate between the low-PI condition than in the high-PI condition. In contrast, there was no difference in response times or accuracy between the low- and high-PI conditions when there were only four items. Halford et al. reported a second experiment that used rhyme categories rather than semantic categories, and also included lists of six and eight items. Again, the response times for the 4-item lists did not differ between the low-PI and high-PI conditions, but did for the 6-, 8-, and 10-item lists. Similar results—evidence of PI when there are more than four items and no evidence with four or fewer items—have been reported by others (e.g., Cowan, Johnson, & Saults, 2005; Tehan & Humphreys, 1995; Wickens, Moody, & Dow, 1981).

There are, however, three papers—Atkinson, Herrmann, and Wescourt (1974), Monsell (1978), and McElree and Dosher (1989)—that did report PI on trials that had as few as two items. The various studies differ in many ways, so it is difficult to determine which factors are critical in obtaining an effect of PI. Tehan and Humphreys (1996, p. 719) note that PI will be "observed only if interfering and target items are subsumed by the same cue." One possibility for the many instances of failing to find effects of PI is that the cues used to create the interference by the experimenter might not be used by the subjects or might be used in a different way. For example, McElree and Dosher (1989, Experiment 2) found effects of PI with lists containing two, three, or four items. Unlike the aforementioned studies, McElree and Dosher used a probe that was the same word as one of the items in a fairly recent list.

Most of these studies include additional variables and become quite complex in their design; thus, it is not always clear what additional factors are being introduced. Hanley and Scheirer (1975) also found evidence of proactive interference with short lists, but they had a far more simple design. They, too, used a version of the standard Sternberg task, but they used letter pairs or number pairs. (A number pair is simply a two-digit number.) On each trial, three letter pairs were presented sequentially. At test, a probe (a letter pair) was shown, and the subject was asked to indicate as quickly as possible whether that item was in the set of three just shown. Four trials were conducted with letters, and then four trials were conducted with numbers. This pattern of alternation continued throughout the experiment. Trial 1 was thus a low PI trial, and Trial 4 was thus a high PI trial. Hanley and Scheirer found that response times increased as subjects received more trials; that is, previous trials interfered with processing of the current three letter pairs. Although one could argue that the subjects needed to store 6 items (in the case of letters), one cannot make that claim for numbers. Thus, even if one considers only the case with three numbers, it is well below the limit of four items ascribed to the focus of attention (cf. Cowan, 2000).

One final demonstration of proactive interference for items that could plausibly be said to be in the focus of attention or some other putatively PI-immune store concerns the acoustic confusion effect (Conrad, 1964). This effect refers to the finding that lists of similar-sounding items are harder to recall than otherwise comparable lists of dissimilar-sounding items. For current purposes, it is an example of both proactive and retroactive interference: The item at Position 1 can interfere with the item at Position 2 and 3 (PI), and the item at Position 3 can interfere with the items at Positions 1 and 2 (RI). Most importantly, only PI can affect the final item in the list.

Baddeley, Lewis, and Vallar (1984, Experiment 3) had subjects listen to lists of two, three, four, five, six, and seven similar-sounding or dissimilar-sounding letters. Dissimilar-sounding lists were better recalled than similar-sounding for lists of 4 or more items. No errors were made with list lengths of two. The data when the list length is three is suggestive of an effect: there were more errors for three-item lists of similar-sounding letters than dissimilar-sounding letters in the slow condition (one item every 1.5 s), but not in the fast condition. However, Baddeley et al. did not report their results as a function of serial position. It is possible that (almost) perfect performance at the first position is masking an effect observable at the final position. Consistent with this account, Roodenrys and Miller (2008) found better recall of a three-item list of dissimilar-sounding items than similar-sounding items. Most importantly, this difference was observable at the final position, where only proactive interference could be playing a role.

3.3.4 Possible Exceptions

There is one possible exception to the principle that all memory is cue driven. We have shown, earlier, that even when there are only three or four items to be remembered, a number within the capacity of the focus of attention (Cowan, 2000), cueing effects are observed. However, not all theorists set the capacity limit at four, and some set the limit as low as a single chunk (Jonides et al., 2008) or a single item (e.g., Garavan, 1998; McElree, 2001; Verhaeghen & Basak, 2005).[5] We could find no studies in which only a single item needed to be remembered and evidence of red-integration, cueing effects, or PI was obtained. A strong prediction, based on our principle, is that if an appropriate experiment is conducted, then the various types of cueing effects should be observable.

If it turns out that there is a real exception to the cue-driven principle, the implications for our approach are not too severe. One could make the argument, harkening back to William James, that the focus of attention with a capacity limit of only one item is not memory proper.[6] For example, in most versions, saying that an item is currently the focus of attention is essentially the same as saying an item is currently being processed. If one did want to agree that this really is memory proper, then it could be seen as a special case: The principle would hold for all memory regardless of the type of information, the type of processing, the hypothetical system supporting the memory, or the time scale, as long as there was more than a single item to be remembered.

---

[5] Verhaeghen, Cerella, and Basak (2004) allow for the capacity to increase from 1 to 4 items with as little as 10 hr of practice.
[6] We raise this issue again in Chapter 10.

3.4 Chapter Summary

There is near unanimity in the view that memory is cue driven. The one area in which this view is contested concerns a particular form of memory that is characterized by highly restrictive capacity limitations. Although there are many studies in which redintegrative effects, cueing effects, or PI effects have not been observed when items are thought to be stored in this particular form of memory, one can find a few studies in which these effects have been found. It is always potentially problematic to establish that something does not exist; an easier approach is to assume the absence of something and then offer a positive illustration. Thus, if one assumes the absence of redintegrative effects, cueing effects, and PI effects, the positive examples offered earlier should be sufficient to argue against the view that some types of memory are never cue driven. Although the cue-driven principle states that all memory is cue driven, it does not require that such effects be observable in every single experiment; it is very easy to manipulate a nominal cue that turns out to differ from the functional cue. With appropriate manipulations, however, such effects are readily observed in a wide variety of paradigms.

CHAPTER

The Encoding–Retrieval Principle

If you inquire then deeply enough what particular sensation you have in a given case, you always find it necessary to take account of the manner in which, and the reasons why, it was experienced at all.

—Angell (1906, p. 67)

4.1 Principle 2: The Encoding– Retrieval Principle

The most commonly cited principle of memory, according to the literature search we reported in Chapter 1, is the encoding specificity principle (Tulving & Thomson, 1973). Our version of this is called the encoding–retrieval principle to emphasize that memory depends on the relation between the conditions at encoding and the conditions at retrieval. The name "encoding specificity" leaves "retrieval" out of the name, suggesting that the most important aspect is the encoding.[1] Thus, our version of this principle states that memory depends on the relation between the conditions at encoding and the conditions at retrieval.

---

[1] Note that, even though it is not indicated by the name, Tulving and Thomson's (1973) definition of the encoding specificity principle *does* include retrieval: "... the encoding specificity principle: What is stored is determined by what is perceived and how it is encoded, and what is stored determines what retrieval cues are effective in providing access to what is stored." (p. 353)

4.2 Encoding Specificity

An appreciation for the importance of the encoding–retrieval interaction came about as the result of studies that examined the potency of various cues to elicit items from memory. A strong cue is a word that elicits a particular target word most of the time. For example, when most people hear the word *bloom*, the first word that pops into their head is often *flower*. A weak cue is a word that only rarely elicits a particular target. When people hear *fruit*, they respond with *flower* only about 1% of the time. A reasonable prediction seems to be that strong cues should be better than weak cues for eliciting the correct item. However, this inference is not entirely correct because it fails to take into account the relationship between the encoding and retrieval conditions. For example, Thomson and Tulving (1970) reported an experiment in which they manipulated what cues were present at study and test. Some target words were presented alone at study, and some were presented along with a weak cue. At test, there were three cue conditions: no cue, a weak cue, or a strong cue. The results, shown as the probability of recalling the correct target word, are displayed in Table 4.1.

When there was no cue present at study, a strong cue at test led to better performance (0.68) than either a weak cue (0.43) or no cue (0.49). However, when there was a weak cue present at study, the weak cue at test led to better performance (0.82) than a strong cue (0.23). The important aspect of this result is that the effectiveness of even a long-standing strong cue depends crucially on the processes that occurred at study and the cues available at test.

This basic idea became the foundation of the transfer-appropriate processing framework. Transfer-appropriate processing can be seen as both a processing view (as described in Chapter 2) and also as a functional statement in that it fundamentally describes "what memory is doing" (Toth & Hunt, 1999, p. 255).

TABLE 4.1 The Proportion of Items Correctly Recalled as a Function of the Presence or Absence of Various Types of Cues at Study and Retrieval

	Retrieval Cue		
Study Cue	None	Weak	Strong
None	0.49	0.43	0.68
Weak	0.30	0.82	0.23

Note: Data from Thomson & Tulving (1970). *Journal of Experimental Psychology, 86*, 255–262.

4.3 Transfer-Appropriate—Not Similar—Processing

Taken literally, all that transfer-appropriate processing requires is that the processing done at encoding be appropriate given the processing that will be required at test; it permits processing that is identical and permits processing that is similar. It also, however, permits processing that is completely different as long as it is appropriate.

As Nairne (2002a) points out, however, many proponents of this view act as if the name were "transfer similar processing" and express the idea as requiring a "match" or "overlap" between study and test. One reason for this emphasis on matching and similarity might be that in the Thomson and Tulving (1970) data, the best performance is indeed in the condition in which the cues match (i.e., weak cues at both study and test). However, just because increasing the match sometimes leads to enhanced retention does not mean that it is the match that is the critical variable. Nairne offers an extensive analysis that shows that any formulation of transfer-appropriate processing that requires a match between encoding and retrieval is proposing an account that is fundamentally flawed: "The overall match *per se* doesn't predict anything about retention—memory might improve, stay the same, or get worse" (Nairne, 2002a, p. 393). That is, one can easily set up situations in which the degree of match is improved and memory retention is worse, or the degree of match is decreased and memory is better, or the degree of match is changed (either increased or decreased) and it has no effect on retention. Match, then, is simply not the critical variable in determining memory performance.

Here, we add two more examples to those already noted by Nairne (2001, 2002a) that show why match is not predictive. The first is an existence proof that shows it is possible to construct a plausible account of memory in which the "match" between the cue and the desired memory does not predict recall. As the "match" between the cue and the target increases, performance can either increase, stay the same, or decrease. The second is an empirical example.

4.3.1 The Irrelevance of Match: Theoretical Example

We use the feature model (Nairne, 1990) for the existence proof. A complete understanding of the model is not necessary in order to illustrate that the degree of match between the cue and target is irrelevant to overall levels of performance.[2] The model gets its name from the fact that items in memory are represented as vectors of features, a common assumption in many models of memory (e.g., Hintzman, 1991). At its core, the model is based on a version of Luce's (1963) choice rule, which states that the probability of sampling a particular item in memory, M_j, given a particular cue, C_i, is given by the similarity between the cues and the item divided by the sum of the cues to other possible responses:

$$P_s\left(M_j \mid C_i\right) = \frac{S_{ij}}{\sum\limits_{k=1}^{n} S_{ik}}$$

Similarity, here, is derived from the relative number of mismatching features, m.

$$S_{ij} = e^{-m_{ij}}$$

The measure of mismatch between cue i and memory j, m_{ij}, is defined as the number of features that mismatch divided by the number of features compared.

Table 4.2 shows three items (Target and Alternates 1 and 2) stored within the feature model. In this example, each item has 10 features and each feature can take a value from 1 to 5. The table also shows three different retrieval cues (Cue 1, Cue 2, and Cue 3). The cues also have 10 features, which can take values from 1 to 5. However, the cues also include missing features, represented by a value of 0.

The three cues vary in the degree of "match" to the target. According to transfer similar processing, Cue 2 is the best retrieval cue for the target because it is the best match (i.e., the most similar): 7 out of 10 features have the same value. Within the feature model, however, Cue 3 is the best retrieval cue, even though it is the worst match: only 3 out of 10 features have the same value. Table 4.3 shows why this is the case.

Cue 1 has five features that match those of the target (features three through seven), and therefore, five mismatching features. The proportion of mismatching features is thus 0.5, and the similarity between Cue 1 and the Target is

$$S_{ij} = e^{-0.5} = 0.607$$

---

[2] The interested reader is referred to Nairne (1990) and Neath (2000) for details.

TABLE 4.2 Feature Values for 3 Items Stored in the
Feature Model (Target and Alternates 1 and 2), and
Feature Values for 3 Different Cues

	Feature Number									
	1	2	3	4	5	6	7	8	9	10
Target	1	2	3	4	5	1	2	3	4	5
Alternate 1	1	2	3	5	4	1	2	3	4	4
Alternate 2	1	2	3	1	2	3	4	1	2	3
Cue 1	0	0	3	4	5	1	2	0	0	0
Cue 2	1	2	3	4	5	1	2	1	2	3
Cue 3	0	0	0	4	5	0	0	0	0	5

Note: The shaded areas show overlap between the cues and the target.

TABLE 4.3 The Number and Proportion of Mismatching Features
Between the 3 Cues and Each of 3 Possible Targets Shown in
Table 4.2, as well as the Resulting Similarity and Probability of
Sampling

		Number of Mismatching Features	Proportion of Mismatching Features	Similarity	Probability of Sampling
Cue 1	Target	5	0.50	0.607	0.402
	Alt. 1	7	0.70	0.497	0.329
	Alt. 2	9	0.90	0.407	0.269
Cue 2	Target	3	0.30	0.741	0.367
	Alt. 1	5	0.50	0.607	0.301
	Alt. 2	4	0.40	0.670	0.332
Cue 3	Target	7	0.70	0.497	0.403
	Alt. 1	10	1.00	0.368	0.299
	Alt. 2	10	1.00	0.368	0.299

Note: Note how a high similarity value (0.741) does not necessarily result in a high probability of sampling.

Cue 1 has seven mismatching features with Alternate 1, so the similarity between the two is $e^{-0.7}$, or 0.497. Cue 1 has nine mismatching features with Alternate 2, so the similarity between the two is $e^{-0.9}$, or 0.407.

The probability of sampling the Target, given Cue 1, is 0.402:

$$P_s\left(T \mid C_1\right) = \frac{S_{ij}}{\sum_{k=1}^{n} S_{ik}} = \frac{0.607}{0.607 + 0.497 + 0.407} = 0.402$$

In this example, then, a cue that matches half of the features of the target will sample that item 40.2% of the time.

Now, consider Cue 2. This is a better match to the target, as only three features mismatch. The similarity between Cue 2 and the Target is $e^{-0.3}$, or 0.741. However, it is also more similar to the Alternative items. Because of this, Cue 2 will sample the target less often than Cue 1, only 36.7% of the time.

Finally, consider Cue 3. This is the worst match with the target as there are seven mismatching features. The similarity between Cue 3 and the Target is $e^{-0.7}$, or 0.497; however, it is also the least similar to the alternatives. Therefore, Cue 3 will sample the target slightly more often than Cue 1, 40.3% of the time.

Thus, the feature model can readily produce cases in which increasing the match between a cue and target causes performance to get worse and decreasing the match causes performance to get better. Nairne's (2002a) example showed how increasing the match resulted in identical performance; here, we have shown how increasing the match can also increase or decrease performance. The point is that it is not the match that is the key ingredient. The retrieval conditions include other possible responses, and these other items can affect performance. The most accurate description, then, is that it is the relation between encoding and retrieval that matters, not the degree of match or similarity.

4.3.2 The Irrelevance of Match: Empirical Example

Simulations can be convincing, but empirical demonstrations are perhaps even more powerful. To those empirical demonstrations already noted by Nairne (2001, 2002a), we add one more. Gardiner, Craik, and Birtwistle (1972) used a version of the Brown–Peterson task, named after Brown (1958) and Peterson and Peterson (1959). In a typical Brown–Peterson task, people see three items and are then engaged in some unrelated activity to prevent rehearsal. Finally, the subjects are asked to recall the items. The typical finding is that performance systematically decreases as more trials are experienced, with substantial decreases being observed with as few as four trials (Keppel & Underwood, 1962).[3]

The experiment reported by Gardiner et al. (1972) differed from the more usual Brown–Peterson tasks in two important ways. First, the three to-be-remembered items came from the one of two categories, each of which could be subdivided into two further categories. For example, games can be either indoor or outdoor games; flowers can be either

---

[3] The buildup of proactive interference is discussed in more detail in Chapter 5.

wild or garden flowers. Second, different conditions received different cues, but all prior to retrieval. For example, on Trial 1, all received the cue "games" and then saw three examples, followed by some distracting activity. Trials 2 and 3 were identical, except that the cue was not repeated. On all of these trials, the to-be-remembered items came from the category "games." Unknown to the subjects, all of the games were actually outdoor games; on Trial 4, the to-be-remembered items were still games, but now were indoor games. (Other subjects were switched in the reverse direction, and still others received the flowers manipulation.) On Trial 4, the control group still received no cue. The experimental group saw the items, performed the distractor activity, and then received the cue "indoor games" immediately prior to retrieval.

In the control group, performance on Trial 4 was slightly worse than on Trial 3, the usual finding in Brown–Peterson tasks. In the experimental group, however, performance on Trial 4 was significantly better than on Trial 3. The important point is that subjects in the experimental group were presented with new information at retrieval that was not available at encoding; therefore, there was a decrease in the match between encoding and retrieval. Because of this, it is likely that the processing done at encoding and retrieval differed in the experimental group, but the different processing done at retrieval was more appropriate than the processing done at encoding.

The data from Gardiner et al. (1972) are consistent with the idea that performance can improve if the conditions at retrieval differ from the conditions at encoding as long as the conditions at retrieval are appropriate. Nairne (2001, 2002a), offers many other examples also consistent with this account. Later, we offer yet another example when we discuss the circumstances in which an item can be a worse retrieval cue for itself than some different item.

4.4 Implications of Principle 2

As Tulving (1983, p. 239) noted, the dynamic relation between encoding and retrieval conditions prohibits any statements that take the following forms:

1. "Items (events) of class X are easier to remember than items (events) of class Y."
2. "Encoding operations of class X are more effective than encoding operations of class Y."
3. "Retrieval cues of class X are more effective than retrieval cues of class Y."

Absolute statements that do not specify both the encoding and the retrieval conditions are meaningless because an experimenter can easily change some aspect of the encoding or retrieval conditions and greatly change the memory performance. We view each of the foregoing three statements as a corollary (in the sense of a natural consequence or result) of Principle 2.

4.4.1 Corollary A: Items Do Not Have Intrinsic Mnemonic Properties

Many articles and textbooks state that "pictures are easier to remember than words."[4] When a recognition test is used and the measure of memory is the number of items correctly recognized as being on the list, pictures are indeed remembered better than words, the so-called picture superiority effect (e.g., Paivio, Rogers, & Smythe, 1968). However, the statement "pictures are easier to remember than words" is correct only some of the time because there are studies in which words are easier to remember than pictures.

As one example, Weldon and Roediger (1988; see also Roediger & Weldon, 1987) used an indirect test (word fragment completion) and incidental learning rather than a standard recognition test. In this kind of task, there are two phases. In phase 1, the subjects were exposed to the items, both words and pictures. Phase 2 was the actual test, and it required two groups: an experimental group that was in phase 1 and a control group that was not in phase 1. The test consisted of word fragments, and the subjects were asked to complete the fragment with the first word that popped into their head. For example, if they saw the word fragment $t \_ b \_ g g \_ n$, a solution would be *toboggan*. The measure of memory, priming, was the difference between the mean proportion of fragments completed by the experimental group and the mean proportion completed by the control group. Weldon and Roediger found that word fragments that could be completed to form a word that had been shown in phase 1 were more likely to be completed than those fragments that could be completed to form the name of a picture that had been shown in phase 1. Using word fragment completion as the task and priming as the measure, words are remembered better than pictures. Weldon, Roediger, and Challis (1989) replicated this experiment and showed that a word superiority effect could be found with direct tasks provided the cues available at test are appropriate to the encoding instructions. Other studies have confirmed the idea that the usual picture superiority effect is

---

[4] References omitted to protect the guilty.

due to encoding–retrieval interactions rather than an inherent mnemonic advantage for pictures over words (McBride & Dosher, 2002).

According to Corollary A, then, one cannot say that one kind of stimulus, such as a picture, is inherently more memorable than another kind of stimulus, such as a word, unless one specifies the encoding and retrieval conditions.

4.4.2   Corollary B: Processes Do Not Have Intrinsic Mnemonic Properties

Just as with items, one cannot make absolute statements about the mnemonic properties of various types of processes. According to the levels of processing framework (Craik & Lockhart, 1972), deeper types of processing, such as semantic or meaning-based processing, will lead to better memory performance than more shallow types of processing, such as processing items based on how they look or sound. Thus, if you rate words for pleasantness—a deep task because you need to think about what the word means and consider the word's various connotations—you will recall more items on a free recall test than if you judged whether the words contained a particular letter (Hyde & Jenkins, 1973). However, if the test is changed, shallow processing can lead to better performance than deep processing.

For example, Morris, Bransford, and Franks (1977) presented sentences in which a word was missing. In one condition, subjects judged whether a target word made semantic sense if filled in the blank. For example, the sentence might be "The (blank) had a silver engine" and the target word might be *train*. In a different condition, subjects judged whether the target word rhymed with another. In this case, the sentence might be "(Blank) rhymes with legal" and the target word might be *eagle*. Two different tests were used. One test was a standard recognition test, in which a target word was presented and subjects were asked whether it had been seen previously. The second test was a rhyming recognition test, in which subjects were asked whether a word rhymed with one of the target words. With a standard recognition test, the deeper encoding process (whether the word fit in the sentence) led to better performance than did the more shallow encoding process (whether the word rhymed). However, with the rhyme recognition test, the shallow processing led to better performance than did the deep processing.

Corollary B, then, holds that one cannot say "deep processing is better than shallow processing" or, more generally, that one type of processing is better than another unless the encoding and retrieval conditions are specified.

4.4.3 Corollary C: Cues Do Not Have Intrinsic Mnemonic Properties

Just as with items and processes, one cannot make absolute statements about the mnemonic properties of retrieval cues. It might seem reasonable that the best memory cue for an item is the item itself, a so-called copy cue. That is, if we wanted to find out whether you remembered seeing the word *chair* on a list, we would use a cue that included a copy of the item we were interested in. However, this argument has been invalidated using a procedure known as "recognition failure of recallable words." In this paradigm (e.g., Nilsson, Law, & Tulving, 1988; Wallace, 1978; Watkins & Tulving, 1975), the subject studies a list of word pairs in which the first word in the pair is a weak cue of the second word; for example, *glue* might be paired with *chair*. Then, a word that is a strong cue is given, such as *table*, and subjects are asked to write down as many word as they can that are associated with *table*. A recognition test is then given in which a copy cue (the word *chair* itself) is used, and subjects often fail to recognize this item as one of the words on the original list. The final test is cued-recall, where *glue* is the cue. Now, subjects are quite likely to recall the word they earlier failed to recognize. *Chair* is not always an effective cue when trying to remember *chair*.[5]

According to Corollary C, then, one cannot say that copy cues are the most effective cue or, more generally, that one type of cue is better than another unless one specifies both the encoding and retrieval conditions.

4.4.4 Corollary D: Forgetting Must Be due to Extrinsic Factors

According to Corollary A, items do not have intrinsic mnemonic properties. This implies that forgetting is not due to the intrinsic mnemonic properties of items or, to state Corollary D, forgetting must be due to extrinsic factors. In most areas of memory research, forgetting is seen as due to retrieval failure, often ascribed to some form of interference. There are, however, two areas of memory research that propose that forgetting is due to an intrinsic property of the memory trace, namely, decay.

It should be noted at the outset that most theorists who propose that items in memory decay do not specify how this works in any detail. The two most common accounts view decay as either a mathematical convenience in a model, in which a parameter t is associated with time and

---

[5] A related finding is that presenting the to-be-remembered items to the subject at test does not necessarily reinstate item information (Neath, 1997).

leads to worse performance, or as some loss of information, in which it is unclear exactly what aspect of memory is decaying and what parts remain. In principle, a decay theory of memory could be proposed that is specific and testable, such as a process analogous to radioactive decay, in which it is understood precisely what is lost and what remains. Thus far, no such decay theory exists.

Decay is posited as the forgetting mechanism in only two areas of memory research, sensory memory and short-term/working memory. A detailed critique of these areas is beyond the scope of the current chapter; rather, the reader is referred to a recent review by Nairne (2003; see also Crowder & Surprenant, 2000; Neath & Surprenant, 2003). Here, we briefly review both applications of decay theory.

4.4.4.1 Forgetting in Sensory Memory

The evidence for sensory memory as a separate memory system is not nearly as strong or compelling as it used to appear. Indeed, as reviewed in Chapter 2, almost all versions of the multiple memory systems account of memory omit sensory memory as a separate system.

Rather than positing a separate memory system for sensory information, most researchers now emphasize the difference between two forms of persistence, stimulus persistence and information persistence (see, e.g., Coltheart, 1980). A typical visible persistence task might involve a synchrony judgment: A stimulus is presented, followed by an interval of variable duration, and then followed by a signal, such as a tone. The subject is asked to adjust the signal so that its appearance coincides with the disappearance of the stimulus. If the subject adjusts the signal such that it appears 150 ms after the true offset of the stimulus, then one can infer that the original stimulus persisted for 150 ms. In contrast, a typical information persistence task would involve trying to extract some information from the original stimulus. The standard Sperling (1960) partial report task involves presenting a matrix of stimuli (usually letters) for a brief period (around 50 ms). After a variable delay, a signal is presented that indicates which part of the matrix should be recalled. Performance in this partial report condition is compared to performance in a whole report condition, in which all the information in the matrix is recalled. When the matrix is shown for 50 ms, the partial report advantage lasts approximately 500 ms. Recent experimental work suggests, contrary to most conceptions of sensory memory, that visible persistence tasks and information persistence tasks are not measuring the same thing (Loftus & Irwin, 1998).

Most likely, stimulus persistence is not part of memory, as most people would define that term. Rather, there is an emerging consensus that it is the result of a particular continuing pattern of neural activity in response to the original stimulus. One key finding that argues against decay here is the inverse duration effect: Stimulus persistence decreases with increases in stimulus duration (e.g., Bowen, Pola, & Matin, 1974). It is hard to conceive of a form of forgetting where the longer you are exposed to a stimulus, the faster the forgetting.

Whereas stimulus persistence is best thought of as not memory, information persistence is now increasingly viewed as the same type of memory as short-term/working memory in that it shows the same patterns of item and order errors as well as output interference and category cueing effects (Nairne, 2003; Neath, 2005; Neath & Surprenant, 2003).[6] Given that information persistence is best described as resulting from the same type of memory as short-term/working memory, there is thus only one type of memory left in which decay is proposed as a mechanism for forgetting, and we examine this next.

4.4.4.2 *Forgetting in Short-Term/Working Memory*

One reason that time-based forgetting, such as decay, is often invoked is the common belief that short-term/working memory is immune to interference, especially proactive interference (e.g., Cowan, 2000). This is simply not so. The suffix effect (Crowder, 1967; Dallet, 1965) is a retroactive interference effect. Recall of the last item in a list of auditorily presented items is impaired if the list is followed by a stimulus suffix, an irrelevant item that is the same on every trial and that does not need to be recalled or processed by the subject. The acoustic confusion effect (Conrad, 1964), the finding that lists of similar-sounding items are harder to recall than lists of dissimilar-sounding items, is an example of both proactive and retroactive interference in short-term/working memory. The first item in the list is affected by retroactive interference; the final item is affected by proactive interference; the other items are potentially affected by both RI and PI. As a third example, Tehan and his colleagues (e.g., Tehan & Humphreys, 1996, 1998; Tolan & Tehan, 1999) have developed a task in which PI can be observed in short-term memory settings. Subjects are asked if an instance of a particular category was seen on the immediately preceding list of four items. They are to ignore any instances prior to the most recent list. However, if there are either semantically similar or phonologically similar items in the preceding list, PI can be observed. Thus, interference effects are readily observed in the short term. Chapter 3 reviewed additional evidence illustrating that PI can be observed in such tasks.

The idea of a separate short-term memory has been challenged almost since it was first proposed (e.g., Melton, 1963) and has continued to be

---

[6] Or as we have rephrased this elsewhere, "the bit that's sensory isn't memory, and the bit that's memory isn't sensory" (Surprenant & Neath, 2008, p. 37).

challenged (e.g., Crowder, 1982; Neath & Surprenant, 2008; Surprenant & Neath, 2008). Recently, Nairne (2002b) provided a critical evaluation of the current "standard model" of short-term/working memory (e.g., Baddeley, 1986; Burgess & Hitch, 1999; Cowan, 1995; Shiffrin, 1999). In this version, permanent knowledge is activated, and the collective set of activated items is defined as short-term memory. The activation decays over time and can be offset by refreshing the decaying items through rehearsal. The key finding supporting this idea is that words that take less time to pronounce are recalled better than otherwise equivalent words that take more time to pronounce (Baddeley, Thomson, & Buchanan, 1975). This effect has been characterized as "the best remaining solid evidence" for decay offset by rehearsal (Cowan, 1995, p. 4).

This result is not without controversy: Lovatt, Avons, and Masterson (2000) have shown that this result holds only for one particular set of words. When other sets of words are used, the time-based word length effect is not observed. In fact, there is only one set of words that produces the effect, and eight other sets that should produce the effect do not do so (see Neath, Bireta, & Surprenant, 2003).[7]

Another finding historically used to support time-based decay comes from the Brown–Peterson paradigm. In this task, subjects are given three items (usually consonants) to remember, and then are prevented from rehearsing by engaging in a distractor task. The original finding was the recall of the items (in the correct order) decreased the longer the distractor duration. This was interpreted as showing that when rehearsal is prevented, items will decay over the course of 20–30 s. However, these findings are better conceived as supporting an interference rather than decay explanation (see Neath & Surprenant, 2003, pp. 125–135, for a detailed review). The two key findings problematic for a decay explanation are the buildup and the release from PI (see also the discussion of this in Chapter 5). Decay predicts the same decrease for the same duration of distractor activity. Interference predicts differential effects depending on the presence or absence of interfering items. Numerous studies support the interference predictions and disconfirm predictions made on the basis of a decay view (e.g., Keppel & Underwood, 1962; Gardiner, Craik, & Birtwhistle, 1972; Turvey, Brick, & Osborn, 1970).[8]

As a final example, Cowan, Saults, and Nugent (1997) presented data that suggested that the absolute amount of time that has passed before a memory test takes place does have an effect on subsequent performance. Their task involved comparing pure tones to determine

---

[7] For explanations of the word length effect without the concept of decay, see Hulme et al. (2006) and Neath and Nairne (1995).

[8] The experiment reported by Baddeley and Scott (1971) is often taken as showing decay in the Brown–Peterson paradigm. However, Neath (2006) showed how SIMPLE, a model with no decay, easily accounts for the results through the concept of inter-item interference.

whether they have the same or different frequency, and the main variable manipulated was the duration between various tones. However, Cowan, Saults, and Nugent (2001) performed further analyses to take into account an explanation based on differential distinctiveness (see Chapter 8). After ensuring that relative distinctiveness was held constant, Cowan et al. concluded that "we have failed to find clear evidence of decay in a situation that has often been viewed as one of the simplest paradigm cases for decay, namely in two-tone comparisons" (p. 326).

4.4.4.3 Forgetting due to the Passage of Time

Cohen's (1985) second law of memory states that the longer something has to be retained in memory, the less the likelihood that it will be remembered. Kihlstrom's (1994, p. 338) time-dependency principle states that "the memorability of an event declines as the length of the storage interval (i.e., between encoding and retrieval) increases." Both of these statements are incorrect.

Principle 2 states that memory depends on the relation between encoding and retrieval. Because of this, you cannot make absolute statements about memory unless you fully state the conditions at encoding and retrieval. It is trivially easy to construct an experiment in which memory for an item does not change or even gets better the longer the retention interval. Here, we provide only eight examples, although there are numerous other examples; a more complete review and discussion are offered by Capaldi and Neath (1995) and Bjork (2001).

Reminiscence is the name given to the finding that after repeated testing, new items will continue to be recalled (Payne, 1987). For example, on the first test, a given item might not be recalled. Time passes, and further study is not allowed. On test two, the item is now recalled. Spontaneous recovery is a second example of a phenomenon defined as better memory after more time has elapsed when there is no opportunity for further study. Although usually used to refer to effects apparent in conditioning in animals (i.e., after extinguishing a response, the response reappears after a delay), the same pattern of results is observable in humans (Wheeler, 1995).

A third example concerns the shift from recency to primacy. For example, Neath (1993) presented a list of four items followed by a probe recognition test in which the subject was asked to indicate whether the probe was in the list. When there was no delay between the end of presentation and the test, recall of the final item was excellent, whereas recall of the first item was quite poor. As the duration of the retention interval increased, memory of the final item decreased but memory for the first item increased. This effect has been replicated numerous times with many different kinds of stimuli (e.g., Knoedler, Hellwig, & Neath, 1999).

A fourth example concerns the reminiscence bump (Conway & Pleydell-Pearce, 2000). When people are asked to recall events from their life, they typically recall very few memories from infancy and early childhood. There is an increase, known as the reminiscence bump, for events that occurred between the ages of about 10–30, in that more events are recalled from this period than either earlier or later. For current purposes, events from this period are older than events from middle age, but they are recalled better.

A fifth example is the ratio rule in free recall (Glenberg Bradley, Kraus, & Renzaglia, 1983; see also Bjork & Whitten, 1974). The ratio rule relates the recency effect in free recall to the ratio of the duration of the inter-item presentation interval (IPI) and the retention interval (RI). Of key importance is that it is a ratio. That is, if the size of the recency effect is proportional to the ratio of the IPI divided by the RI, then the units of time do not matter: The ratio of 1 s to 1 s is the same as the ratio of 10 s to 10 s and that of 2 weeks to 2 weeks.

A sixth example concerns the continual distractor task. In this paradigm, the subject is presented with a to-be-remembered item, and then engages in some distracting activity before receiving the next item. Neath and Crowder (1990) showed that the total time an item had to be remembered was unrelated to subsequent recall. For example, the recall test occurred 56 s after presentation of the first item in both the I and D1 conditions, yet recall was substantially better in the latter condition than the former. The conditions differed in the distribution of distractor activity. Similarly, the first item in the control condition had to be retained for only 32 s, but this did not yield better performance than in D1.

A seventh example comes from the Brown–Peterson paradigm, in which a person is asked to remember three items for anywhere between 3 to 30 s. On the very first trial, performance is equivalent in the two conditions (Keppel & Underwood, 1962). That is, remembering something for 30 s does not lead to worse memory than remembering something for 3 s.

A final example comes from a modified Brown–Peterson paradigm used by Unsworth, Heitz, and Parks (2008). In the trials of interest, the subjects saw three consonants, and then were asked to count backwards for 8 s or 16 s before being asked to recall the three items. In one case, there was a 60 s gap between the end of one trial and the beginning of the next; in the other, there was a standard 1.5 s. The key finding is that performance in the 16 s condition (when it followed the 60 s gap) was better than in the 8 s condition (when it followed the 1.5 s gap). That is, memory was better when an item had to be retained for 16 s than when it had to be retained for half that time.

Of course, the key feature in this and most of the previous examples is that a memory trial is not performed in isolation: not only do the factors at encoding and retrieval play a role, but also factors on previous trials. A detailed explanation of these kinds of situations is given in Chapter 8 in conjunction with the relative distinctiveness principle.

You might be tempted to say, yes, well, there are occasions in which the passage of time is either uncorrelated with or even negatively correlated with memory performance, but on average, you do worse with longer retention intervals. However, this confirms that the putative principle—the memorability of an event declines as the length of the storage interval increases—is not correct. As McGeoch (1932, pp. 355–356) put it, because time and forgetting are not correlated to the extent implied by principle, "even if it were true in some cases, [it] is not the general law which it purports to be." One can make statements about the effects of absolute time, but only to the extent that one specifies both the conditions at encoding and those at retrieval.

4.5 Chapter Summary

The idea that one has to consider the relation between the conditions at encoding and those at retrieval has important implications. As noted by Tulving (1983), it means that items do not have intrinsic mnemonic properties, processes do not have intrinsic mnemonic properties, and cues do not have intrinsic mnemonic properties. It further follows that forgetting cannot be due to an intrinsic mnemonic property, such as time-based decay. Similarly, memory cannot be said to be worse the longer the information has to be remembered. These kinds of statements do not take into account the relation between the conditions at encoding and those at retrieval. Eight examples that illustrate no change or even better memory after a longer interval were provided.

Finally, thinking of the relation between encoding and retrieval offers a way of understanding why dissociations (and double dissociations) are found. For a multiple systems theorist, an individual might fail on one task but succeed on another because the knowledge to perform each task resides in a different memory storage unit, and one unit is destroyed and another remains intact. However, if we allow that different types of information are useful (different cues, different processes) for different types of tasks, and if we assume that subtle changes from encoding to retrieval can greatly affect performance, it is clear that dissociations are not only possible, but are in fact inevitable (Van Orden, Pennington, & Stone, 2001). According to this view, a double dissociation shows only that there were differences in the relation between the conditions at encoding and retrieval between the two conditions, groups, or people.

The Cue Overload Principle

It is not the load but the overload that kills.

—**Spanish Proverb**

5.1 Principle 3: The Cue Overload Principle

According to Principle 1, all memory is cue driven; according to Principle 3, cues are subject to overload. Watkins and Watkins (1975, p. 443) noted that cue overload is "emerging as a general principle of memory" and defined it as follows: "The efficiency of a functional retrieval cue in effecting recall of an item declines as the number of items it subsumes increases." As an analogy, think of a person's name as a cue. If you know only one person named Katherine, the name by itself is an excellent cue when asked how Katherine is doing. However, if you also know Cathryn, Catherine, and Kathryn, then it is less useful in specifying which person is the focus of the question. More formally, a number of studies have shown experimentally that memory performance systematically decreases as the number of items associated with a particular retrieval cue increases (e.g., Bower, 1970; Earhard, 1967, 1977; Mathews, 1954; Tulving & Pearlstone, 1966).

5.2 Explanatory Power

The cue overload principle is an excellent example of a principle that offers explanatory power. In many situations, a decrease in memory performance can be attributed to cue overload. This may not be the ultimate explanation, as cue overload itself needs an explanation, but it does serve to link a variety of otherwise disparate findings together. As Watkins (2001, p. 192) notes, having the general principle unexplained may not be ideal, but "is a less disorderly state of affairs than one involving multiple unexplained phenomena." Here, we consider three examples of how the cue overload principle offers an explanation for a variety of otherwise disparate results.

5.2.1 Buildup of and Release From Proactive Interference

Watkins and Watkins (1975) first used cue overload as a way of explaining the buildup of proactive interference in the Brown–Peterson paradigm (Brown, 1958; Peterson & Peterson, 1959). In this paradigm, subjects see three items (e.g., three consonants or three words) and are then given a distractor task to prevent rehearsal and recoding. The distractor activity is chosen to minimize any interference with the to-be-remembered items; when letters are the stimuli, the distractor task is something like counting backwards by 3s or by 7s. Following the distractor period, the subjects are asked to recall the three items in order. Peterson and Peterson (1959) found that after 18 s of distracting activity, three consonants were recalled only 10% of the time.

Subsequent research showed that analyzing the data in this way obscured an important finding. Instead of averaging over dozens or scores of trials, Keppel and Underwood (1962) scored performance on the first few trials separately. What they found was that performance systematically decreased from Trial 1 to Trial 3. On Trial 1, performance was almost perfect even after 18 s of distractor activity: the proportion of items correctly recalled was 0.97. On Trial 2, this dropped to 0.69, and on Trial 3, it dropped further to 0.56. According to a cue overload interpretation, the category of the to-be-remembered items is a significant retrieval cue. It is as if the subject were asking at test, "What were the three letters I just saw?" As more trials occur, the number of potential responses increases. The cue, in this case, letters, becomes less and less helpful, as there are more and more letters to choose from. The number of items subsumed under the category name increases, and performance decreases.

The cue overload account makes a prediction about what happens when the type of to-be-remembered information is changed on Trial 4. Consider the case in which subjects receive three trials, each of which uses consonants as the to-be-remembered stimuli. In the control condition, they receive consonants on the fourth trial as well. In the experimental condition, the type of stimuli is changed to three numbers. Performance on the fourth trial is dramatically increased relative to the control condition

(Wickens, 1970; Wickens, Born, & Allen, 1963).[1] This increase in performance on Trial 4 is termed release from proactive interference. According to cue overload theory, subjects can now use a different, nonoverloaded cue ("What were the three numbers I just saw?"). Importantly, if Trial 4 is followed by more trials with numbers, PI builds up again (Wickens, 1970). These results have been replicated numerous times.

One key prediction from the cue overload perspective is that if the subject is unaware that the category has changed, there will be no release from PI even if the category does change. Gardiner, Craik, and Birtwistle (1972) examined this hypothesis using two categories of items, each of which could be divided into subgroups. Some subjects received types of games, others types of flowers. Unnoticed by the subjects, the first three trials were all indoor games (or wildflowers), and the fourth trial was outdoor games (or garden flowers). All subjects received this subtle change in categories, but only two of the groups were informed of the change. One group was informed prior to presentation of the fourth trial (the presentation group), and the other group was informed after presentation of the fourth trial but prior to retrieval (the retrieval group). Nothing extra was said to the control subjects. Consistent with the cue overload explanation, the control subjects continued to be affected by the buildup of PI on Trial 4, as to them there was no category change: If the change is unnoticed, then the presumed cue used will be the same as on previous trials and there will be no release from PI. Both the presentation and retrieval groups showed an equivalent release from PI. Gardiner et al. argued that this release of PI must be a retrieval effect because that is the only place both the recall and retrieval groups had the category change information at the same time: The retrieval group could still take advantage of the change, even though they were unaware of this subtle change in category at encoding.

5.2.2 List Length Effect

The list length effect is the finding that recall of a given item from a list becomes less likely as the length of the list increases. Assuming that one retrieval cue could be a particular list in a particular context, then cue overload explains this result (Watkins, 2001): the more items subsumed by this cue, the poorer the performance. Although this explanation might seem

---

[1] There are usually two other conditions in these experiments: Control 2 has numbers on every trial, and Experiment 2 has a change from numbers to consonants. This way, one can show it is the change per se that is driving the effect rather than a change from one specific type of stimulus to another.

to be simply a restatement of the effect, the cue overload principle is more abstract than the list length effect. It is the same explanation offered for the buildup and release of proactive interference in the Brown–Peterson paradigm (Section 5.2.1) and the same explanation for the difference in memory performance following deep processing compared to shallow processing (Section 5.2.4). As such, the more abstract principle links the results (see also Watkins, 1979).

A second reason that this is not merely a restatement of the result is that the cue overload principle can be instantiated in a very specific way to show exactly how it might work. For example, Raaijmaker and Shiffrin (1981, p. 130), when describing SAM (Search of Associative Memory), one of the so-called global memory models, state that "the cue overload principle is, in SAM, one of the fundamental bases of retrieval failure from memory." A detailed presentation of the model is not possible here.[2] However, the basic idea can be easily understood. Within the model, it is assumed that the cue is associated not only with the response, but also, residually, to each word in the list. In the equation that describes the probability of sampling a particular item, given a particular cue, the strength of the association between the cue and the target item is in the numerator; the strength of the association between the cue and the other items in the list is in the denominator. Thus, as the list length is increased, the probability of sampling an item for retrieval decreases because, on average, the magnitude of the denominator will increase.

5.2.3 The Fan Effect

The *fan effect* is the name given to the finding that response times increase (and error rates increase) on memory tests when the number of items associated with a probe increases. In an early study, Anderson (1974) had subjects learn a series of 26 statements, each of which took the form *A person is in a location.* (e.g., the professor is in the park; the lawyer is in the church). The person could appear once or twice in the set, and the location could appear once or twice in the set. There were thus four types of sentences: (a) Person once, location once; (b) person twice, location once; (c) person once, location twice; and (d) person twice, location twice. The subjects studied this material until it could all be recalled accurately, after which they were given a speeded recognition test. A sentence was shown, and the subjects were asked to indicate, as quickly as they could, whether it was one of the set they had memorized.

---

[2] The interested reader is referred to pages 364–372 of Neath and Surprenant (2003) for an introductory overview of SAM.

The key finding was that the more times an item appeared, the slower the response time. For sentences in which the subject and location each appeared only once, the mean response time was 1.11 s. For sentences in which both the subject and location appeared twice, the response time was the slowest: 1.22 s. For sentences in which either the subject appeared twice and the location once, or the subject once and the location twice, the response times were in between at 1.17 s. Thus, the time to correctly recognize a sentence increased as the number of facts studied about the person increased, and also as the number of facts studied about the location increased.

According to a cue overload explanation, the less a cue is overloaded, the more likely the cue will result in correct recall. Operationally, this can be manipulated by having subjects focus more on the person or more on the location. Sohn, Anderson, Reder, and Goode (2004) did just this. Subjects were induced to focus on either the person or the location by seeing either a photograph of a person or a grid on which the locations were shown. Consistent with a cue overload explanation, the size of the fan effect was larger for the focused dimension than for the nonfocused dimension (98 vs. 63 ms for the person and location effect when the focus was on the person, and 73 vs. 118 ms for the person and location effect when the focus was on the location).

Once again, then, the cue overload principle provides an explanation that is more general than just a restatement of the finding. The same idea that explains the fan effect is also useful in understanding why recall decreases as list length increases, why proactive interference increases over trials, why release from proactive interference occurs if the type of material is changed, and, as we will see in Section 5.2.4, why the levels of processing effect occur.

5.2.4 Levels of Processing

In a typical levels of processing experiment, the goal is to manipulate how a person processes information. To do this, the experimenter usually does not mention that there will be a memory test so that the subjects do not feel it necessary to rehearse or otherwise come up with their own processing strategy. Instead, the experimenter devises a "cover story" in order to manipulate the type of processing that the subject performs. For a shallow task, the subject might be asked to indicate whether the presented item rhymes with another. For a deep task, the subject might be asked to indicate whether the word makes sense in a particular sentence. After all of the words have been presented, the subject is given a surprise free recall test, in which the goal is to recall as many of the words as possible, or a surprise recognition test, in which a word is shown and the subject is asked to indicate if it was one of the words processed. More words are recalled and recognized following deep processing than shallow processing.

The original idea was based on the assumption that the deeper the level of processing (or analysis), the better the memory (Craik & Lockhart, 1972). Numerous experiments with a wide variety of tasks were reported that were consistent with this idea. But why is deep processing better than shallow? Craik (1979, p. 457) invoked a cue overload explanation: "there is more built-in cue overload for shallow encodings" than for deep encodings. Other factors being equal, there are fewer sounds that could serve as possible cues than meanings. Thus, sounds are more likely to become overloaded than meanings, resulting in a less useful cue.

This account works even when the level of processing is manipulated at both study and test. As described in Chapter 4, both encoding and retrieval conditions need to be considered in any memory task. The study by Morris, Bransford and Franks (1977; outlined in Section 4.4.2) is the classic demonstration of this. Morris et al. (1977) gave subjects two orienting tasks at study: one that focused attention on surface features of the items (rhyme) and another that focused on deeper analysis of the items (meaning). At test there were two different tasks, a rhyme recognition task where information about rhyming words on the study test was queried and a standard recognition test, relying on meaning-based information. With the standard recognition test they replicated the levels of processing effect; memory was best for the items encoded in a deeper, more meaningful manner. However, the rhyming test led to the opposite pattern; better recall of the items that were encoded shallowly than those that were encoded deeply.

The key issue here, however, concerns the comparison between performance when there was deep processing at both study and test and when there was shallow processing at both study and test. In the experiment reported by Morris et al. (1977; see also Fisher & Craik, 1977; Nelson, Wheeler, Borden, & Brooks, 1974), the deep-deep condition led to better memory than the shallow-shallow condition. This is consistent with the cue overload account because, all else being equal, the shallow cues will have more pre-experimentally associated items than the deep ones.

This account makes possible several testable predictions. First, it should be possible to construct a situation in which deep and shallow cues are equated and the levels of processing effect disappears. Nelson and Brooks (1974) did just this. Of most relevance to the cue overload account, they created a set of rhyme cues and synonym cues that were equated for set size. To do this, they collected normative data. A large group of subjects were asked to write down the first word they thought of that was a synonym of a target word. In the rhyme condition, the instructions were almost the same, except that the word should rhyme with the target. Set size was estimated from the number of different responses given to each target word. Using this measure, the mean set size for rhymes was 6.83 and the mean set size for synonyms was 6.42. In a subsequent free recall test using these stimuli, the levels of processing effect disappeared.

A second prediction concerns what happens when a deep cue is subjected to more overload than a shallow one. Parkin (1980) tested this by manipulating the level of processing of an interpolated task. Subjects were first asked to study a memory set of six items that all belonged to the same category (e.g., musical instruments). Then, one of two types of interpolated task occurred. In the semantic condition, the subject was given a particular subcategory (e.g., string instruments) and was asked to judge whether the next set of six items belonged to this subcategory. None of the items were in the memory set, but all belonged to the same higher-level category as the memory set. In the nonsemantic condition, the subjects saw exactly the same items as in the semantic condition, but rather than judging category membership, they reported the number of syllables in each word. Finally, the subjects were asked to recall the memory set. The proportion of items recalled from the memory set was better following the nonsemantic interpolated task (0.83) than following the semantic interpolated task (0.61). The explanation offered was that the most likely retrieval cue was the initial category (i.e., musical instruments), and that this cue would subsume more items when the interpolated task focused on category membership than on the number of syllables.

According to our view, then, it is not so much deep versus shallow processing that is critical, but rather the extent to which the cues are overloaded. Cue overload is a more fundamental[3] explanation than levels of processing. Again, it is not a complete explanation, as that requires a discussion of the relation between the encoding and retrieval conditions, the subject of our previous principle and Chapter 4.

5.3 Objections to Cue Overload

The cue overload principle can be, and has been, questioned on a variety of grounds. Here, we focus on two such issues. First, it might seem as if this principle violates an idea we introduced in Chapter 4, that cues do not have intrinsic mnemonic properties. Second, it has been argued that cue overload explanations of forgetting apply only in controlled laboratory settings and not in "real life."

---

[3] We were tempted to say "deeper"!

5.3.1 Violation of the Encoding–Retrieval Principle

In the preceding chapter, we argued that one corollary of the encoding–retrieval principle is that cues do not have intrinsic mnemonic properties. At first glance, one might think that the statement that cues are subject to overload implies that cues have an intrinsic mnemonic property, to wit, a capacity limitation. This interpretation of the principle, as described in this chapter, and as described in other papers (e.g., Wolters & Verduin, 1982), is not correct.

The easiest way to illustrate why the cue overload principle does not ascribe an intrinsic mnemonic property to a cue is by considering what would be necessary, experimentally, to demonstrate cue overload. First, there must be some encoding condition in which a cue and an item are associated. Second, there must be some other encoding condition in which the same cue is associated with a different item. Finally, there must be a retrieval attempt in which the cue is used. Cue overload would be shown when, for example, an experiment in which there are fewer encoding episodes in which a given cue is associated with different items results in better performance than an otherwise comparable condition with more such episodes. Thus, in its most simple incarnation, cue overload refers to the relation between the conditions at two study episodes and one retrieval episode. Changes in either the encoding or retrieval episodes could magnify or mitigate the effects of cue overload. At the heart of cue overload, then, is the relation between the conditions at (possibly multiple) encodings and those at retrieval.

Another way of making the same point is to consider a numerical example. A version of Luce's choice rule (see, e.g., Luce, 1959, 1963, 1977) can be seen as a form of cue overload. Part of the choice rule involves an estimate of the degree of association between a cue and some possible response. In order to avoid cumbersome circumlocutions, we use the term *strength* to describe this relation on a scale from 0.0 to 1.0. We intend the account to be as theoretically neutral as possible, and the term *strength* is not meant to imply anything special.

$$P_{ij} = \frac{S_{ij}}{\sum\limits_{k=1}^{n} S_{ik}}$$

The probability that cue i will elicit item j—P_{ij}—depends on the strength of the relation between cue i and item j, S_{ij}, divided by the sum of the strengths between cue i and the other n possible response items. Other factors being equal, the probability that a particular cue will elicit a particular response will decline as n increases (as long as the strength between the cues and items is greater than zero).

For example, consider a cue, A, and three possible items, J, K, and L. If Cue A is associated perfectly with item J (i.e., $S_{AJ} = 1.0$) and is not associated at all with the other items (i.e., $S_{AK} = 0.0$ and $S_{AL} = 0.0$), the probability that cue A will elicit item J is 1.0:

$$P_{AJ} = \frac{1}{1+0+0} = 1.0$$

If cue A becomes slightly associated with a second item, K (i.e., $S_{AK} = 0.1$), P_{AJ} decreases to 0.91 even if S_{AJ} remains unchanged:

$$P_{AJ} = \frac{1}{1+0.1+0} = 0.91$$

If cue A becomes slightly associated with a third item, L ($S_{AL} = 0.1$), P_{AJ} further decreases to 0.833.

$$P_{AJ} = \frac{1}{1+0.1+0.1} = 0.83$$

Cue overload, then, is not an intrinsic mnemonic property of the cue itself; rather, it is a property of the relation between the cue and one or more items as a consequence of the interaction between the encoding and retrieval conditions.

5.3.2 Relevance of Cue Overload

Perhaps the most serious challenge to the cue overload principle is the claim that it may not be relevant to forgetting in everyday life; indeed, according to Wixted (2005, p. 7), "the only reason to believe that cue-overload effects play any role at all in everyday forgetting is that almost everyone can point to a few examples from their own lives." In our view, this statement is misleading because of the overly narrow way in which Wixted defines cue overload.

Wixted (2004a, 2005) identifies cue overload effects with performance on one specific type of paired associate test, usually referred to as an A-B, A-C test. Although there are a number of variations on this task, the typical procedure is to have subjects learn a list of paired associates (the A-B list) and then learn a second list with the same cues but different responses (the A-C list). Memory for the A-C list is tested by presenting the A term as a cue and asking for the appropriate item from the C list. Performance is worse compared to a condition in which the A-B list had not been learned, and the explanation is usually to invoke proactive interference. After reviewing the literature on this one task, Wixted concludes that cue overload due to proactive interference is observable only when the learning trials are massed; with distributed trials, such effects are not seen. "If learning [outside of the laboratory] is typically distributed, these results suggest that PI may not be a major source of forgetting in everyday life" (Wixted, 2004a, p. 240).

The major problem with this analysis is linking cue overload to this one type of test. Not only does it ignore cue overload due to retroactive interference using essentially the same paradigm (e.g., testing for B items rather than C), but it also ignores the fact that cue overload is observable in many other paradigms, several of which were described earlier. If one admits that cue overload is not exclusively related to proactive interference designs using only the A-B, A-C methodology, then there are no grounds to dismiss cue overload as one factor involved in everyday forgetting.

5.4 Chapter Summary

The cue overload principle states that the effectiveness of a cue will decrease the more items it subsumes. For example, if you need to remember to take a certain book to work tomorrow, you might imagine yourself locking the door to your house, carefully putting the keys away in your bag, and turning to leave. You would then imagine yourself cursing creatively as you have to fish out your keys, unlock your door, and re-enter the house to get the book you need. This cue is an excellent mnemonic to remember the book.[4] If you need to remember both the book and a DVD you need to return to the rental store, the cue would work less well. If you also add a bill that you need to mail, and more coffee for the machine in your office, the cue will work even less well.

The cue overload principle is an excellent example of how one can relate the findings of multiple paradigms at a more abstract level. In this chapter, we have examined only a few examples: the results from studies examining list length effects, the buildup and release from proactive interference, the fan effect, and the levels of processing effect. Many other paradigms have also invoked this principle, ranging from environmental context-dependent memory effects in recognition (Rutherford, 2004) to sentence processing (Van Dyke & McElree, 2006) to the effects of midazolam (a benzodiazepine) on memory (Reder et al., 2007). In all of these cases, performance decreases as the cue is overloaded. Rather than having a list of unrelated effects, we can put them all together as examples of a higher-level explanation.

---

[4] An even better mnemonic would be a brightly colored note taped to the door through which you will leave the house. It turns out that writing the information down is the mnemonic most often suggested by memory experts, from Plato to the present (Park, Smith, & Cavanaugh, 1990).

The Reconstruction Principle

From the content point of view the original never is and never can be literally duplicated. Functions, on the other hand, persist as well in mental as in physical life.

—J. R. Angell

6.1 Principle 4: The Reconstruction Principle

Memory, like all other cognitive processes, is inherently constructive. Information from encoding and cues from retrieval, as well as generic information, are all exploited to construct a response to a cue. Work in several areas has long established that people will use whatever information is available to help reconstruct or build up a coherent memory of a story or an event (e.g., Bartlett, 1932). However, although these strategies can lead to successful and accurate remembering in some circumstances, the same processes can lead to distortion or even confabulation in others (Estes, 1997). There are a great many studies demonstrating the constructive and reconstructive nature of memory, and the literature is quite well known. We begin by briefly reviewing the noncontroversial aspects of this area before expanding it into what might be seen as slightly more adventurous territory: semantic memory, immediate or short-term memory, very short-term memory, and sensory or iconic memory. If this property of memory is to be considered a principle by our definition, it should hold across all domains of memory.

6.2 Classic Demonstrations

A classic example of reconstructive memory concerns the ability to reproduce a simple line drawing. (See Figure 6.1.) Carmichael, Hogan, and Walter (1932) presented simple line drawings to subjects and told half of the subjects that the drawing looked like one particular object and told the other half of the subjects that the drawing looked like a second, different object. For example, one group of subjects might be told that the drawing resembled a pair of eyeglasses whereas the other group was told the drawing looked like a set of dumbbells. At a later test, the subjects were asked to draw the original figure as accurately as possible. Examples of reproduced figures can be seen in Figure 6.1. Most subjects changed the figure so that it looked more like the verbal label. The idea is that adding a verbal label provided another cue that was available at test, but the label was only partially helpful (i.e., it said only what the object was like, not what the object was). At test, the cue misled the subjects into reconstructing a drawing that made sense given the cue, but differed from the original drawing (see also Moore, 1910).

Perhaps the most well-known early study of reconstruction in memory was reported by Bartlett (1932). Bartlett asked English college students to reproduce an unfamiliar North American Native folktale entitled "The War of the Ghosts." The story is rather incoherent to Western ears and includes some supernatural events. Bartlett reported that with repeated retrievals the subjects "regularized" the story, making it follow the structure or schema of the more familiar Western fairy tale. Surprisingly, over the years there have been very few attempts to duplicate this result, and some questions have been raised about its replicability. However, Bergman and Roediger (1999; see also Wheeler & Roediger, 1992) conducted a close replication and repeated Bartlett's results: The critical variables are an unfamiliar story schema and repeated testing over long intervals.

These data and many others have been interpreted as showing the influence of preexisting knowledge structures or "schemas" that we develop to help us organize our knowledge and predict the events in particular situations. Schemas are idiosyncratic, active, dynamic, and constantly changing as new experiences are encountered. These properties that make them so flexible and adaptable also make them rather hard to study in a rigorous fashion, although some serious attempts have been made (e.g., Rumelhart, Smolensky, McClelland, & Hinton, 1986). Nonetheless, it is clear that recall of events is deeply influenced by a tendency to reconstruct them using whatever information is relevant and to repair holes or fill in the gaps that are present in memory with likely substitutes.

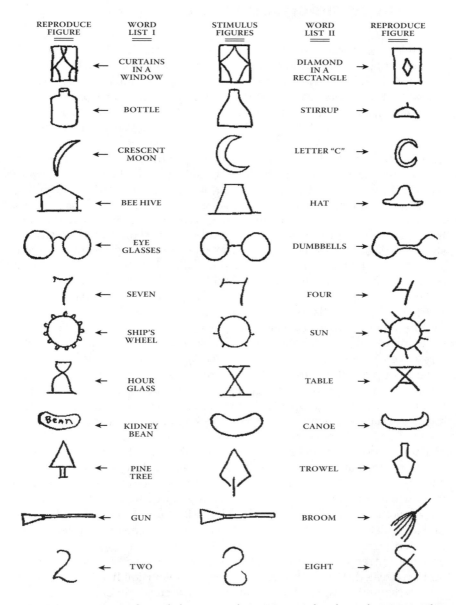

REPRODUCE FIGURE	WORD LIST I	STIMULUS FIGURES	WORD LIST II	REPRODUCE FIGURE
	← CURTAINS IN A WINDOW		DIAMOND IN A RECTANGLE →	
	← BOTTLE		STIRRUP →	
	← CRESCENT MOON		LETTER "C" →	
	← BEE HIVE		HAT →	
	← EYE GLASSES		DUMBBELLS →	
	← SEVEN		FOUR →	
	← SHIP'S WHEEL		SUN →	
	← HOUR GLASS		TABLE →	
	← KIDNEY BEAN		CANOE →	
	← PINE TREE		TROWEL →	
	← GUN		BROOM →	
	← TWO		EIGHT →	

FIGURE 6.1 Examples of drawings from Carmichael et al. (1932). The middle figure is the presented stimulus, and the left and right drawings are reproduced versions from subjects given the label from List 1 (left) or List 2 (right).

6.3 The Misinformation Effect

Another well-known example of this principle involves eyewitness memory. Loftus and Palmer (1974) asked subjects to watch a film that included a car accident. After seeing the film, the subjects were asked, "How fast were the cars going when they _____ each other?" The researchers varied the intensity of the verb that described the collision, using *smashed, collided, bumped, hit,* and *contacted.* When the verb was *smashed,* the estimates averaged 41 mph; when the verb was *contacted,* the estimates averaged 32 mph. A follow-up question asked whether there was broken glass. Nearly one third of the subjects who had heard the verb *smashed* said "yes," but only one tenth of those who heard the verb *contacted* said there was broken glass. There was actually no broken glass. Clearly, the verb used led to the subjects' reconstructing their memory to be consistent with the speed implied by the verb. Many other studies show similar findings. For example, subjects will say "yes" more often to a question like "Did you see *the* broken headlight?" than "Did you see *a* broken headlight?" (Loftus & Zanni, 1975).

People can also "remember" entire episodes that did not happen (Ceci, 1995; Hyman & Pentland, 1996). This can be demonstrated in the laboratory by picking an episode (such as getting lost at a shopping mall) and ensuring that it did not happen to the subject. Then, a confederate, usually a relative or close friend, starts reminiscing about events that did occur. After a couple of these, the confederate reminisces about an event that did not occur. Although the subjects might not recall the event at first, they will usually begin to supply their own details very soon and within a few days, will have a memory that is rated as vivid and as accurate as a genuine memory (Loftus, 1993).

Even if most of a memory is accurate, making a mistake about one small piece of information can render it inaccurate. Baddeley (1990) relates one such case. Donald Thomson, an Australian psychologist, was picked up by police and identified by a woman as the man who had raped her. His alibi was that he had been on a television talk show at the time and that he had an assistant police commissioner as a witness. The police interrogator reportedly responded with "Yes, and I suppose you've got Jesus Christ and the Queen of England, too!" (Baddeley, 1990, p. 27). Later released and exonerated, Thomson found out that the television had been on when the woman was raped. Her memory was accurate enough to identify Thomson, but she made an attribution error: she attributed the face she remembered to her attacker rather than to the person on television.

These examples illustrate the dynamic nature of memory and how people reconstruct a memory based on a combination of information available both at encoding and retrieval. The name given to a drawing can alter how it is subsequently reproduced, the words used in questions can affect what is recalled, and events can be recalled that were not present at encoding. As the Loftus and Palmer (1974) verb study shows, once a particular memory has been constructed, it can affect subsequent recollections: People who thought *smashed* implied *fast* also thought they saw broken glass; people who thought *contacted* implied slow thought they did not see broken glass.

6.4 Reconstruction in Semantic Memory

Reconstructive processes are not restricted to memory for particular episodes or stories. Generic or semantic memory is also quite susceptible to these effects. According to a multiple memory theorist, if a person cannot remember anything about the episode in which the information was learned, the information is in semantic memory. Memory for song lyrics often meets this criteria: You may know the words and sing along, but you do not know when you learned the lyrics.

Hyman and Rubin (1990) gave subjects the titles and first lines of Beatles' songs and were asked to recall the rest of the song. Although subjects failed to recall four fifths of the lines, of the lines that were recalled, 70% were recalled perfectly, 20% were recalled with only one or two words incorrect, and 10% were recalled with changes to three or more words. Evidence for reconstruction comes from several different analyses. First, Hyman and Rubin also included a perception condition, in which people were asked to transcribe the lyrics. Compared to the memory sample, the perception sample made far fewer errors of any kind. When the perception sample were asked to recall the songs five days later, more errors were made than during transcription. Second, when people made errors of recall, the misrecalled item generally fit in with the song and "rarely violated the thematic, rhythmic, and poetic constraints of the songs."

Hyman and Rubin (1990, p. 213) conclude that "song recall is based on the same constructive processes as story recall, with the addition of more constraints that make recall more accurate. "The reconstruction process is characterized by "multiple constraints working together … to efficiently direct word selection."

6.5 Reality Monitoring

Given that memory is a reconstructive process, it should not be surprising to find that there is a large literature showing that people have difficulty distinguishing between memories of events that happened and memories of events that did not happen (see, for example, Conway, 1997). In a typical reality monitoring experiment (cf. Anderson, 1984; Johnson & Raye, 1981), subjects are shown pictures of common objects. Every so often, instead of a picture, the subjects are shown the name of an object and are asked to create a mental image of the object. The test involves presenting a list of object names, and the subject is asked to judge whether they saw the item (i.e., judge the memory as "real") or whether they saw the name of the object and only imagined seeing it (i.e., judge the memory as "imagined"). People are more likely to judge imagined events as real than real events as imagined.

The likelihood that a memory will be judged as real rather than imagined depends upon the vividness of the memory in terms of its sensory quality, detail, plausibility, and coherence (Johnson & Raye, 1981). What this means is that there is not a firm line between memories for real and imagined events: if an imagined event has enough qualitative features of a real event it is likely to be judged as real.

One might argue that all of the foregoing research involves reconstruction of meaningful, coherent events. If our principles are to be general, they must be applicable to all forms of memory, including those more traditional memory paradigms developed for use in the laboratory such as recall and recognition of arbitrary materials. In the following text, we summarize some of the relevant data on reconstructive processes in such situations.

6.6   Deese/Roediger/McDermott Procedure

Based on a series of studies by Deese (1959a, 1959b), Roediger and McDermott (1995) presented subjects with lists of words, such as *thread, pin, eye, sewing, sharp, point, pricked, thimble, haystack, pain, hurt,* and *injection.* All these words are related to *needle,* which does not appear on the list, but which was recalled approximately 40% of the time. Following recall, the subjects were given a recognition test and were asked to indicate on a scale of 1 to 4 whether each item was from one of the lists. A rating of 4 meant they were sure the word was on the list, a rating of 3 meant they thought the word was probably on the list, a rating of 2 meant the word was probably not on the list, and a rating of 1 meant the word was definitely not on the list. On average, the words that were on the list were given a rating of 3.6, whereas words that were neither on the list nor related to words in the list were given a rating of 1.2. The critical words, which were related but were not on the list, received a mean rating of 3.3, not significantly different from words that were actually on the list. In a subsequent experiment, the subjects were asked to make a remember/know judgment (cf. Tulving, 1985b). In this procedure, subjects are given a recognition test and are asked to indicate whether they actually remember the information (have a conscious recollection of the information's occurrence on the study list) or just somehow know the answer (know that the item was on the list but have no conscious recollection of its actual occurrence). Surprisingly, the proportion of studied items that received a remember judgment (0.79) was almost identical to the proportion of critical lures that received a remember judgment (0.73).

Sommers and Lewis (1999) replicated the Deese–Roediger–McDermott (DRM) results effect using phonological rather than semantic associates. The critical lure in this case shared phonemes with the presented items but was not associated in terms of the meanings of the words. As in the semantic overlap case above, subjects were as likely to falsely recall and recognize the critical unpresented item as an item that was actually presented on the list. Sommers and Lewis (1999) explained this result by appealing to the concept of phonological priming.

The Roediger and McDermott (1995) study spurred a flurry of activity using this method, now called the DRM procedure. There are literally dozens of replications of the basic effect and hundreds of extensions that include populations such as children, older adults, and individuals diagnosed with schizophrenia and depression. Numerous variables including modality of presentation, warnings that there will be a related lure, and effects of practice have all been shown to affect the results to one extent or another. A general conclusion is that it is a very robust effect and, although it can be prevented, it is difficult to do so.

Thus, it is extremely easy to demonstrate reconstruction in a memory task in which the to-be-recalled items do not form a coherent episode. One might still argue, however, that the words in the DRM procedure are all related so we have not yet demonstrated reconstructive processes in a traditional list-learning paradigm in which the items are specifically chosen to be unrelated to one another. In addition, all of the studies so far can be classified in the systems view as arising from "long-term" memory, albeit from both episodic and generic memory. In order for our principle to be general we need to demonstrate it in a task that purportedly utilizes another memory system entirely, short term, working, or immediate memory. Some of the relevant data from that literature are summarized in the section following.

6.7 Recognition Without Identification

Peynircioğlu (1990) reported that individuals could recognize words as being previously presented on lists even though they could not identify them. Her technique, called "recognition without identification"

(Cleary & Greene, 2000) involved presenting subjects with a long list of study items. At test, the subjects were given a fragment of a word and asked to complete it with a valid English word. Then, even if they were not able to complete the fragment successfully, they were asked to rate their confidence that the word represented by the fragment had been presented on the study list. The results showed that recognition ratings were significantly higher for those words on the study list, compared to non-studied items, even if the fragment was not completed. This result was subsequently replicated (Cleary & Greene, 2000) and extended to include a perceptual identification task (Cleary & Greene, 2004, 2005).

Cleary and Greene (2004) also reported recognition without iden-tification in false recognition of unpresented associates of list items using a modified Deese–Roediger–McDermott procedure (Roediger & McDermott, 1995). They presented subjects with a list of words (e.g., *bed, rest, doze, snore, nap*) all associated with an unpresented critical lure (e.g., *sleep*). At test, words were flashed on a screen for 50 ms, preceded and followed by a pattern mask. Subjects were asked first to try to identify the word and then, even if the word was not identified, to give a rating of their confidence that the word had been presented in the study epi-sode. The results showed that recognition ratings of a nonidentified word were higher if the word was a critical associate of one of the test lists than if it was an unrelated word. Cleary and Greene (2004, 2005) argued that these recognition ratings were based on judgments of familiarity. According to their argument, some diffuse, global feeling of familiarity is engendered by even the small amount of information gleaned from a perceptual identification task. This familiarity is then the basis of the recognition judgment.

If these recognition ratings are based on a feeling of familiarity, then we should be able to observe the same effects as a result of response bias based on spurious feelings of familiarity to nonpresented items. Familiarity can be generated by statistical regularities such as word fre-quency, strength of trace such as concreteness, or experimentally induced by requiring unscrambling of the stimuli (the so-called "revelation effect"; Watkins & Peynircioğlu, 1990). Greene (2004) developed what he called a "counterfeit list" procedure in which subjects were told that they were going to be seeing a list of words presented subliminally. In reality, no words were presented; the stimuli were pattern masks flashed on the screen. At test, subjects were given lists of words that varied (depending on the experiment) in frequency, concreteness, and whether the stimuli had to be unscrambled or were intact. Remember that no stimuli were pre-sented in the study phase so any "old" responses were false alarms. False alarm rates were higher for high frequency words than for low, for highly concrete words than for low, and for words that had to be unscrambled rather than those intact. These studies demonstrate an almost pure effect of reconstruction in recognition; individuals are responding to unspecific feelings of familiarity rather than a specific event.

6.8 Reconstruction in Immediate Memory

Although not usually termed "reconstruction" there are many examples of distortions in recalling lists that were only just presented. In our view, these should be explained by the same principle as the ones discussed above.

6.8.1 Redintegration

As mentioned in Chapter 3, the term "redintegration" in the memory field has mainly been used to refer to the finding that recall accuracy in immediate memory tasks is heavily influenced by long-term, pre-existing knowledge. Thus, *ceteris paribus*, lists of more frequent words are recalled better than less frequent words, words are recalled better than nonwords, nonwords consisting of more frequent phonotactic frequency are recalled better than those that consist of less frequent arrangements of phonemes, and so on (see Thorn, Gathercole, & Frankish, 2005 for a review). We also note that these are exactly the same variables that affect lexical access in a variety of priming paradigms (see Just & Carpenter, 1987 for a review), identified by systems theorists as arising from either semantic memory or the perceptual representation system (see Chapter 2).

Many theories of immediate memory explain these influences of long-term knowledge by appealing to a process in which previously acquired knowledge helps reconstruct or fill in the gaps in an incomplete memory trace at recall. According to this type of explanation, each one of the above effects is due to the fact that this reconstruction or redintegration only assists in recall if there is some preexperimental information that can be used to make the trace whole again. Thus, for example, words have an advantage over nonwords because there is lexical knowledge that can be tapped in the process of reconstructing a degraded trace whereas less knowledge exists for nonwords. In terms of the language used in the reconstruction literature summarized previously, there is a schema that can be used to fill in the gaps in words that is not present for nonwords.

One influential model of redintegration is Schweickert's (1993) multinomial processing tree model (see Chapter 3). According to this model, the probability of correctly recalling an item is a function of the probability of recalling an undegraded trace plus the probability of the item being successfully redintegrated from a degraded or incomplete trace.

The probability of redintegration is a function of the amount of preexisting knowledge that can be brought to bear in reconstructing the item. Thorn et al. (2005) extended this model to include two influences of long-term knowledge in immediate recall: first a process that activates incoming representations in short-term memory to a higher or lower level, depending on preexisting knowledge, and second, a redintegration process that operates similarly to that described by Schweickert (1993). As Thorn et al. (2005) point out, Schweickert's model implies that long-term knowledge does not influence the undegraded traces—it has its effects only on a trace that is incomplete. This assumption is also implicit in Cowan's (2000) embedded process model: Items that are already within the focus of attention are already retrieved, in a sense, and so do not need to be redintegrated. We have already presented, in Chapter 3, evidence against this view that items in the focus of attention are not cue driven, are not retrieved, and are not susceptible to redintegration. We add more evidence below after first considering the types of errors made when redintegration fails.

6.8.2 Regularization of Errors

One hallmark of reconstructive processes is that in many circumstances they aid in memory retrieval because they rely on regularities in the world. If we know what usually happens in a given circumstance, we can use that information to fill in gaps that may be present in our memory for that episode. This will lead to a facilitation effect in some cases but will lead to errors in cases in which the most probable response is not the correct one. However, if we take this standpoint, we must predict that the errors that are made when using reconstructive processes will not be random; in fact, they will display a bias toward the most likely event. This sort of mechanism has been demonstrated many times in studies of schema-based representations (e.g., Bower, Black, & Turner, 1979; Loftus & Palmer, 1974), and language production errors (Dell, Reed, Adams, & Meyer, 2000) but less so in immediate recall.

Nevertheless, there are a few reports indicating that this prediction holds for immediate recall. Mayzner and Schoenberg (1964) showed that lists of consonants made up of high-frequency bigrams were recalled better than those that made up of less frequent bigrams, similar to the results reported above in the section on redintegration. More important, for present purposes, were the errors that were made: When adjacent items were transposed, the resulting sequence was overwhelmingly more frequent than the original. Very few transpositions were found in the condition in which all of the bigram frequencies were high.

Although this seems like clear evidence in favor of a bias toward regularization in errors, Botvinick and Bylsma (2005) noted a difficulty in interpreting these data. They argued that the stimuli were constructed in such a way that any inversion, even a random one, would result in a more frequent bigram than the original. To avoid this problem, they constructed two artificial grammars in which the transitional probabilities between adjacent items could be completely controlled. In one of the grammars, the probabilities were manipulated such that some sequences were more likely to occur than others. In the second, control grammar, all sequences were equally probable. After extensive training, lists of six items were presented and participants were asked to reconstruct the order of the list immediately after presentation. The results showed that there was a bias toward the more probable sequence in the biased grammar and, furthermore, that this bias could not be explained by random processes. Botvinick and Bylsma (2005) conclude, as we argue in this chapter, that the process of regularization in immediate memory is indistinguishable from that described by Bartlett (1932).

6.8.3 Building a DOG from a DART, a MOP, and a FIG

One theory of immediate memory, Cowan's (1999) embedded-processes view (see Chapter 3), assumes that if an item is currently being processed or is in the focus of attention, then it can be output directly from the short-term store. In this case, no decay or degradation of the trace has occurred and so redintegrative processes should not be necessary. Within Cowan's model, a maximum of four items can be included in the focus of attention at any one time, although items that have recently been in focus retain residual activation for a short amount of time. Thus, in order to explain redintegrative processes, Cowan assumes that those items that are reconstructed are outside the focus of attention and are partially degraded. Similarly, Schweickert's model, described in Chapter 3, includes the probability that an item will be recalled intact with no opportunity for redintegration. If this is true, it might pose a problem for the generality of our principle.

However, Tehan and Humphreys (1998) provided a very clever demonstration of reconstructive processes in immediate memory in a situation in which it was unlikely that the target item was out of the focus of attention or had degraded enough to require redintegration processes. They presented subjects with lists of four items each (see Figure 6.2). After some trials participants were shown an exclamation point which told them to forget the just-presented list and remember the subsequent list. At test, a category cue appeared and participants were instructed to recall the item on the most recent list that belonged to that category. Note that the lists themselves were only four items long; certainly not long enough to strain

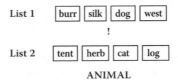

FIGURE 6.2   A sample trial sequence from Tehan and Humphreys (1998).

the capacity of short-term memory or be out of the focus of attention. Critical trials consisted of a two-list sequence in which one of the words on the first list was semantically related to the target word on the second list (i.e., *dog* on list 1, *cat* on list 2). In addition, some of the words in the second list were phonologically related to the critical foil from the first list (i.e., *dog* on list 1, *log* on list 2). Given the cue "animal," the participant has semantic information in addition to phonological information that can act to bias the response toward the foil (*dog*) rather than the target (*cat*). Using this method, Tehan and Humphreys were able to decrease correct recall and show that the interfering foil was more likely to be recalled than the target. They were also able to demonstrate proactive interference when list 2 contained the items *dart, mop, fig*, and *cat*. The idea is that the phonemes /d/, /o/, and /g/ all occurred, and were subsequently reconstructed into *dog*.

Although Tehan and Humphreys (1998) interpreted this finding as showing that proactive interference occurs in immediate recall (see Chapter 3 for a discussion of this), we argue that it also supports the idea of reconstruction processes at work even when lists are substantially below memory span. Again this meshes with the literature on lexical access—preexisting knowledge structures (schemas, if you will) are involved in every aspect of processing a word from perception to recall.

6.8.4 False Memory in Short-Term/ Working Memory Tasks

There have been a number of recent demonstrations of false memory in what would be considered a test of items still within working memory or the focus of attention (Baddeley, 1986; Cowan, 1995). For example, Coane, McBride, Raulerson, and Jordon (2007) used a modified Sternberg task to examine false alarms to critical lures in short-term memory. In a Sternberg task, the subject is given a list of items to hold in memory, a probe item is then presented, and the subject is asked to determine as quickly as possible whether the probe was in the memory set. Accuracy is generally quite high in this paradigm so response times are also recorded.

Coane et al. (2007) compared performance on lists of words taken from the DRM lists described above to lists of unrelated words varying from three to seven items. Although accuracy for the three-item lists was at ceiling levels, response times for the critical lures were significantly slower than unrelated items at all list lengths. Atkins and Reuter-Lorenz (2008) reported similar results with four-item lists. Thus, short-term/working memory is not immune to reconstruction.

6.9 Reconstruction in Very Short-Term Memory

One way of probing very short-term memory is to use so-called RSVP or rapid serial visual presentation. In this task a list of items (usually words or letters) is presented extremely rapidly (about 150 ms per item) one at a time. Thus, an entire list of six items can be presented in under a second. There are a number of notable results reported using this technique not the least of which is that any words can be reported at all. However, for the present purposes the main finding of interest is the phenomenon of "repetition blindness." Repetition blindness refers to the finding that subjects are less likely to report two occurrences of the same word in an RSVP list than they are to report two unrelated words (e.g., Kanwisher, 1987).

The usual explanation of this effect (and the reason it is called "repetition blindness") is that as each word is encountered it activates a representation of some concept (a "type"). At the same time a memory is formed of a particular instance of that type (a "token"). When reporting the list, an individual retrieves the set of tokens activated by the initial list presentation. Kanwisher (1987) suggested that if two tokens of the same type are presented in rapid succession, the second occurrence of a word is not "tokenized" and thus is not retained. This explanation relies on a deficit at encoding of the second word.

However, Masson, Caldwell, and Whittlesea (2000) argued that repetition blindness is not due to an encoding deficit but, instead, can be accounted for by the same reconstructive processes described by Bartlett (1932). In a series of studies, Masson et al. (2000) manipulated the orthographic similarity of two words in an RSVP list. In one experiment they showed that the probability of reporting one word (i.e., "lust") in the list was greatly enhanced when an orthographically similar word (i.e., "lost") was presented later in the list, compared to a control condition in which all of the words were dissimilar. In another experiment Masson et al. presented a nonword early in the list followed by an orthographically similar word. In this case, report of the second word was enhanced, showing a retroactive effect of reconstruction. They went on to perform a number of other manipulations in which they were able to selectively enhance or depress performance by manipulating the relationship between the target items. Masson et al. argue that "the act of remembering, including recall of the contents of an RSVP list, is a reconstructive one that operates on retrieved fragments of experience and inference about what plausibly might have occurred" (p. 19).

More recently Campbell and Fugelsang (2002) showed that repetition blindness only occurs if the to-be-reported stimuli are words. In fact, repetition of nonwords within a list can actually lead to higher report of the second token. They also showed that making the repeated word distinct from either the first presentation or from the rest of the list (by making it brighter or changing its location) makes it more likely that two occurrences will be reported. Campbell and Fugelsang (2002) argue that repetition blindness reflects the contribution of preexisting memory representations.

6.10 Reconstruction in Iconic Memory

A final consideration for this principle is in the area that has generally been called *sensory memory*, specifically *iconic* memory. In the prototypical experiment of this type, subjects are shown a brief (50 ms) display of letters and asked to report which letters were in the display. Sperling (1960) noted that people were able to report only four or five letters correctly. However, some of the subjects said that they felt as if they had seen the entire display but that it faded away before they could report more than about four letters. To test this intuition, Sperling developed what he called the "partial report" technique. Sperling reasoned that if there were more letters available immediately after presentation, then asking a subject to report only part of the total display would allow him to estimate the number of letters available to the subject at that particular time. Thus, if the subject is asked to recall one row of the display, whatever percentage of correct performance achieved on that particular row should represent the percentage of the whole display that was available. Subjects were given an auditory cue indicating the to-be-reported row over delays ranging from –100 ms (the cue was given 100 ms before the display) to 1000 ms (the cue was given one second after the display had terminated). The results showed that the estimated number of letters available in a display of 12 letters was about 9 immediately after the display went off and decreased in a relatively linear manner up to 1 sec when it became about the level of whole report.

Originally these results were thought to show the operation of a specialized memory system that can hold a great deal of visual information for a brief period of time until it can be recoded into primary memory. The information persisted for less than a second before fading away. However, today most researchers agree that there are two aspects to visual sensory memory, information persistence, probably due to residual neural activity, and informational persistence, probably based on your garden-variety memory processes (Nairne, 2003). If this is the case then we should be able to show reconstructive processes within the traditional paradigms used for demonstrating iconic memory.

Sperling (1967) reported that errors in a typical partial report experiment were often based on acoustic or phonological confusions. For example, *P* might be reported when *C* would have been the correct answer. Thus, the types of errors generally made in the research on iconic memory are precisely the same types of errors found in immediate recall. Mewhort and Leppman (1985) presented displays very similar to those shown by Sperling. Rather than reporting all of the letters, as in the Sperling experiments, the task was to indicate whether a particular letter appeared at all in the display. The data showed no decrease in accuracy as a function of the delay interval for this type of information. However, a condition in which the subject was asked to indicate the position of a probe item in the display, accuracy decreased at about the same rate as reported by Sperling (1960). Thus, what is being forgotten is location information—where an item was—rather than item information—what items were present (see also Mewhort, Campbell, Marchetti, & Campbell, 1981). This mirrors a great deal of research in memory that has shown that memory for position is more fragile than memory for the item itself (e.g., Healy, 1974; Nairne, 1992).

Other similarities between iconic memory and memory "proper" can be found, such as frequency and familiarity effects (Mewhort, 1972; Mewhort, Merikle, & Bryden, 1969), effects of orthographic structure and experience (Lefton & Spragins, 1974), and different results when using letters, numbers, familiar geometric forms, and unfamiliar geometric forms (Dick, 1974). The ordering of the "decay" of these types of information is precisely what would be predicted from the research on memory proper: The more familiar and meaningful the information, the less likely it is to show an effect of retention interval.

Dick (1974) reported that the pattern of errors in such a task shows that the most frequent source of errors in iconic memory is an inversion error in which the subject reports the item in the position immediately to the left or the right of the target item. Again, this is the same pattern found when looking at position-error gradients in any memory task on any time scale (Nairne, 1992). In addition, these data show the same reconstructive effects that have been reported in all types of memory tasks.

6.11 Chapter Summary

We argue that reconstruction is not restricted to the case of meaningful, connected events and is not restricted to one or even two hypothetical memory systems but can be easily demonstrated in all types of memory situations. Although acknowledging the effects of previous experience and knowledge on more classic immediate memory tasks is not our insight (see Masson, Caldwell, & Whittlesea, 2000; Underwood & Schultz, 1960; Whittlesea, 1997), inclusion of these in discussions of the reconstructive nature of memory is not common. However, the sections above demonstrate that this principle meets our criterion of being a general principle in that it applies regardless of the time scale or putative memory system.

We show that memory is reconstructed regardless of the time scale, the materials, and the processing. In addition to the classic demonstrations of reconstruction in meaningful prose, we show how it affects every single aspect of memory from the moment the information is interpreted by the cognitive system. Each time an event is recalled, the memory is slightly different. Because of the interaction between encoding and retrieval, and because of the variations that occur between two different retrieval attempts, the resulting memories will always differ, even if only slightly.

CHAPTER

The Impurity Principle

The truth is rarely pure and never simple.

—Oscar Wilde (*The Importance of Being Earnest*, 1895, Act I)

7.1 Principle 5: The Impurity Principle

In this chapter we discuss the idea that a task or a process can be a "pure" measure of memory, without contamination from other hypothetical memory stores or structures, and without contributions from other processes. Our impurity principle states that tasks and processes are not pure, and therefore one cannot separate out the contributions of different memory stores by using tasks thought to tap only one system; one cannot count on subjects using only one process for a particular task; and one cannot, therefore, use logical subtractive methods. Our principle follows from previous arguments articulated by Kolers and Roediger (1984) and Crowder (1993), among others, that because every event recruits slightly different encoding and retrieval processes, there is no such thing as "pure" memory.

7.2 Tasks and Processes

The fundamental issue is the extent to which one can determine the contribution of a particular memory system or structure or process to performance on a particular memory task. There are numerous ways of assessing memory, and many different ways of classifying tasks. Typically, some event or set of items is presented to the subject followed by a series of questions. The encoding can be either intentional, in which the subject knows there is a memory test that will follow and intends to remember the material, or incidental, in which the subject is unaware that there will be a later memory test and does not intentionally try to remember the material. Similarly, at test the subject can be asked to relate the cues back to the learning episode, a direct test of memory, or may be unaware that the test is related to the encoding episode, an indirect test of memory (see Table 7.1).

Craik (1983) suggested that many commonly used tests can also be classified with respect to how much environmental support they provide or how much self-initiated activity they require (see Table 7.2). Craik argued that the differences in memory performance between elderly and young populations were related more to the amount of environmental support available than to the putative memory system tapped by that task. Here, we emphasize two related variables that are at work: whether the test requires identification of a particular encoding context and whether the test includes a more specific cue or a more general cue.

TABLE 7.1 One Way of Categorizing Memory Tasks

		Retrieval	
		Indirect Test	**Direct Test**
Encoding	Incidental	Cell 1	Cell 2
	Intentional	Cell 3	Cell 4

Note: Encoding can be incidental or intentional, and retrieval can be via a direct or an indirect test.

TABLE 7.2 The Amount of Environmental Support Typically Accompanying Various Memory Tasks

Task	More Environmental Support
Word fragment completion	↑
Relearning	
Recognition	
Cued recall	
Free recall	
Remembering to remember	
	Less environmental support

Note: Craik (1983). *Philosophical Transactions of the Royal Society of London B*, 302, 341–359.

A free recall test typically provides little environmental support. A list of items is presented, and the subject is asked to recall which items were on the list. Say the list included the words *greyhound, table,* and *broccoli.* The subject knows all of these words prior to the presentation of the list, and will know these words after the experiment is over. The experimenter simply says, "Recall the words that were on the list," and it is up to the subject to identify which list is being referred to, how many items need to be recalled, and then discriminate the items that were on this particular list from those that were not. This is an example of memory for an item in context.

A typical recognition test provides more environmental support. Although a comparable list of items might have been presented, and although the subject is asked again about memory for an item in context, the subject is provided with a more specific cue, and knows exactly how many items to respond to.

Some tests, such as word fragment completion and general knowledge questions, offer more environmental support. These tests provide more targeted cues, and often the cues are unique; moreover, neither of these tests requires the reinstatement of a particular context. For both tests, it does not really matter whether a specific encoding context is consciously remembered, although it can be a useful piece of information. For example, if you are given a word fragment and asked to complete it with the first word that pops in your head, you are free to try a variety of strategies. You might just try random words, or you might think back to the first part of the experiment you were in and see if any of those words fit the fragment. In one case, you are ignoring a particular learning episode, in the other you are not, and different results might obtain (e.g., Bowers & Schacter, 1990). Very different types of processing can be used by subjects even when given the same type of test or cue. People will use any and all processes to help them answer a question.

In contrast to both standard free recall and recognition tests, immediate memory tests (e.g., digit span) generally do not require contextual information at all. In a typical test of this type, a person is given six or seven items (often letters or digits) in random order, and is then asked to recall them in the order in which they were presented. Because so little time has elapsed from the end of list presentation to the beginning of the retrieval attempt, the context is unlikely to have changed and so the subject is likely to be still in her or his original encoding state. Thus, although this is memory for an item in context, the subject is likely to be in the same context at test. If recall is delayed, then it is more likely that contextual reinstatement will be necessary, so it is likely that results will differ between immediate and delayed recall. It should be noted that delaying recall in this fashion can confound the effect of time and the need to reinstate context.

The picture becomes a little more complicated, however, when one tries to include an account of how processing might differ. One common processing distinction involves the aspects of the stimulus that are focused on or are salient at encoding and retrieval: Subjects can focus more on an item's physical appearance (data driven processing) or on an item's meaning (conceptually driven processing; Blaxton, 1989; Rajaram, 1998; Roediger & McDermott, 1993; Roediger, Weldon, & Challis, 1989).

In general, performance on tasks such as free recall that offer little environmental support is better if the rememberer uses conceptual rather than perceptual processing at encoding. Although there is perceptual information available at encoding, there is no perceptual information provided at test so data-driven processes tend not to be appropriate. Typical recognition and cued-recall tests provide more specific cues, and as such, data-driven processing becomes more appropriate, but these tasks still require the subject to discriminate which items were presented in a particular specific context; this is often better accomplished using conceptually driven processing.

To return to Table 7.2, some tests, such as word fragment completion and general knowledge questions, provide quite targeted and even unique cues and, because neither of these tests requires the reinstatement of a particular context, both offer a high degree of environmental support. In addition, attention to perceptual features of the stimulus at encoding generally results in improved performance. But this does not mean that contextual reinstatement or conceptually driven processing do not play a role. As noted above, although you might just try random words, you might also explicitly think back to the learning context.

In addition to distinctions between data driven and conceptually driven processing, another common distinction is between an automatic retrieval process, which is usually referred to as *familiarity*, and a nonautomatic process, usually called *recollection* (see, for example, Jacoby 1991). Additional distinctions abound. Our point is that very different types of processing can be used by subjects on a particular task, and that tasks can differ from one another on a variety of different dimensions. In short, people can potentially use almost any combination of processes on any particular task.

7.3 Task Purity

From a structural point of view, it has often been assumed that certain tasks tap certain memory systems more than other tasks. The ultimate goal, presumably, is to devise a task that is a pure measure of a particular kind of memory. However, as noted above, two different tasks can vary in far more ways than might originally be apparent, and even one particular task can be solved by a wide variety of different processes. In this section, we review certain tasks that have historically been thought to tap a particular system.

7.3.1 Implicit Versus Explicit

One classic division of memory into implicit and explicit memory systems[1] has been promoted by examining dissociations among tasks. A dissociation occurs when one variable (such as time) has a different effect on two different memory tasks. A classic example of a task dissociation was reported by Tulving, Schacter, and Stark (1982). Tulving et al. showed participants lists of words that were to be rated for pleasantness (incidental learning). After a variable delay, subjects were either asked to recognize the words that had appeared on the list (a direct test) or to complete word fragments with an English word (an indirect test). One hour after the list had been learned, performance was better on the recognition task than on the word-fragment completion task. In contrast, after a delay of one week, performance on the word-fragment completion task was essentially identical to that on the immediate test but recognition was substantially worse. The authors interpreted this result as demonstrating that the time between encoding and retrieval had different effects on explicit and implicit memory. They further speculated that this is because there are separate systems responsible for storing these different types of information.

Such task dissociations have been demonstrated many times with both normal and clinical populations. For example, individuals diagnosed with anterograde amnesia perform about the same as control subjects on a variety of indirect memory tasks such as fragment completion, but are severely impaired on direct tasks requiring conscious recollection such as recognition or recall (e.g., Warrington & Weiskrantz, 1974). The most common interpretation of such data is that these different tasks rely on different memory structures that are functionally independent and can be separately damaged.[2]

One problem with much of the early literature was a confound between the type of processing and the type of task. Different tasks induce the rememberer to focus on different aspects of the stimuli and available cues both at encoding and at retrieval. Based on the principles of

---

[1] We can substitute *nondeclarative* and *declarative* for *implicit* and *explicit*.

[2] The conclusion that dissociations (and double dissociations) among tasks provide sufficient evidence for separate systems has been strongly debated (see, for example, Roediger, Rajaram & Srinivas 1990; Van Orden, Pennington, & Stone, 2001).

transfer-appropriate processing, changes in the cues between study and test can have different effects depending on the aspect of the stimulus that was attended to at encoding (see Roediger & McDermott, 1993). Most implicit tasks, such as word fragment completion, include cues about the physical appearance of the stimulus at test, and because of that will be well supported by attention to the physical aspects at encoding. Such a task, then, will tend to induce data-driven processing. In contrast, many explicit tests such as free recall require the use of internal conceptual or meaning-based cues because there are none present at test. These tasks induce conceptually driven processing.

Blaxton (1989) devised an experiment that directly contrasted the predictions of an account based on such a transfer-appropriate processing theory with a systems account. She unconfounded memory tasks with the type of processing: Not only did she have the standard data driven indirect task used to assess implicit memory and the standard conceptually driven direct task used to assess explicit memory, but she also had a conceptually driven indirect task and a data driven direct task. Importantly, the structuralist and the processing frameworks make opposite predictions: The systems view predicts that the two explicit (direct) tasks will differ from the two implicit (indirect) tasks (regardless of the type of processing), whereas the transfer-appropriate processing account predicts that the two data-driven tasks will differ from the two conceptually driven tasks (regardless of the type of conscious knowledge needed to perform the tasks). The data supported the transfer-appropriate processing view. These results, and many others, question not only the assumption that certain tasks are pure measures of implicit memory, but that a particular kind of memory is being tapped at all.

7.3.2 Episodic Versus Semantic

Episodic memory and semantic memory differ primarily in whether the rememberer is aware of the original learning episode. For example, if asked who is the only Nobel Prize laureate who also played first-class cricket, you might remember sitting in a comfy chair, with a nice cup of freshly brewed coffee at your side, perusing Chapter 3 of this book, and reading this fact for the first time. Being aware of the encoding episode suggests that the information is in episodic memory. In contrast, you might be an expert on cricket (or literature), and might just "know" this information, in the same sense that you might "know" that there is a Nobel Prize for literature, but you are unaware of the episode during which you acquired this information. In this case, the information is in semantic (or generic) memory.

One way of examining the relative contributions of episodic and semantic memory is through a procedure called the Remember/Know paradigm (Gardiner, 1988; Tulving, 1985b). In this procedure subjects are asked to give a "remember" response to all those items for which they can explicitly bring to mind the episode in which the item was learned. There must be conscious awareness of the specific learning episode in this case. However, if the subjects think the item was on the list but cannot consciously recall learning that particular item in the learning phase, they are instructed to give a "know" response. Tulving (1985b) asked subjects to learn lists of paired words in which the second word was a member of the category described by the first word, for example, *a fruit— pear*. Three successive tests were used: free recall, cued recall with the category name as a cue, and cued recall with the category name plus the first letter of the target. For each item recalled, the subjects were asked to indicate whether they actually "remembered" its occurrence in the list or whether they simply "knew" on some other basis that the item was a member of the study list. Tulving found that the proportion of "remember" judgments decreased across the three tests indicating a decrease in autonoetic (self-knowing) conscious awareness across the different tests. Theoretically, although the task itself is not solely tapping one system, one can estimate the relative contributions of these systems for each task using such a method.

Many dissociations have been reported using the remember/know methodology. Gardiner and colleagues have shown effects on "remember" but not "know" judgments for a number of manipulations including levels of processing, the generation effect, frequency effects, divided attention, and test delay (Gardiner, 1988; Gardiner & Java, 1990; Gardiner & Parkin, 1990). These results have been interpreted as showing that the "remember" judgments arise from an episodic process of effortful recollection whereas the "know" judgments reflect a contribution of a different system. From a systems point of view, these two types of responses are being controlled by different memory systems.

One problem, however, was noted by Hamilton and Rajaram (2003). According to multiple systems theorists, the proportion of "remember" judgments should be highest for free recall, which is considered to rely more on conscious recall of a particular episode, and then systematically decrease for other types of tests such as cued recall and ultimately word fragment completion. Hamilton and Rajaram showed that, even though overall levels of recall differed among different tasks such as free recall, cued recall, and recognition, the proportion of "remember" versus "know" responses stayed quite constant. That is, certain tasks did not appear better tuned to tapping a particular system. Moreover, Hamilton and Rajaram showed that "remember" (and therefore also "know") responses were not influenced by the type of processing engaged in at study (conceptual versus perceptual): both perceptual and conceptual cued recall elicited the same proportion of "remember" responses as paired-associate recall. Thus, even the most "intentional" form of memory task, free recall, involves a combination of conscious episodic retrieval and some other process, perhaps something like familiarity or fluency. Importantly, at least in terms of the "remember/know" procedure, the relative contributions of familiarity and recollection appear to be the same regardless of the memory test. Thus tests or tasks do not tap only one particular memory system.

7.3.3 STM (and WM) Versus LTM

Short-term memory originated in the 1950s from apparent discrepancies observed when researchers began to move away from multitrial learning episodes to single trials. A complete review of STM versus LTM is beyond our current remit; the interested reader is referred to Surprenant and Neath (2008; see also Neath & Surprenant, 2008). Rather, here we focus on one particular task that has long been held to be a measure of short-term (and then working) memory: immediate serial recall.

Immediate serial recall is basically synonymous with memory span. In one the first reviews of this topic, Blankenship (1938, p. 2) noted that "memory span refers to the ability of an individual to reproduce immediately, after one presentation, a series of discrete stimuli in their original order."[3] The primary use of memory span was not so much to measure the capacity of a short-term memory system, but rather as a measure of intellectual abilities (e.g., Bolton, 1892; Watkins, 1915). Early on, however, it was recognized that memory span, whatever it was, varied as function of a large number of variables (Blankenship, 1938), and could even be increased substantially by practice (Martin & Fernberger, 1929). Nonetheless, memory span became increasingly seen as a measure of the capacity of a short-term memory system that was distinct from long-term memory. Generally, most individuals can recall about 7 ± 2 items (Miller, 1956) or the number of items that can be pronounced in about 2 s (Baddeley, 1986) without making any mistakes.

Does immediate serial recall (or memory span) measure the capacity of short-term (or working) memory? The currently available evidence suggests that it does not. First, there is a growing recognition that long-term memory plays a role, as revealed by such phenomenon as redintegration (see Chapter 3). Second, when the memory span procedure is adapted to measure long-term memory (primarily by delaying the test for 5 min), one finds the same "capacity limitation" as in the short-term case (Nairne &

---

[3] Blankenship concluded his review with the following (pp. 18–19): "Though 146 references are listed in the bibliography, it is appalling to note how little real knowledge there is in the field of memory span. … Probably the one thing most experimenters do agree on is a functional definition of memory span."

Neath, 2000). This, of course, makes no sense, as the capacity of any long-term memory system has to be larger. What it suggests is that the limit in the short-term case is not a fixed capacity. Rather, we suggest elsewhere (Neath & Surprenant, 2008) that the limit has to do with distinctiveness and is in accordance with our relative distinctiveness principle (see Chapter 8).

A third problem arises if one takes memory span seriously as a measure of capacity. What should happen when the capacity limit is exceeded? Beaman (2006) used a serial recall task and showed that as list length increased, the proportion of items recalled decreased (as had been shown many times before). However, he also showed that the mean number correct actually increased with list length. This is important because it shows that the number of items that can be recalled is larger than the presumed capacity of the memory system. Beaman argued that a simple capacity explanation of short-term memory could not account for these data.[4] One could postulate that under these conditions, there are contributions from a long-term memory system, but this would only reinforce our point that memory span is not a pure measure of short-term or working memory.

The main difficulty in attempting to construct a "pure" measure of immediate memory capacity is that, just as Ebbinghaus (1885) observed, the influence of previously acquired knowledge is impossible to avoid. There are numerous contributions of long-term knowledge not only to memory span and immediate serial recall (e.g., Thorn, Gathercole, & Frankish, 2005) but to other short-term tasks as well (see *Interactions Between Short-Term and Long-Term Memory in the Verbal Domain*, Thorn & Page, 2008).

7.4 Process Purity

As we have already discussed, people can solve a particular task in many different ways; indeed, several processes might contribute to performance on a single task. Here, we focus on the idea that there are at least two processes that can operate in any given situation, one that requires an effortful, nonautomatic processing (generally termed *recollection*) and another that is automatic and faster (generally termed *familiarity*). Thus, processes themselves are not pure measures of memory.

7.4.1 Process Dissociation

Jacoby (1991) argued against the idea of equating certain tasks with certain underlying memory systems and, instead, developed a way of measuring

---

[4] Beaman's (2006) explanation was in terms of Nairne's (1990) feature model.

the contribution of automatic processes of familiarity and more effortful processes of recollection in tasks thought to tap implicit and explicit memory. His process-dissociation procedure sets up a situation in which the two processes work together in one condition but work in opposition in a second condition.

For example, let us consider an experiment reported by Jacoby, Toth, and Yonelinas (1993).[5] In Phase 1 of the experiment, subjects heard a list of words. In Phase 2 they read a list of words in one of two between-subjects conditions: a full-attention condition in which no concurrent task was required, and a divided-attention condition in which subjects were asked to monitor an auditory stream for repeated digits. At test, subjects were given word stems written in red or green ink consisting of a few letters, and were asked to complete each stem with a valid English word. The subjects were instructed to complete the green stems with a word they encountered in either Phase 1 or 2 of the experiment. If they could not remember a word, they should just complete the stem with the first word that comes to mind. This is the inclusion condition: both recollective and automatic processes are working together to produce a response. In the exclusion condition, subjects were asked when they encountered a red stem to think back to the words they encountered in Phases 1 and 2 and complete the stems with any word they could think of that was NOT presented. In this condition, then, recollective and automatic processes are working in opposition. The results are shown in Table 7.3.

The observed data can be used to estimate the contribution of two different processes. More formally, in the inclusion condition the probability of responding with a studied item is the probability of conscious recollection (R) plus the probability that a word came to mind automatically (A) if the recollective process failed ($1-R$).

TABLE 7.3 The Probability of Completing the Stem With a Studied Item on Both Inclusion and Exclusion Tests for Experiments

	Performance Component			
	Read		Heard	
Attention	Inclusion	Exclusion	Inclusion	Exclusion
Full	0.61	0.36	0.47	0.34
Divided	0.46	0.46	0.42	0.37

Note: "Read" and "Heard" correspond to whether the item came from Phase 1 or Phase 2 of presentation. Based on data reported in Jacoby, Toth, & Yonelinas (1993). *Journal of Experimental Psychology: General, 122,* 139–154.

[5] This section is adapted from material presented in Chapter 5 of Neath and Surprenant (2003) and is incorporated with permission of the copyright holder, Wadsworth.

$$Inclusion = R + A(1-R)$$

In the exclusion condition a studied word will only be produced if recollection fails but the word came to mind automatically anyway.

$$Exclusion = A(1-R)$$

Replacing A(1-R) in the first equation with Exclusion, we get

$$Inclusion = R + Exclusion$$

or

$$R = Inclusion - Exclusion$$

We can also solve for A:

$$A = Exclusion/(1-R)$$

Using the values in Table 7.3, we can calculate estimates of R and A in the various cells. These are shown in Table 7.4. Divided attention was designed to minimize the effect of conscious recollective processes, because the subject was required to attend to the irrelevant vigilance task, and so the estimate for R in the divided attention task is 0. In contrast, divided attention should not affect the automatic component, and the estimates of A are identical in the full and in the divided attention conditions.

Additional evidence consistent with this view that at least two processes are required comes from an extensive analysis of over 30 years of research on recollection and familiarity in recognition by Yonelinas (2002). His findings are summarized in Table 7.5. Overall, encoding manipulations lead to similar effects on both recollection and familiarity, although there is often a larger change for recollection. However, manipulating

---

TABLE 7.4 Estimates of the Contribution of Recollective and Automatic Processes for the Words That Were Read, Calculated from the Data Presented in Table 7.3

Attention	Estimate	
	Recollection	**Automatic**
Full	0.25	0.47
Divided	0.00	0.46

Note: Based on data reported by Jacoby, Toth, & Yonelinas (1993). *Journal of Experimental Psychology: General, 122*, 139–154.

TABLE 7.5 Summary of the Effects of Encoding Manipulations and Retrieval Manipulations on Recollection and Familiarity

	Recollection	Familiarity
Encoding Manipulations		
– Shallow versus deep processing	Larger increase	Smaller increase
– Read versus generate	Larger increase	Smaller increase
– Full versus divided attention	Larger decrease	Smaller decrease
– Shorter versus longer study Duration	Increase	Increase
Retrieval Manipulations		
– Full versus divided attention	Large decrease	No effect
– Same versus different perceptual match (verbal)	No effect	Large decrease
– Same versus different perceptual match (nonverbal)	Decrease	Decrease
– No delay versus short delay	No effect	Rapid decrease
– No delay versus long delay	Decrease	Decrease
– Less fluency versus more fluency	No effect	Large increase
– Change response criterion	No effect	Large effect

Note: The terms "increase" and "decrease" refer to the effect on performance relative to the appropriate control condition. Based on Yonelinas (2002). *Journal of Memory and Language, 46,* 441–517.

conditions at retrieval produce a different pattern of results in which the manipulation can affect each process differently.

Jacoby and others argue that such data require a dual process theory of memory in which recollection and familiarity are due to the operation of two underlying processes, although others disagree (see Erdfelder & Buchner, 1998). In general, the effects of familiarity can be considered as a continuous process of building evidence for a particular response, whereas recollection is better thought of as a threshold process. Regardless of the model, however, it is clear that recognition memory, in particular, and most likely all memory tasks, are supported by at least two different processes. This is exactly what the impurity principle predicts.

7.4.2 Processes and Subprocesses

The impurity principle states that tasks and processes are not pure measures of memory. This means more than just stating, as shown by process dissociation, that there are multiple processes involved in a single task. It also means that the types of processing identified—data driven and conceptually driven, recollection and familiarity—are not necessarily pure themselves.[6]

Masson and MacLeod (1997) showed in an exhaustive series of experiments that data-driven or conceptually driven processes are not pure measures of memory. Recall that, in general, generation has a large effect on recollection but a smaller effect on familiarity. That is, generated words are recognized much better than words that are simply read. In contrast, in a masked word identification task, read words are recognized more easily than generated words (Jacoby, 1983). Thus, consistent with the transfer-appropriate processing view, the data-driven task of masked word recognition is helped when the "data" are present at encoding (read condition) compared to a condition in which the actual physical stimulus is not presented (generate condition). Masson and MacLeod (1997) found that this result occurs only when the generate task involves antonyms (i.e., hot c__?). Other various generating tasks, such as definition completion (the orange vegetable a rabbit eats c__?) resulted in equal priming for both generated and read items.

In a further sequence of studies Masson and MacLeod (1997) introduced what they called a "read-associate task" in which subjects were asked to read a word (according to their framework, this engages both perceptual and conceptual processes) and then to produce an associate to that word (additional conceptual processes). They compared the results of such a condition to "regular" read and generate conditions using Jacoby's process dissociation framework discussed above. Note that in the read-associate task the subject is getting both the data and the conceptually driven components of processing. Thus, this should result in better perceptual priming for the word compared to a generate condition in which the physical stimulus was not presented and identical priming to the regular "read" condition. However, they found that the estimates for the automatic contribution in the read-associate condition were identical to those of the generate condition: much more of an influence of controlled compared to automatic processing. Masson and MacLeod's interpretation of this result is that there is an automatic or involuntary activation of conscious memory which is masked in the generate condition *just because* the event itself is remembered better than in the read condition. Recall that in the exclusion condition, the instructions ask the subject not to recall the item if they can recall it as having been presented before. Therefore, even if the automatic influences are equal, the controlled influences will overpower the fluency estimate because the conscious recollection passes

---

[6] Roediger, Buckner, and McDermott (1999) have proposed a hybrid approach called "components of processing" that combines task analysis and data from functional imaging to map particular components of various tasks onto brain areas. Although an overview of this account is beyond the scope of this chapter, the basic idea behind their view is consistent with the impurity principle

a high threshold. They then replicated the study using the remember/ know procedure. Masson and MacLeod argued that the procedures for separating out automatic and conceptual processes are not valid because the processes themselves are not pure measures of memory.

Our impurity principle predicts that when distinctions are made between types of processing (e.g., conceptually driven versus data driven; familiarity versus recollection; automatic versus conceptual; item specific versus relational), each of those individual processes will not be pure measures of memory. A procedure analogous to that used by Masson and MacLeod (1997) can reveal the impurities.

7.5 Subtractive Logic in Neuroimaging

A final implication of the impurity principle concerns the use of subtractive logic. In essence, if neither the minuend nor the subtrahend are pure measures of memory, the difference is likely to be contaminated also.

Over the past 20 years great strides have been made in noninvasive techniques for measuring brain activity. In particular, PET and fMRI studies have allowed us to obtain an on-line glimpse into the hemodynamic changes that occur in the brain as stimuli are being processed, memorized, manipulated, and recalled. However, many of these studies rely on subtractive logic that explicitly assumes that (a) there are different brain areas (structures) subserving different cognitive processes and (b) we can subtract out background or baseline activity and determine which areas are responsible for performing a particular task (or process) by itself. There have been some serious challenges to these underlying assumptions, which we discuss below.

Historically, the basic idea for the subtractive method is credited to F. C. Donders (1868–1969). Until Donders' work, most philosophers and early psychologists believed that thought was instantaneous. However, Donders reasoned that if mental events take time, the more complex a task, or the more steps needed to complete it, the longer it should take. He also suggested that a more complex task builds on and must include the steps required to complete a simple task as one of its components. Armed with this idea, he was able to show that a simple response to the presence of a stimulus was faster than deciding what the stimulus was and choosing a response. Given that the choice task included the time taken to respond to a simple stimulus, Donders subtracted the time it took to do the simple response time from the choice response time in order to gain a relatively pure estimate of the time it takes to make a choice between two stimuli—factoring out the time taken to perceive the stimulus and to make the motor response embodied in the simple response time. This simple idea was the beginning of mental chronometry (e.g., Posner, 1978) and task analysis in human factors (e.g., Proctor & Dutta, 1995). This method has been used extensively in cognitive psychology, although it is not without its detractors (see, e.g., Van Zandt & Ratcliff, 1995).

In the field of neuropsychology the same logic is used, however, it is not based on the time taken to complete a task but rather on the neural substrates of each process. A basic assumption is that there is some baseline activation that is present all of the time and that the baseline is built upon by adding more activation. Thus, when the baseline is subtracted out, what is left is a relatively pure measure of the brain areas that are active in completing the higher-level task.

One assumption of this method is that adding a second component to the task does not affect the simple task. However, this assumption does not always hold true. For example, Jennings, McIntosh, Kapur, Tulving, and Houle (1997) performed PET scans on the same subjects while they were performing semantic living/nonliving judgments and letter judgments in which they decided whether a target word contained a particular letter. According to subtractive logic, the pattern of activity while doing the letter judgment task can be subtracted from the semantic task. The remaining areas of activation will show the area of activation associated with the semantic aspect of the task, having taken out all of the activity generated by reading the letters in a word and making a yes/no decision. In this study, rather than having just one response mode, as is usually the case, Jennings et al. had three response modes for each task: a mouse click, a spoken yes/no response, and a silent thought response. According to subtractive logic, we can take out the effect of the responses just by subtracting them out. The behavioral data showed the expected pattern of levels of processing regardless of the response mode: more words were remembered after making living/nonliving judgments than in the letter search task. However, in the PET scan data, after subtracting out the letter judgment task for each response mode, there were different levels of activation of the same areas for the three different response modes and, more troubling, there were some areas uniquely activated when one response mode was used compared to the others. Thus, the semantic task itself (and presumably the baseline, too) differed, based on the ultimate response mode required.

Even if the additive factors logic were correct, these studies often assume that a task is a pure measure of one process or another. For example, one of the tasks that is used quite extensively in the neuroimaging literature is the n-back task. In this task the subject is asked to indicate whether a stimulus was repeated n items back. For example, subjects should respond "yes" in a two-back task to the string B P G D G because G was repeated two items back. This task is supposed to be a good measure of working memory because it requires the active maintenance and manipulation of information and can be used with both verbal and non-verbal stimuli. According to Baddeley's (1986) working memory model, the central executive is involved in all working memory tasks and controls the allocation of resources to the subordinate, slave systems. The subordinate systems are responsible for a limited number of domain-specific functions. Thus, the central executive will be involved in all working memory tasks but each subordinate system is only involved if the task requires the maintenance and rehearsal of a certain type of information. Logically, then, if we compare two working memory tasks that require the activation of different slave systems, the activation they have in common is due to the activation of central executive. Using this logic and the n-back task with different materials, tapping different slave systems, researchers have argued for a large prefrontal lobe component in executive functioning in working memory compared to more posterior regions for the different slave systems within the model. This is interesting in that those areas identified with the central executive had previously been identified as being associated with spatial processing. One conclusion, then, is that these areas are associated with domain-general processes, not spatial processes, per se.

However, Meegan, Purc-Stephenson, Honsberger, and Topan (2004) questioned the assumption that the n-back task is a pure measure of working memory processes, uncontaminated by other processes. They used the interference logic outlined by Brooks (1968) and conducted three behavioral studies in which they found significant interference in a verbal n-back task from a spatial response mode. In addition, there were significant eye movements during the n-back task that grew larger as the task became more difficult. They concluded that the n-back task is not purely a working memory task and, instead, it involves the spatial system, perhaps playing a supportive part in rehearsal. Similarly, Cabeza, Nyberg and colleagues (Cabeza, Dolcos, Graham, & Nyberg, 2002; Cabeza, Dolcos, Prince, Rice, Weissman, & Nyberg, 2003; Naghavi & Nyberg, 2005) have reported substantial overlap in the activation of brain areas during episodic memory retrieval and working memory as well as visual attention and conscious visual perception tasks. These broader investigations suggest that these areas are involved in general cognitive processing and are not uniquely associated with memory performance.

Again, the point is that humans will utilize whatever resources they can recruit in order to perform a task. Individuals using different retrieval strategies (e.g., visualization, verbalization, lax or strict decision criteria, etc.) show very different patterns of brain activation even when performing the same memory task (Miller & Van Horn, 2007). This makes it extremely dangerous to assume that any task is made up of purely one process. Even though many researchers involved in neuroimaging do not make task purity assumptions, these examples "illustrate the widespread practice in functional neuroimaging of interpreting activations only in terms of the particular cognitive function being investigated (Cabeza et al., 2003, p. 390)." Although it is tempting to assume that the brain is organized according to categories identified by cognitive science, it is more likely that, as suggested by Friston, Price, Fletcher, Moore, Frackowiak, and Dolan (1996), "the structure of the cognitive components (functional model) and the brain's physiological implementation are not isomorphic" (p. 98). We do not mean to suggest that these studies have no value—they clearly do add to our knowledge of how cognitive functioning works—but, instead, would like to urge more caution in the interpretation of localization studies, which are sometimes taken as showing that an activated area is where some unique process takes place.

7.6 Chapter Summary

There have been numerous critics of the idea that a task or a process can ever be a "pure" measure of memory, without contamination from other processes (Crowder, 1983; 1993; Jacoby, 1991; Restle, 1974). Even while paying lip service to these criticisms, many researchers still act as if a task taps one or just a small number of memory systems (episodic, semantic, etc.) or processes (data driven, conceptually driven, etc.). However, as we have demonstrated here, even using logical and computational methods, it is difficult if not impossible to separate out contributions of one memory system or one process. In some senses this is an antiprinciple rather than a principle, per se. However, it is an important factor in memory research because it sets a fundamental limitation on how research can be interpreted and, as such, we argue, fits our criteria for a principle in that it follows from viewing memory as a function.

The Relative Distinctiveness Principle

If you take cranberries and stew them like applesauce they taste much more like prunes than rhubarb does.

—Groucho Marx

8.1 Principle 6: The Relative Distinctiveness Principle

The relative distinctiveness principle states that performance on memory tasks depends on how much an item stands out "relative to the background of alternatives from which it must be distinguished" at the time of retrieval (Fisher, 1981, p. 310). It is important to keep in mind that one of the determinants of whether an item is more or less distinct at the time of retrieval, relative to other items, is the relation between the conditions at encoding and those at retrieval (the encoding retrieval principle). It is meaningless to talk of an item's being distinct (or not) in the absence of a specification of the encoding and retrieval processes and the nature of the competing items.

8.2 The Von Restorff Effect

There has been a long history of distinctiveness as an important concept and research topic in memory, with numerous early studies examining both "distinctiveness" and "vividness" (e.g., Burnham, 1888; Calkins, 1894; Jersild, 1929; Koffka; 1935; Van Buskirk, 1932). Perhaps the most well-known example of distinctiveness is the isolation or von Restorff effect (named after Hedwig von Restorff, 1933). In the typical isolation experiment, there are two types of lists. The control list features words presented (for example) in black against a white background. The experimental list is identical to the control list in all respects except that one of the items is made to stand out in some fashion: it could be shown in green instead of black, in a larger font size, with a large red frame around it, the word *trout* could appear in a list in which all the other items are names of different vegetables, or any number of similar manipulations. The much-replicated result is that the unique item (the isolate) is remembered better than the item in the same position in the control list. For example, Huang and Wille (1979) presented subjects with lists of 17 words followed by a free recall test. All words were in black except for the isolate, which was in red. The isolate could occur in either the 2nd, 9th, or 16th position. The results are shown in Figure 8.1.

The control condition showed the standard asymmetrical serial position function seen with free recall: There was an extended recency effect (good recall of items in later serial positions relative to items in the middle of the list) and a smaller primacy effect (recall of items in the first few serial positions). The isolate was recalled better than its control counterpart regardless of its position in the list. The von Restorff effect is reliably obtained with many kinds of tests, including delayed free recall, serial recall, serial learning,

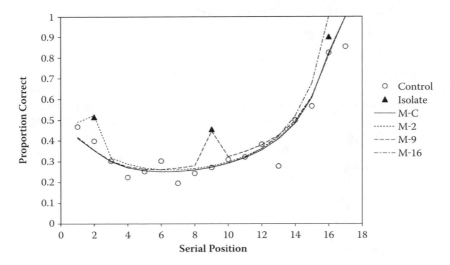

FIGURE 8.1   Proportion of items recalled as a function of serial position. The isolate could occur in the 2nd, 9th, or 16th position. The lines show the predictions of SIMPLE, discussed below, fitting the control data (M-C), and the isolate conditions when it occurred in the 2nd (M-2), 9th (M-9), and 16th (M-16) position. Data reprinted with permission from Huang and Wille (1979). *The Journal of General Psychology*, *101*, 27–34. Copyright © 1979 Heldref Publications.

recognition, and many others. It is also readily observable with nonverbal stimuli (Guérard, Hughes, & Tremblay, 2008), and is observed when the subjects are children (Howe, Courage, Vernescu, & Hunt, 2000), young adults (Huang & Wille, 1979), and older adults (Bireta, Surprenant, & Neath, 2008).

One explanation for this effect is that it is due to surprise: Additional attention is given to the item that differs from its neighbors. Although consistent with the subjective experience, there are many examples of the isolation effect where attention cannot be invoked as an explanation. In particular, this explanation does not explain such effects when the isolate occurs at the first or second position (Bone & Goulet, 1968; Kelley & Nairne, 2001; von Restorff, 1933).[1] When the subject sees the first item, it is not known whether it stands out or not, as there are no other items to compare it to. When the second item is shown, at most the subject can determine that they differ; however, it is still not clear which item is the odd one out. It is only when there are at least three items that the subject can know which one was odd. Moreover, because there are no known differences between isolation effects observed at the first or second position in a list and those at later positions, it seems implausible to invoke an explanation based on attention or surprise. Indeed, the surprise account should predict that when the isolate occurs as the first item, subjects should recall the second item better than when the isolate is much later in the list because it should have evoked a surprise response. This is not seen in the data.

The distinctiveness explanation holds that at retrieval, the isolated item stands out from the other list items. A visual analogy is that a particular red item is easier to see among a field of black items than an otherwise identical black item would be. Although more attention may have been given to the red item at the time it was seen, such additional attention is not necessary. A more detailed account of this explanation is offered later in this chapter.

8.3 Distinctiveness in Short-Term/Working Memory

The typical von Restorff experiment uses a long list of items (a dozen or more), well beyond the capacity limit most multiple memory theorists impose on short-term or working memory. However, the same basic

---

[1] Many authors cite Pillsbury and Rausch (1943) as showing a von Restorff effect when the first item in the list is the isolate. This is a misreading of their experiment. Their stimuli "were presented in random order" (p. 294); the isolated item could have occurred in the first position by chance, but no data are reported that reveal whether this resulted in a von Restorff effect. Similarly, there is no relevant evidence reported by Bellezza and Cheney (1973): They asked their subjects to rehearse the isolated items more than the nonisolated items.

isolation effect is readily observable in experiments that are typically designed to examine short-term or working memory. For example, Kelley and Nairne (2001) had subjects read out loud six-item lists of words. Immediately following list presentation, the subjects were given a free reconstruction of order test in which the same six words were shown, but this time in a new random order. The subjects' task was to rearrange the words so that they were in their original presentation order. There were two isolation manipulations: In one condition, the isolate was shown in a larger font size, and in a second condition, the isolate was shown in a smaller font size. This was to rule out an explanation based on ease of perceptual processing. If the items in the larger font size were better recalled, one explanation might be that these items were easier to process. However, this argument would not explain why items that are harder to perceive would be better recalled. Kelley and Nairne had isolates occur equally often at each serial position, and therefore could construct and plot a composite list. The results are shown in Figure 8.2.

It is important to note that the magnitude of the effect is essentially constant over every position, including the first position. This is further evidence against an attentional account. It is also important to note that there is no apparent difference between rendering one item unusual by making it larger, or by rendering it unusual by making it smaller. What matters is that the isolate differs, not that it is easier to process. Similar effects have been reported in other short-term paradigms (e.g., Cunningham, Marmie, & Healy, 1998). Again, the distinctiveness account readily explains the results in the exact same way as when the effect occurs in situations

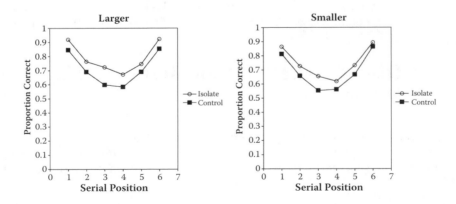

FIGURE 8.2   The isolation effect is observed (1) in a typical short-term memory task and (2) in all serial positions, including the first position. Data from Experiment 2 of Kelley & Nairne (2001). *Journal of Experimental Psychology: Learning, Memory, and Cognition, 27,* 54–66.

beyond the capacity of short-term or working memory: the unusual item (whether smaller or larger) stands out from the other items.

8.4 Instantiating the Principle

Thus far, we have appealed only to an intuitive notion of what it might mean to be distinct: A red item is distinct when it is embedded in a list of black items, the word *table* is distinct when it is embedded in a list of types of fish. In other situations, however, it may not be as obvious whether an item stands out or, if it does, the degree to which it stands out. Before presenting other examples of distinctiveness in various types of memory, we make the principle more precise by instantiating it within a specific model.

There have been many mathematical and computational models based on the idea of distinctiveness (see Neath & Brown, 2007, for a review). Here, we focus on one particular model that includes elements from many of the earlier models (e.g., Baddeley, 1976; Murdock, 1960; Neath, 1993). Brown, Neath, and Chater (2007; see also Neath & Brown, 2006) proposed a model called SIMPLE, which stands for Scale Independent Memory and Perceptual Learning. The model is scale independent in the sense that it applies equally to short-term/working memory as long-term memory: the time scale is irrelevant to the operation of the model. The basic idea is that memory is best conceived as a discrimination task. Items are represented as occupying positions along one or more dimensions and, in general, those items with fewer close neighbors on the relevant dimensions at the time of retrieval will be more likely to be recalled that items with more close neighbors.

8.4.1 SIMPLE and Absolute Identification

The easiest way to present the ideas behind SIMPLE is by way of an absolute identification task (for more details, see Neath, Brown, McCormack, Chater, & Freeman, 2006). Consider the two sets of lines shown in Figure 8.3. If you were in the control condition, you would be shown all nine lines in the top part of the figure, one at a time. Then, for each test trial, you would be shown one line by itself and asked to indicate its number. If you were in the isolate condition, the exact same procedure would be followed except that you would see the lines in the bottom part of the figure.

Figure 8.4 shows the results of an unpublished experiment that used these stimuli. The left panel shows performance in the control condition and the right panel shows performance in the isolate condition. In the control condition, performance is best for the end items and worst for the

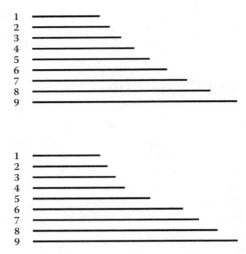

FIGURE 8.3 Two sets of stimuli. The upper set vary by a fixed percentage (i.e., line 2 is 15% longer than line 1). In the lower set, Line 5 is 27% longer than line 4 and 27% shorter than line 6; all other lines differ by 11%.

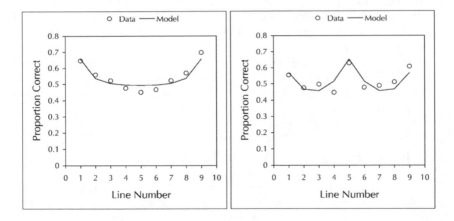

FIGURE 8.4 Proportion of lines correctly identified as a function of line number (see Figure 8.3). The circles show the data, the lines show the fit of SIMPLE.

middle item. In distinctiveness terms, Line 1 and Line 9 have no neighbors on one side (i.e., there is no Line 0 or Line 10), whereas Line 5 has 4 neighbors on each side. In the isolate condition, performance is best for the middle item, next best for the end items, and worst for the remaining items. Although Line 5 still has neighbors on each side, it has no close neighbors. Line 1 and Line 9 have only 1 neighbor, but it is a close neighbor.

To fit SIMPLE to these data, we first assume that the lines are represented on a dimension that corresponds to length: the lines do not really vary systematically in any other dimension. In SIMPLE, the underlying psychological dimension is typically log-transformed; that is, the line of 3 cm is represented by a value of 1.099 on the internal dimension.[2] The other values are shown in Table 8.1. Note that on a log scale, all items in the control condition differ by 0.140 (taking into account rounding).

In SIMPLE, then, items are represented on a log-transformed dimension, and the particular dimension depends on the stimuli and the situation. In the absolute identification task, the subject is asked to indicate the test stimulus' number. In the model, this is the same as saying that a cue is presented (in this case, the actual line) and the subject has to retrieve the correct number (in this case, the stored representation that is most similar to the cue and indicate its number). This is described by Equation 8.1: The probability of responding with item i, R_i, when given the cue for stimulus j, c_j, is a ratio of the similarity between item i and cue j ($\eta_{i,j}$) divided by the sum of the similarity between cue j and all the other items that are potential responses.

$$P\left(R_i \mid C_j\right) = \frac{\eta_{i,j}}{\displaystyle\sum_{k=1}^{n} \eta_{j,k}} \tag{8.1}$$

How is similarity defined? The similarity, $\eta_{i,j}$, between two log-transformed memory representations, M_i and M_j, is given by Equation 8.2:

$$\eta_{i,j} = e^{-c\left|M_i - M_j\right|} \tag{8.2}$$

Ignore the parameter c for a moment. This equation has the effect that items that are very close on a psychological scale have a similarity that approaches 1.0 (because when $|M_i - M_j| = 0$, the equation reduces to $e^0 = 1$), whereas items that are very distant on the scale have a similarity that approaches 0.0 (because as $|M_i - M_j|$ approaches infinity, the equation reduces to $e^{\infty} = 0$). This is quite typical of many models (e.g., Shepard, 1987).

TABLE 8.1 The Length (in Centimeters) and the Corresponding Log-Transformed Values for Each Line Shown in the Top Half of Figure 8.3

Line	1	2	3	4	5	6	7	8	9
Length	3.000	3.450	3.968	4.563	5.247	6.034	6.939	7.980	9.177
Log value	1.099	1.238	1.378	1.518	1.658	1.797	1.937	2.077	2.217

---

[2] See the discussion in Brown et al. (2007) for the use of a log transform rather than, for example, a power function. Of relevance here, a log transform keeps the number of parameters to a minimum.

The main free parameter in SIMPLE is c, and this affects the rate at which similarity reduces with psychological distance. The effect of this parameter is that the probability of correctly identifying a given item is determined most strongly by its immediate neighbors; more distant neighbors have less influence. The effect of changing parameter c is shown in Figure 8.5: When c is smaller (i.e., 0.5) a difference on the psychological scale of 0.5 results in a computed similarity value of 0.78. As c increases, the same difference between two memory representations results in less and less similarity. When c is 5, a difference on the psychological scale of 0.5 results in a computed similarity value of 0.08.

To fit the data, the log values shown in Table 8.2 are used to calculate the similarity of each item to every other item. For example, the similarity between Line 1 and Line 2 is

$$\eta_{1,2} = e^{-c|1.099-1.238|} \tag{8.3}$$

With c set to 7.65, the similarity is 0.343. This is done for all combinations. Then, a probability matrix is generated, shown in Table 8.2, which indicates how likely it is that each item will be retrieved given a particular cue.

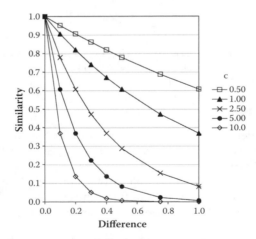

FIGURE 8.5   When c is small (e.g., 0.50), a difference of 1.0 between two items results in substantial similarity (i.e., 0.6 on a scale of 0.0 to 1.0). As c increases, this same difference results in less and less similarity until (in this particular example), as c becomes closer to 10.0, similarity decreases to 0.0. Reprinted with permission from Neath and Brown (2006). SIMPLE: Further applications of a local distinctiveness model of memory. *The Psychology of Learning and Motivation, 36,* 201–243. Copyright © 2006 Elsevier.

TABLE 8.2 The Probability That a Particular Line Will Be Recalled, Given Each Cue

	Line 1	Line 2	Line 3	Line 4	Line 5	Line 6	Line 7	Line 8	Line 9
Cue 1	0.657	0.225	0.077	0.027	0.009	0.003	0.001	0.000	0.000
Cue 2	0.184	0.536	0.184	0.063	0.022	0.007	0.003	0.001	0.000
Cue 3	0.059	0.173	0.504	0.173	0.059	0.020	0.007	0.002	0.001
Cue 4	0.020	0.058	0.170	0.495	0.170	0.058	0.020	0.007	0.002
Cue 5	0.007	0.020	0.058	0.169	0.492	0.169	0.058	0.020	0.007
Cue 6	0.002	0.007	0.020	0.058	0.170	0.495	0.170	0.058	0.020
Cue 7	0.001	0.002	0.007	0.020	0.059	0.173	0.504	0.173	0.059
Cue 8	0.000	0.001	0.003	0.007	0.022	0.063	0.184	0.536	0.184
Cue 9	0.000	0.000	0.001	0.003	0.009	0.027	0.077	0.225	0.657

Note: For this computation, c was set to 7.65. The diagonal represents correct responses.

Figure 8.4 shows that the model does a good job of accounting for the data. The sole difference between fitting the control and the isolate data is the values of the lines; the value of the one free parameter is the same for the two conditions. According to the model, the increased performance in the isolate condition is due to increased relative distinctiveness of the fifth item compared to the uniform condition. Similar experiments have been conducted with stimuli that varied systematically along other dimensions including frequency (Hz), weight (g), and numerosity (number of stimuli). For each dimension, the results were similar to the predictions shown in Figure 8.4 (Neath et al., 2006).

According to SIMPLE, the same idea explains the isolation effect in both absolute identification and isolation effects observed in free recall and serial recall, whether short-term or working memory is playing a role or not. Performance depends on the extent to which an item stands out relative to the background of alternatives from which it must be distinguished at the time of retrieval. In order to apply SIMPLE to the isolation effect observed in free recall shown in Figure 8.1, however, some additions to the model are necessary.

8.4.2 SIMPLE and Free Recall

In the typical free recall task, the experimenter chooses a set of to-be-remembered words that are equated for frequency, familiarity, concreteness, and so on. Thus, in the usual case, the only systematic variation is when the item occurred. According to SIMPLE, items in a free recall task are represented on a temporal dimension (Brown, Morin, & Lewandowsky, 2006). The zero point is the time the item is retrieved, and each item's value is the time until retrieval.

As an example, consider a list of nine items presented at a rate of one item per second. The items vary systematically only in terms of the time of presentation, so the underlying representational dimension is assumed to be temporal. We further assume that recall of the first item begins 1 s after presentation of the final item. Thus, at this stage in recall, Item 9 has a temporal value of 1 to reflect the 1 s that elapsed between its presentation and initiation of recall. Item 8 has a temporal value of 2 because it was presented 2 s before the initiation of recall. Item 7 has a temporal value of 3 because it was presented 3 s before the initiation of recall, and so on. These values are shown in Table 8.3. These temporal values are then log transformed, resulting in the values shown in the row labeled Log 1 in the table. This corresponds to the log values at the time of recall of the first item.

What complicates the matter is that free recall is a dynamic process: It takes time to recall each item. For simplicity, in this example we assume that recall of each item takes 1 s. After the first item is recalled, the temporal values are updated (TV2) and again log transformed. The line "Log 2" gives these values at the time of recall of the second item. After the second item is recalled, the temporal values are again updated (TV3) and log transformed, resulting in the line "Log 3." Note that what is happening is that items are moving closer together, but the change is greatest for items at the end of the list.

For most free recall experiments, researchers do not report the order of output or the time taken to produce each response. When temporal output times (Surprenant, Neath, & Brown, 2006) and order of recall (Brown et al., 2007) are actually measured, SIMPLE does, in fact, make accurate predictions. However, the model also makes quite accurate predictions when some simplifying assumptions about temporal output are made. For a nine-item list, we might assume an average output time of 5 s.

TABLE 8.3 At the Time of Recall of the First Item, the Items Have the Temporal Values Shown in the Row Labeled TV1

	Item								
	1	2	3	4	5	6	7	8	9
TV1	9	8	7	6	5	4	3	2	1
Log 1	2.197	2.079	1.946	1.792	1.609	1.386	1.099	0.693	0.000
TV2	10	9	8	7	6	5	4	3	2
Log 2	2.303	2.197	2.079	1.946	1.792	1.609	1.386	1.099	0.693
TV3	11	10	9	8	7	6	5	4	3
Log 3	2.398	2.303	2.197	2.079	1.946	1.792	1.609	1.386	1.099

Note: Because recall of that first item takes time, the temporal values need to be updated for recall of the second item (TV2)

Another difference between absolute identification and free recall is that in the latter task, people rarely recall all of the items; that is, they often omit responses. As described so far, SIMPLE makes no omissions. One way of implementing omissions in SIMPLE is to decrease the probability of responding if the probability of responding as calculated in Equation 8.1 is below some threshold. Equation 8.4 does just that.

$$P_o = \frac{1}{1+e^{-s(P-t)}} \tag{8.4}$$

The probability of output, P_o, is related to the initial probability calculated according to Equation 8.1, P, in the following way. There are two parameters: t is a threshold, and varies between 0 and 1. The other parameter, s, affects the noisiness of the threshold. For example, if t were set to 0.8 and s were very large, the model would approximate a system that recalled (with 100% probability) all items with relative strengths greater than 0.8 and omitted (with 100% probability) all items with strengths less than 0.8. As s becomes smaller, the transition from low to high recall probabilities becomes more gradual.

There are thus three free parameters, c, s, and t. With c set to 5.95, s set to 9.09, and t set to 0.52, SIMPLE produces the output probability matrix shown in Table 8.4.

The final difference we will consider between absolute identification and free recall is how to interpret the output probability matrix. In absolute identification, a response was correct only if the response to the cue for Line X was Line X. All other responses were errors. In free recall, however, it does not matter which cue elicits a particular item as long as the item was on the list. So, if the response to the cue for Item 1 is Item 1, that is a correct response. However, if the subject is trying to retrieve the

TABLE 8.4 The Output Probability Matrix for Free Recall of a Nine-Item List When the Average Output Time Is Assumed to Be 5 s

	Item 1	Item 2	Item 3	Item 4	Item 5	Item 6	Item 7	Item 8	Item 9
Cue 1	0.274	0.083	0.034	0.019	0.013	0.011	0.009	0.009	0.009
Cue 2	0.058	0.168	0.054	0.025	0.015	0.011	0.010	0.009	0.009
Cue 3	0.025	0.048	0.141	0.044	0.021	0.013	0.010	0.009	0.009
Cue 4	0.016	0.023	0.044	0.140	0.040	0.019	0.012	0.010	0.009
Cue 5	0.012	0.015	0.021	0.043	0.156	0.038	0.017	0.011	0.009
Cue 6	0.010	0.012	0.014	0.020	0.043	0.191	0.037	0.016	0.011
Cue 7	0.009	0.010	0.011	0.013	0.019	0.044	0.257	0.037	0.014
Cue 8	0.009	0.009	0.010	0.011	0.013	0.019	0.046	0.392	0.036
Cue 9	0.009	0.009	0.009	0.009	0.010	0.012	0.018	0.056	0.719

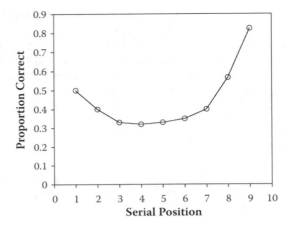

FIGURE 8.6 Predicted proportion correctly recalled for the 9-item free recall example.

fifth item (i.e., is using the cue for Item 5) but happens to recall Item 4 instead, that is still a correct response. The reason is that in free recall, all the experimenter cares about for scoring purposes is whether an item was recalled. In SIMPLE, then, the probability of recalling an item in free recall is the sum of the probabilities of that particular item being recalled due to any cue. We simply sum the columns, and the resulting probability, capped at 1.0 if necessary, is the prediction. Figure 8.6 shows the result. There is the classic asymmetry, due to the logarithmic compression of the temporal values. There is an additional slight benefit for the first and last items due to the lack of a neighbor on one side. Keep in mind that recall of each item is a function of its relative distinctiveness along, in this case, a temporal dimension. In absolute identification, correct performance was also a function of each item's relative distinctiveness, but along a dimension corresponding to length rather than time.

8.4.3 SIMPLE and the von Restorff Isolation Effect

We can now fit the Huang and Wille (1979) data shown in Figure 8.1. The basic idea is that the to-be-remembered items are represented on two dimensions rather than just one. The first dimension is the usual temporal dimension, and the second dimension represents (in this case) the color of the item. Adding a second dimension requires changing Equation 8.2. Following Nosofsky (1992) and others, an attentional parameter, W, is introduced to weight each dimension, with the constraint that the weights must sum to 1.0. For the case of two dimensions, time and color, the similarity between i and j will be given by:

$$\eta_{i,j} = e^{-c(W_T|T_i-T_j|+W_C|C_i-C_j|)}$$ (8.5)

where T_i and C_i are the values of item i in memory on the temporal and color dimensions, respectively, and W_T and W_C are the respective weights. All black items get a value of 1 on the color dimension, but the red item gets a value of 2. The average output time is assumed to be 9 s. The other parameters were set as follows: $c = 8.45$, $s = 16.08$, $t = 0.36$, and $W_T = 0.94$ (and thus $W_C = 1 - W_T$). The results are shown in Figure 8.1. Not only does SIMPLE capture the performance in the control condition well, but it also accurately shows the enhanced recall of the more distinct item. Brown et al. (2007) show how SIMPLE accounts for other isolation data.

According to SIMPLE, then, not only is the isolation effect due to relative distinctiveness, but the general shape of the serial position curve is due to relative distinctiveness. In general, free and serial recall produce a function in which the first few items are well-recalled (the primacy effect) and the last few items are well recalled (the recency effect), but items in the middle are recalled less well. The magnitude of primacy and recency effects can be affected by many different manipulations, and depending on the experimental design, one can observe almost all possibilities, from almost all primacy to almost all recency. The thing that all have in common, however, is that the experimental manipulation has caused some items to be more distinct at the time of retrieval than other items.

8.4.4 SIMPLE and Serial Recall

Several recent papers have suggested that whereas people do seem to be using a temporal dimension in free recall (Brown et al., 2006), they may not do so in serial recall tests (Lewandowsky, Duncan, & Brown, 2004; Lewandowsky, Brown, Wright, & Nimmo, 2006). Serial recall requires the subject to recall the items in the same order in which they were presented. Given this emphasis, it seems reasonable that serial position might be the primary dimension. But when is position used and when is time used? Currently, it seems as if temporal information is used if it is available and useful (or predictable).

In studies in which items are presented at a constant rate, it is unclear whether subjects are using a temporal or positional dimension. In studies where items are not presented at a constant rate it is possible to infer whether the temporal information is affecting recall. For example, Neath and Crowder (1996) presented some lists with a decreasing temporal interval between items (e.g., 400 ms between Item 1 and Item 2, 200 ms between Item 2 and 3, 100 ms between Item 3 and 4, and so on), and some with an increasing temporal interval (the reverse of the decreasing). As predicted by SIMPLE, recall was sensitive to these manipulations: In those parts of the list in which items had increased relative distinctiveness, performance was better, and in those parts of the list in which items had reduced temporal distinctiveness, performance was worse.[3] This differential performance indicates that subjects were aware of and did use the temporal information. In SIMPLE terms, the major dimension was temporal.

However, when the varying temporal intervals are not predictable, one does not see performance change as a function of temporal distinctiveness (e.g., Lewandowsky et al. 2006). This suggests that subjects are not representing the information on a temporal dimension. In these cases, a version of SIMPLE in which items are represented on a dimension corresponding to serial position fits the data well.

8.5 Distinctiveness in Sensory Memory

The relative distinctiveness principle applies in situations that use a time scale commonly found only in studies of sensory memory.[4] Consider a five-item list of consonants presented at a rate of approximately one item every 50 ms. One second elapsed between the offset of the final item and the appearance of the test. The test was a standard serial reconstruction of order task in which five buttons appeared on the screen displaying the letters that had appeared on that trial in a new random order. The subject's task was to click on the five buttons in the original presentation order. In this test, omissions were not possible.

The data are shown in the Figure 8.7 as filled squares. Each panel shows the proportion of times the indicated item was recalled in each of the five possible positions. Primacy and recency effects are evident, and the position error gradients are typical: when an item is recalled in the wrong position, it is mostly likely to be recalled in an adjacent position. This procedure produces serial position curves and position error gradients that look almost identical to those observed in standard immediate serial recall (e.g., Nairne, 1992), as well as those observed when the time scale is on the order of weeks (see Neath & Brown, 2006); the time scale in the current experiment, however, is measured in milliseconds.

---

[3] Neath and Brown (2006) show the fits of SIMPLE to this type of data.
[4] A complete description of the experiment is available in Neath (2005). This example was first presented in Neath and Brown (2006).

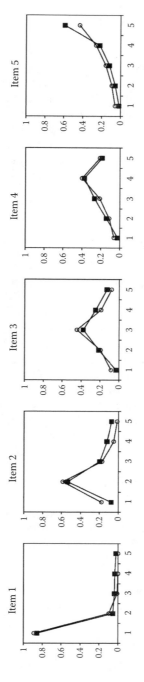

FIGURE 8.7 Proportion of times each item was recalled in each position (black squares) and predictions of SIMPLE (white circles) for data collected in a sensory memory paradigm. Reprinted with permission from Neath and Brown (2006). SIMPLE: Further applications of a local distinctiveness model of memory. *The Psychology of Learning and Motivation, 36*, 201–243. Copyright © 2006 Elsevier.

Because the temporal intervals were predictable, we use the temporal version of SIMPLE to fit these data. For simplicity, the final (fifth) item is presented 1 s prior to the retrieval. Each succeeding item is an additional 0.05 s earlier. Thus, the first item is presented 1.2 s prior to its attempted retrieval. Recall of all five items takes time. On the plausible assumption that each retrieval takes 1 s, the second item is retrieved 2.15 s after presentation, although it occurred 1.15 s prior to the recall attempt of the first item. With this assumption and with c set to 51.86, SIMPLE produces an appropriate pattern of results, as shown as open circles in the top panel of Figure 8.7.[5] SIMPLE produces serial position curves and appropriate error gradients in iconic-like paradigms for the same reason it produces them at longer intervals, relative distinctiveness on the dimension (or dimensions) on which the items are represented.

8.6 Distinctiveness in Semantic Memory

In this section, we give two examples of how the relative distinctiveness principle can be observed in semantic memory. In both cases the probability of making a correct response (or the probability of making an error) is related to the similarity among items and the similarity is affected by how close the items are on the dimension(s) of interest.

The first example applies SIMPLE to recall of the order of verses in well-known hymns.[6] By most multisystem accounts of memory, such information should be in the semantic memory system rather than in the episodic memory system. Maylor (2002) recruited subjects from a denomination in which the same versions of the hymns have been used since 1933 and one which routinely sings all verses of a hymn. The subjects were given 6 verses from a hymn and were asked to reconstruct the original order. Maylor was careful to choose hymns in which there were no cues in each verse as to the order. Each subject received 18 hymns, and the results are shown in the left panel of Figure 8.8.

The results have all the hallmarks of data from an episodic memory task involving sensory, working, short-term, or long-term memory: there are clear primacy and recency effects, and the error gradients show that when a verse was placed in the wrong order, it was most often placed in an adjacent position.

To simulate these results, we first assumed an underlying dimension of 1 to 6. With $c = 2.28$, SIMPLE produced the results shown in the

---

[5] It is also possible to fit these data with a positional version of SIMPLE (Lewandowsky et al., 2004).

[6] This simulation is reported in detail in Neath and Brown (2006).

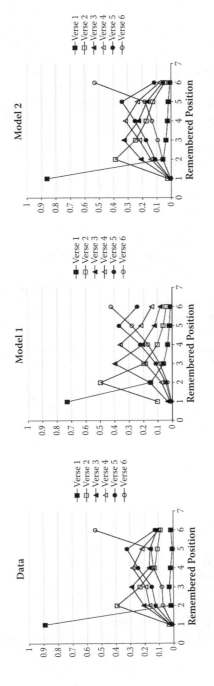

FIGURE 8.8 Proportion of hymn verses recalled in each possible position (left panel) and predictions of two versions of SIMPLE (right two panels). Data reprinted with permission from E. A. Maylor (2002). Serial position effects in semantic memory. Reconstructing the order of verses of hymns. *Psychonomic Bulletin & Review, 9,* 816–820. Copyright © 2002 Psychonomic Society. Model fit reprinted with permission from Neath and Brown (2006). SIMPLE: Further applications of a local distinctiveness model of memory. *The Psychology of Learning and Motivation, 36,* 201–243. Copyright © 2006 Elsevier.

middle panel of Figure 8.8. Although similar to the data, the results from SIMPLE differ in two ways: recall of the first and last items is lower and recall of the middle items is higher than in the data. Maylor (2002, p. 819), pointed out that it is likely that the first verse is slightly more familiar to her subjects because it is included in the announcement of the hymns. If we adjust the values on the underlying dimension such that the values are 1, 4, 5, 6, 7, 12 (rather than 1, 2, 3, 4, 5, 6) and set c to 1.99, SIMPLE produces results much closer to the data, as shown in the right panel of Figure 8.8. Although the adjustment of dimensional values may appear somewhat post hoc in this example, a more comprehensive approach could make use of an independently derived scaling solution to derive the items' locations in psychological space. We return to this issue a little later.

The second example looks at a very different kind of task, the accuracy in determining which of two numbers is the larger. Parkman (1971) presented pairwise combinations of the numerals 1 through 9, and asked subjects to make fast responses to indicate which member of the pair was the larger. Subjects were reliably faster and more accurate when there was a large numerical difference rather than a small numerical difference between the presented digits. We focus here on the error data. Subjects made approximately 7% errors when the digits differed by only one (e.g., 4 versus 3, or 8 versus 7), and progressively fewer errors as the difference became greater (e.g., 2 versus 7, or 9 versus 3). The proportion of errors that were produced for each difference value are shown in Figure 8.9, together with the predictions of the SIMPLE model of the task (described below).

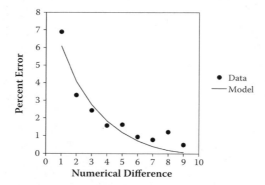

FIGURE 8.9 The percentage error in judging which of two digits is the larger as a function of the numerical difference of the digits (data points) and the fit from SIMPLE (line). Data from Experiment 1 of Parkman (1971). Parkman, J. M. (1971). Temporal aspects of digit and letter inequality judgments. *Journal of Experimental Psychology, 91*, 191–205.

Although many detailed models of number representation have been proposed, our aim here is simply to demonstrate that the principles embodied in SIMPLE—primarily the relative distinctiveness principle— can account for the numerical difference judgment data illustrated in Figure 8.9 as these data represent a clear case of retrieval from long-term (semantic) memory. There exists evidence that suggests that the internal representations of magnitudes are represented as log transformed versions of the actual magnitudes (e.g., Gallistel & Gelman, 1992; for review see Dehaene, 1997). The SIMPLE model, like others, assumes that psychological number representations are logarithmically transformed versions of the actual number magnitudes. In addition, we assume that the probability of making an incorrect decision of which number is bigger is related to the similarity of the two items. Thus, in this simulation, we do not model the decision process itself, but show that the pattern of errors is directly related to the similarity of the numbers that are compared.

We computed the similarity matrix as described earlier. Because Parkman (1971) used all combinations of numbers that differed by 1 (and 2, and 3, and so on), we computed the average similarity between adjacent numbers. We then did the same for all numbers separated by 2, and so on. These average similarity values are then scaled proportionally to reflect percentage errors. With the c parameter was set to 2.19, the model produced the function shown in Figure 8.9. Essentially, the more distinct the numbers were from each other, relative to the other numbers being used, the more accurate was the judgment.

8.7 Distinctiveness in Implicit Memory

It has been claimed that distinctiveness effects are observed only in explicit memory (e.g., Mulligan, 1996; Weldon & Coyote, 1996). Indeed, Smith and Hunt (2000, p. 442) concluded that "distinctive processing does not affect performance in the absence of intentional memory instructions." If this statement is correct, then it would severely limit the distinctiveness principle.

We suggest that the search for distinctiveness effects in implicit memory tasks is similar to the search for interference in implicit memory tasks (discussed in Chapter 3): What is important is whether the information that is supposed to be distinct (in the former case) or interfere (in the latter) is relevant to the task. If it is not relevant, then the effects will not be seen.

Consistent with this claim, Geraci and Rajaram (2004) devised an implicit task in which the distinct information was relevant to processing at test and observed effects of distinctiveness. The experiment is fairly complex, so it is worth presenting it in detail in order to make the results clear. The presentation phase was incidental: there was no mention of any up-coming memory task. Rather, subjects were asked to press the space bar on a computer keyboard after they had read words presented on a computer screen. There were two types of lists. In the "distinct" lists, one item was semantically different from the others (e.g., *trout, herring, shark, table, catfish, perch, salmon, tuna*). In the "common" lists, all items were unrelated (e.g., *opium, cookies, sponge, table, salmon, Iroquois, spokes, four*). Note that for some subjects, the word *table* was distinct whereas for others, it was common. After the lists had been presented, the subjects participated in an unrelated distractor task.

There were two types of tests, one designed to be direct (or explicit), in which direct reference was made to the learning episode, and one designed to be indirect (or implicit), in which no mention was made of the learning episode. For the direct test, subjects saw a category label (e.g., *fish*) followed by a possible category exemplar. They were asked to read both and respond "yes" if the exemplar had been studied and "no" if the exemplar had not been studied. For the indirect test, subjects saw the same items at test, but were told to respond "yes" if the exemplar belonged in the category and "no" if it did not. Following the indirect test, subjects were questioned as to whether they were aware of the manipulation that some of the exemplars had been in the previous list. Data from those subjects who responded that they were aware of the relation was not included in the following analysis.

Given the type of tests used, response times were analyzed (see Table 8.5). The direct test, which required that the subjects refer back to the learning episode, showed the expected distinctiveness effect: response times to the distinct items were faster than to the common items (1495 versus 1550 ms). Critically, the same pattern was also observed in the indirect test: faster responding to distinct than common items (1486 versus 1545 ms). The important point is at the time of retrieval, the subjects in the implicit condition were required to process both the category and the exemplar; in other studies, no such processing was needed at test and thus no distinctiveness effect was observed. In this experiment, the distinctiveness manipulation was relevant to the task, and there was a distinctiveness effect.

TABLE 8.5 Mean Response Time (in Milliseconds) to Respond if the Test Item Had Been Studied (Direct Test) or if the Test Item Belonged in a Particular Category (Indirect Test)

	Distinct Items	Common Items
Direct test	1495	1550
Indirect test	1486	1545

Note: Data from Geraci and Rajaram. (2004). *Journal of Memory and Language, 51*, 217–230.

A similar conclusion holds for the von Restorff or isolation effect and incidental learning. In his comprehensive review of the isolation effect, Wallace (1965, p. 416) noted that the effect is observed in incidental learning, but only when the key item "was isolated in a manner which was relevant to the learner's task, that is, isolation was directly related to the response required of the subject."

8.8 Underlying Dimensions

In order to claim that an item stands out from other items, it is necessary to describe how the items are represented. In the case of absolute identification of pure tones, it is reasonable to assume that the dimension is frequency. In fitting the Maylor (2002) data, it seems reasonable that the verses could be ordered along a position dimension, but a better fit was obtained using values on the scale that were not uniformly spaced.

Rather than making arguments that a particular assumption about the underlying dimension is reasonable or not, it would be better to try to obtain a more objective (or at least an independent) estimate of the underlying psychological dimensions. One way is to use multidimensional scaling (MDS). A full description of MDS is beyond the scope of this monograph (see Borg & Groenen, 2005). However, a brief overview can be given. At its core, MDS takes measurements of similarity (or difference) among pairs of items and represents them spatially. Oftentimes, two dimensions are all that is needed, in which case the representation can be thought of as a map.

Consider, for example, Table 8.6 which lists approximate distances (in kilometers) between three Canadian cities. The important point is that each city is given a measure of how distant it is from all other cities. This information is fed into a program that does multidimensional scaling. You can think of the process as being analogous to the following. First, a mark representing St. John's is put down in an arbitrary location on a piece of paper. Then, another mark, representing Halifax, is put down. The only constraint in the location is that the distance between the two on paper has to be proportional to the actual distance. Then, a third mark is made for Toronto,

TABLE 8.6 Distances (in Kilometers) Between Three Canadian Cities

	Halifax	St. John's	Toronto
Halifax	0	880	1287
St. John's	880	0	2122
Toronto	1287	2122	0

but this mark has to be proportional to both the distance from Toronto to Halifax and from Toronto to St. John's. The resulting map will indicate the relative locations of the cities, although real-world dimensions may not necessarily be preserved. For example, Toronto may appear to the east of St. John's. The coordinates in the map can serve as a precise measurement of how the cities can are represented, and there are procedures to rotate the dimensions to make them correspond to reality (i.e., make Toronto the westernmost city). The important point, however, is that the representational space illustrates how close or far each city is from the others.

This procedure can be done for stimuli in a memory experiment. First, the experimenter obtains a measure of distance (or similarity). This can come from a ratings task, in which the subject rates the similarity of two stimuli. These values are used as input to MDS, and the program will respond with coordinates, just as with the cities example above. Second, the researcher conducts a memory experiment using the same stimuli that had just been rated for similarity (or dissimilarity). Surprenant, Neath, and Brown (2006) reported the results of an MDS analysis which was then used as the basis for specifying the representation in SIMPLE. Here, we focus on one aspect of their data that was not extensively covered in the original report in order to make several points not only about relative distinctiveness but also about SIMPLE and the assumptions it entails.

The experiment was a standard acoustic confusion (or phonological similarity) study. Subjects (adults aged 62–81) heard a list of either similar-sounding (B, D, G, P, T, V) or dissimilar-sounding (F, K, L, M, R, Q) consonants and were then asked to reconstruct the presentation order. Performance was far lower for the similar-sounding lists than for the dissimilar-sounding lists, the standard result. In addition, we measured how long it took each person to make each response (see Table 8.7). This was done to remove the necessity of having to use estimated temporal values in the modeling.

In order to fit SIMPLE to these data, MDS was used to calculate the underlying dimensions. A two-dimensional solution was possible, and the coordinates are shown in Table 8.8 for both the similar- and dissimilar-sounding items.

TABLE 8.7 Mean Output Times for Each Item

	1	2	3	4	5	6
Dissimilar	1.649	1.494	1.374	1.473	1.653	1.284
Similar	1.812	1.350	1.455	2.448	1.731	1.524

Note: Surprenant et al. (2006). Journal of Memory and Language, 55, 572–586.

TABLE 8.8 Coordinates From a
Two-Dimensional Multidimensional
Scaling Solution

	D1	D2
B	−0.2056	0.6496
D	−0.1529	1.1249
G	0.1013	1.0851
P	−0.2978	0.9117
T	−0.1259	0.9744
V	−0.3109	0.7536
F	1.6853	−0.3078
K	1.6341	−0.4777
L	−1.1718	−1.2541
M	−0.7069	−1.6469
Q	1.3066	−1.1139
R	−1.7555	−0.6988

Three dimensions were used to represent the items: The standard temporal dimension (which used the measured values shown in Table 8.7), and the two dimensions from the MDS solution (shown in Table 8.8). There are four free parameters: c, the main relative distinctiveness parameter, which was set to 6.85; s (7.22) and t (0.57), which implement omissions; and w_t, the weight on the temporal dimension, which was set to 0.92. The other two weights, w_{d1} and w_{d1}, the weights on the coordinates from the MDS solution, were constrained to be equal to each other, and with $w_t = 1 - w_{d1} - w_{d2}$, each was set at 0.04. The data (the symbols) and the fit of the model (the lines) are shown in Figure 8.10.

Thus, there are 12 data points shown, and four free parameters. More importantly, the exact same parameters are used for both the dissimilar and similar conditions. The sole difference between the two conditions is the particular MDS solution. According to this account, similar-sounding letters are not recalled as well as dissimilar-sounding letters because they are represented in a smaller area of psychological space. On average, a given similar-sounding item will have more close neighbors than an otherwise comparable dissimilar-sound item. This will result is less relative distinctiveness and subsequent worse performance.

8.9 Chapter Summary

The relative distinctiveness principle states that performance on memory tasks depends on how much an item stands out relative to the background

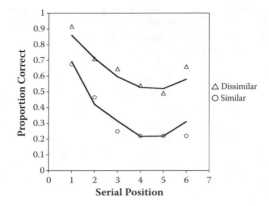

FIGURE 8.10   The proportion of similar- and dissimilar-sounding letters correctly recalled in each position (symbols) and the fit of SIMPLE (lines) when the values for the underlying dimensions were measured rather than estimated. Data from Surprenant et al. (2006). *Journal of Memory and Language, 55,* 572–586.

of alternatives from which it must be distinguished at the time of retrieval. The von Restorff or isolation effect is a clear example of this, but other examples abound. In order to make the notion of relative distinctiveness more precise, it was instantiated in a model of memory called SIMPLE. It is important to note that SIMPLE is not the only way of instantiating the principle, but it was chosen because it highlights the role of distinctiveness in tasks that are often thought to tap sensory memory, working memory, long-term memory, and semantic memory. Although SIMPLE has not yet been applied to implicit memory, distinctiveness effects are also observable in such tasks if they are set up correctly.

The Specificity Principle

I went to a general store, but they wouldn't let me buy anything specific.

—Stephen Wright

9.1 Principle 7: The Specificity Principle

The specificity principle states that those tasks which require the retrieval of a unique piece of information, a single event, or a specific item, seem to be more vulnerable to interference or more likely to result in reduced performance than those tasks that can be completed using generic or gist-based information. Although the principle is intended to capture an empirical regularity seen when different populations are compared (e.g., older versus younger adults, or amnesic versus control subjects), it can also be seen when the same population is compared on different tasks. In one sense, this is our most tentative principle in that, although it captures regularity, there may very well be other important factors, particularly when considering the aging and amnesic literature.[1]

9.2 Levels of Representation

Craik (1983, 1994) noted that the pattern of differences in memory performance between younger and older adults did not fit neatly into the systems categories. In particular, the tasks which older adults tend to do

---

[1] It is perhaps ironic that our most vague principle is the specificity principle.

poorly cut across the proposed episodic and semantic memory systems. According to a structuralist view, this pattern of results is problematic because the episodic and semantic memory systems are categorically and qualitatively different. As such, they are evolutionarily and anatomically distinct, and therefore the two systems develop and decline according to different trajectories. Within this type of framework it is easy to imagine how information in one system might be differentially recallable or might even be destroyed while leaving that in another system entirely intact. The problem is that when the data are examined carefully, this is not the pattern that emerges.

For example, older adults perform worse than younger adults on free recall but not on recognition (Craik & McDowd, 1987), even though both tasks are considered to tap "episodic" or "explicit" memory.[2] Performance on another episodic memory task, cued recall, falls in between recall and recognition, although the size of the age-related difference varies, depending on the demographic characteristics of the sample (Craik, Byrd, & Swanson, 1987). Older adults also experience more tip-of-the-tongue events than younger adults (Burke, MacKay, Worthley, & Wade, 1991) and have more word-finding difficulties in confrontation naming tasks in which, for example, a drawing is shown and the subject is asked to name the object (e.g., Albert, Heller, & Milberg, 1988; Bowles & Poon, 1985). Both of these are, presumably, measures of semantic memory.

Craik (2002a) argued that what older adults find most difficult to retrieve are *specific* pieces of information, whether it be the name of a unique object (semantic memory in the systems view) or the last time a particular story was retold (episodic memory in the systems view). Craik (1983) argued that the results observed with older subjects were related to the amount of environmental support available and the need for self-initiated activity (see Table 9.1). As environmental support decreases, thus requiring an increase in self-initiated activity, the size of the age-related differences increases.

Craik (2002a) elaborated on this continuum and suggested that knowledge might be thought of as being represented in a hierarchy, with the highest levels being abstract, context-free knowledge and the lowest level being specific, almost unique, knowledge. Note that although it might be argued that this is just a restatement of the systems view (with episodic, contextual information at the bottom and semantic, context-free information at the top), it is in fact quite different. Craik does not make a distinction, as is made in the systems view, between first-person autonoetic and general noetic consciousness. Instead, what is important is the uniqueness of the specific piece of knowledge. He also does not argue that these are the result of separate memory systems, but, instead, that they are different

---

[2] Importantly, recognition performance was not at the ceiling nor was recall performance near the floor for either age group.

TABLE 9.1 Memory Tasks Showing Differential Effects of Aging and Levels of Representation

Task	Environmental Support	Self-initiated Activity	Age-related Decrement
Remembering to remember	↑	↑	↑
Free recall			
Cued recall			
Recognition			
Relearning			
Procedural memory			
	Decreases	*Increases*	*Increases*

Note: Adapted from Craik, 1983; 1985.

types of information that are encoded and retrieved with different processes and using different cues (see also Craik, 2002b).

This taxonomy captures much of the existing data regarding what types of tasks are likely to be worse in older as compared to younger adults. For example, item recall is not as affected by aging as order recall (Spencer & Raz, 1995), because according to Craik's view, recalling an item in order usually requires the use of internally generated context cues. Similarly, in comparison to younger adults, older adults have more difficulty remembering the source of a memory (McIntyre & Craik, 1987). Again, situations in which one must recall the source of a particular piece of information generally provide little environmental support and thus require self-initiated activity. As a final example, older adults tend to do quite well on prospective memory tasks that are signaled externally by events in the environment but fare more poorly when performing tasks at a particular time (Einstein, McDaniel, Richardson, Guynn, & Cunfer, 1995). Within Craik's framework, this is because relying on time as a cue involves more self-initiated activity and has less environmental support.

9.3 External Support Versus Specificity

Our principle differs subtly from Craik's framework in that instead of identifying the amount of external or internal support (or perceptual or conceptual processing) as the critical factor, we suggest that the key element is the ability of the cue to constrain the response to a unique item (cf. Bransford, Franks, Morris , & Stein, 1979). Most of the time, environmental support and cue specificity are correlated. For example, in the typical word fragment completion task, there is a great deal of environmental support, and there is only one possible set of letters that can result in a legal completion. In contrast, at the other end of the continuum, a free recall task provides little in the way of environmental support and far fewer constraints on the possible responses. However, it is theoretically possible to construct a situation in which the amount of external support is comparable in two conditions, but the cue gives rise to either a few or many possible responses. We would then predict an age-related difference in the multiple-outcome condition but none in the more constrained response condition.

One study that can be interpreted as supporting our principle was reported by Ryan, Ostergaard, Norton, and Johnson (2001). Ryan et al. tested younger, middle-aged, and older adults using standard direct and indirect stem completion tests. The study phase was always incidental. In the indirect priming test the subjects were told to fill in a three-letter word stem with the first word that came to mind. In the direct cued-recall test, the same word stems were presented but subjects were asked to use the stem to recall items on the study list. The critical manipulations were in the construction of the stimulus lists. One variable was the rank order frequency of the target completion (the words that were presented on the study list) in comparison to other English words that could be used to complete the stem (RF). The second variable was the pronunciation match between the target word and the stem (sound match). The second factor takes into consideration the fact that the pronunciation of a three-letter stem can differ substantially from a word that has the same first three letters. For example, the stem *bar___* is more likely to be completed with the words "bark" or "barn" than "barely" or "baron." Ryan et al. suggested that participants use a strategy of pronouncing the stem and searching the lexicon for a phonological match.

Ryan et al. (2001) showed that when the relative frequency of the target was high, there were no age-related differences on either the direct or indirect test. However, when the relative frequency of the target was low, there were substantial differences between the groups with the young performing the best, the middle-aged in the middle, and the older adults giving the fewest completions from the study list. Sound matching affected priming and cued recall similarly. Importantly, the pattern was the same for both the cued recall and priming conditions. Note that in all the conditions the same amount of external support was provided (three-letter word stems). However, both manipulations of frequency and sound match reduced interference from possible competitors and more precisely constrained the response.

9.3.1 Indirect Memory and Specificity

One area in which our principle might be challenged is with indirect memory tasks. Although older adults tend to do as well as younger on indirect tasks such as priming and the automatic contribution to the remember/know paradigm, it is not invariably the case (see Light, Prull, La Voie, & Healy, 2000 for an extensive review). Our view (and Craik's, 2002a,b) can be interpreted as predicting an ordering of performance on indirect tasks: Given that a conceptual prime provides fewer environmental cues and does not constrain a response as precisely as a perceptual prime, older adults should show worse performance on such a task than in a situation such as perceptual priming in which the cues are entirely present at both encoding and test, and many fewer alternative completions are available. Initially the data on this point were unclear: A meta-analysis performed by Light et al. (2000) described a confusing picture of similarities and differences in semantic and lexical priming for older and younger adults. In particular, contrary to our predictions, Light et al. found that, with some exceptions, older adults tended to perform comparably to young controls on both perceptual and conceptual priming tasks. However, Light et al. noted that there were very few studies that had adequate control conditions and directly tested the conceptual/perceptual priming hypothesis. A more recent study investigating this issue was reported by Stuart, Patel, and Bhagrath (2006).

Stuart et al. (2006) crossed perceptual and conceptual cues with explicit or implicit test instructions. They presented older and younger adults with lists of words and asked them to count the number of vowels in each word (incidental encoding). At test, subjects were either given a word fragment completion task (perceptually driven) or a category exemplar production task (conceptually driven). For example, if the target word on the list had been "lobster," at test subjects were either given "_ob_t_r" and asked to fill in the blanks to create a legal English word, or were given the cue "an edible crustacean." In addition, half of the subjects were given indirect recall instructions ("Answer with the first word that comes to mind") and half were given direct recall instructions ("Use the stimuli presented as cues to recall previously presented items"). In two experiments Stuart et al. found no age differences in the perceptually based tasks. However, as would be predicted by our principle, there were large and significant age-related differences in the conceptual tasks, regardless of the explicitness of the retrieval task. It is worthwhile emphasizing the fact that in the explicit perceptually driven task, there were no age differences. The only difference occurred when the cues given were conceptual (and thus, not uniquely constraining the response), regardless of the recall instructions.

9.3.2 Encoding Specificity

In some senses the encoding specificity principle is a different way of stating our principle. That is, a cue will be useful to the extent to which it was attended to at encoding and is present or reinstated at retrieval. Thus, if older adults have more difficulty with retrieval of specific information, they should show less of an encoding specificity effect. This was confirmed in a series of experiments reported by Rabinowitz, Craik, and Ackerman (1982). Older and younger adults were tested using the procedure developed by Thomson and Tulving (1970) to examine the encoding specificity procedure. In Thomson and Tulving's original experiment words were paired with words that were either weakly or strongly preexperimentally associated with the target. At test, the subjects were given a cue that either matched the one presented at encoding (strong–strong, weak–weak) or mismatched (strong–weak, weak–strong). Thomson and Tulving (1970) showed that when the cues were matched at encoding and retrieval, performance was better than when they mismatched, even when the cue at test was a very strong preexperimentally established associate of the target.

Rabinowitz et al. (1982) replicated this result with younger adults but their group of older adults showed a different pattern: Strong cues were as good a cue as the weak cues even in the condition in which they had not been presented at encoding. Thus, the context-specific cues that aided the younger adults in the weak–weak condition were not used by the older adults. Instead, the older adults used preexperimental knowledge that is less specific to the encoding episode. Rabinowitz et al. also reported this same pattern when younger adults performed the encoding task under conditions of divided attention: Preexperimental strongly associated cues were as good at cuing memory as a weak cue that was present at encoding. Again, general knowledge rather than contextually specific cues were used when processing resources were low or the task was difficult.

Micco and Masson (1992) directly tested the idea that older adults tend to use more general rather than specific cues by using the interpersonal communication paradigm (Begg, Upfold, & Wilton, 1978). This method resembles the old game show *The $10,000 Pyramid* (later *$100,000*) in which one person (the sender) is given a word and then must generate a series of clues that they relate to a second person (the receiver). The receiver must use those clues to determine what the target word is. A twist to Micco and Masson's (1992) procedure was that each target word was given in the presence of either a strongly or a weakly associated context word. The senders were told that the associate was one clue and the clues they provided should be able to provide information that could be used in combination with the context cue. Older and younger adults generated six cues to each target in the presence of both a strongly and weakly associated context word. A different group of older and younger participants were then given these cues and asked to generate the target word. Again, a twist was added so that half of the cue sets were presented along with the context word that was used by the sender to generate the cues and half were presented with the other associate. Cues were provided one at a time and the dependent variable was the number of cues required before the target was produced.

The first result was that the receiver failed to generate the target word more often when the cues were taken from an older adult sender, regardless of the context condition. Thus, on the whole, the cues provided by the older adults were not as useful as those provided by younger adults. However, age of sender interacted with the cue that was present when the sender was generating the cue and the cue that was present when the receiver was attempting to generate the target. In particular, older and younger sender's cues were equally effective when the context cue was a strongly associated word. This suggests that the groups were equally adept at generating cues for the usual or typical meanings of the targets. However, when the targets were presented with the weak associate, the older adults' cues were much less effective than the younger adults' cues. This was the case even when the receiver was a younger person. Thus, the older adults showed deficits when the task required processing of specific features that are not generally associated with the items but were equal to the young adults when the cues were related to the features typically associated with the stimuli.

9.3.3 Gist-Based Versus Item-Based Processing

In addition to recalling fewer correct items than younger adults (errors of omission), older adults are also more likely than younger adults to produce false positive responses in a variety of paradigms (errors of commission). For example, under certain conditions older adults recognize more critical unpresented lures in the Deese–Roediger–McDermott (DRM; Roediger & McDermott, 1995) paradigm (Norman & Schacter, 1997; see Gallo, 2006 for a review). They are also more likely to incorrectly identify a previously-presented name as famous: the "false fame effect" (Dywan & Jacoby, 1990). Similarly, older adults are more likely than younger to report that an imagined event was real (Hashtroudi, Johnson, & Chrosniak, 1990).

There have been a number of reasons put forth to account for these age-related differences (see Schacter, Koutstaal, & Norman, 1997 for a review). One possibility is that older adults simply have more trouble identifying the source of information which then makes internally generated events indistinguishable from actually presented items (e.g., Cohen & Faulkner, 1989). Another explanation, in line with the present principle, is that older adults tend to use a gist-based processing strategy rather than focusing on verbatim memory. The strategy of focusing on the generic aspects of the event or episode will make it difficult to later retrieve specific aspects of the stimuli. As predicted by this analysis, older adults are more susceptible to falsely recognizing the critical lure as having occurred in the Deese–Roediger–McDermott (DRM) paradigm (see chapter 6; Balota, Cortese, Duchek, Adams, Roediger, McDermott, & Yerys, 1999). However, older (and younger) adults can reduce false alarms if the items are given unique cues to help discriminate those items that were presented from others that were not. For example, when pictures were presented with the semantically related lists in the DRM procedure false alarms to the critical lure were greatly reduced (Schacter, Israel, & Racine, 1999; see also Gallo, Cotel, Moore, & Schacter, 2007). Note, however, that hit rates remained lower for the older than younger adults even in the picture encoding condition. Although this is not the conclusion drawn by Schacter et al. (1999), our interpretation of the data relies on the fact that a specific unfamiliar picture is a unique object. The semantic features that are encoded are singular to that picture and are not likely to be those encountered when the generic concept is retrieved (Durso & O'Sullivan, 1983). Thus, encoding pictures along with the words encouraged the older adults to encode the specific features of the items rather than use generic features. Given that fewer generic features were activated at encoding, it makes sense that gist-based errors would be reduced in the form of fewer false alarms. However, the deficit persists in the hit rates because the older adults are less able to retrieve specific episodes.

Tun, Wingfield, Rosen, and Blanchard (1998) manipulated the efficiency of a gist-based strategy using a modified DRM procedure. Older and younger adults were presented with lists of words that were all related to an unpresented critical item. In Experiment 1 the "new" items on the recognition test were all unrelated to the list items, with the exception of the critical lure. This encouraged a gist-based strategy in both younger and older adults: it was an efficient strategy to choose all the items that were related to the list. They found that the difference between younger and older adults disappeared. In Experiment 2, the "new" items included weak associates of the list items. This, then, required the participants to focus on item-specific information in order to successfully complete the task. With this manipulation the age-related difference reappeared: older adults were more likely than younger adults to false alarm to the lures. Tun et al. (1998) argued that older adults rely more on gist-based processing than item-specific processing at recall.

Similarly, Thomas and Sommers (2005) showed that older adults can reduce false memories in a DRM procedure if given the proper contextual support. They presented the to-be-remembered items as the last word in sentences that biased the interpretation of the word either toward the meaning of the critical lure (convergent) or away from the meaning of the critical lure (divergent). Thus, if the critical category was *sleep*, the participants were presented with the sentence, "The weary worker laid down on the *bed*" in the convergent condition and "The boy skipped rocks while standing in the river *bed*" in the divergent condition. Thomas and

Sommers suggested that the context in the divergent condition would make it more difficult for the participants to use gist-based processing and instead would have to rely on item-specific processing in order to make their decisions. Like in the Schacter et al. (1999) study, divergent sentences reduced false alarms for both younger and older adults. Again, correct recall was still worse in the older adults demonstrating that the specific items were still less accessible.

Koustaal (2006) suggested that one difference between older and younger adults is in their ability to flexibly change strategies from gist-based processing to item-based processing, depending on the demands of the task. Koutstaal presented subjects with pictures of common objects. At test, participants were asked to decide whether a stimulus was "old and identical, new but categorically related, or new and unrelated" (p. 84). The type of question varied unpredictably at test. The results showed that both younger and older adults could flexibly change from specific to general processing and back again. However, the older adults still showed more gist-based errors (false alarms to similar items) than the younger adults. She concluded that "younger adults were more adept at resisting responding on the basis of gist when reliance on this form of course-grained categorical information would be inappropriate" (p. 89). Similarly, Willingham (1998) argued that memory will appear to be flexible to the extent to which the changes from study to test are to aspects of the stimuli that are unimportant to the task at hand. Due perhaps to reduced cognitive capacity older adults may appear to encode fewer specific details at encoding and thus are less able to take advantage of specific cues at retrieval.

9.4 Specificity in Amnesia

One of the key findings offered to support fundamentally separate systems, rather than a continuum from generic to specific, is the pattern of memory loss observed in certain types of amnesia. People diagnosed with anterograde amnesia typically demonstrate relatively normal performance on tasks thought to tap short-term memory, such as digit span but are unable to form lasting new episodic memories. In addition, they can learn new skills (procedural memory), and often perform within normal limits on tasks such as perceptual priming. Within this framework this syndrome is characterized by an impairment of one part of long-term memory (episodic memory) but, at the same time, preserved short-term memory and preserved implicit memory.

One alternative explanation of the amnesic syndrome is that amnesics suffer from massive interference from other general material. Warrington and Weiskrantz (1970) are commonly cited as showing that their amnesic patients performed very abnormally on the usual recall and recognition tests but were as good as normal controls on a fragmented letters task. However, what is not generally mentioned is that Warrington and Weiskrantz (1970) concluded that those results were due to the fact that, in the fragmented word task the number of alternative responses are minimal and so incorrect false positive responses are eliminated. In the recall and recognition tasks, however, the ability to suppress task-irrelevant information is critical, and the amnesic subjects are not able to inhibit those responses. Interestingly, in a different report Warrington and Weiskrantz (1970) showed that the number of alternatives that can be used to fill in three-letter stems had a large effect on performance. The stems with more possible completions were less likely to be filled in with the target words from the study list. This is a similar pattern to what was reported above for older adults (Ryan et al., 2001).

In a more recent report, Cowan, Beschin, and Della Sala (2004) examined the role of interference in patients diagnosed with anterograde amnesia. They presented the patients with lists of words or stories and tested verbatim recall both immediately after the material was presented and after 10 minutes or an hour's delay. During the regular interference conditions the subjects were asked to complete a variety of interpolated tasks. In the minimal interference condition subjects were asked to lie down in a darkened, quiet room in order to minimize interference. Although the amnesic subjects showed worse performance than healthy controls in both delay conditions, most (but not all) showed substantial improvement under conditions of minimal interference. Cowan et al. argued that the amnesic subjects could not have maintained the story in short-term or working memory as some of the patients who benefited quite substantially from the minimal interference condition were observed to snore during the unfilled delays. These results are not due to the particular sample of patients tested: Della Sala, Cowan, Beschin, and Perini (2005) replicated this study using a more homogenous group of patients diagnosed with mild cognitive impairment who showed the symptoms of anterograde amnesia without overt dementia. Cowan and his colleagues argued that anterograde amnesia is characterized by an increased susceptibility to retroactive interference. If this is the case, we would predict that amnesic individuals will have impaired short-term memory if they are given distracting information before being asked to recall, thus adding potentially interfering material. This is exactly what occurs (Chao & Knight, 1995; Scoville & Milner, 1957).

In addition to syndromes in which short-term memory is spared and long-term memory is damaged, the opposite pattern can also emerge: semantic and phonological short-term memory deficits accompanying relatively spared long-term memory. Again this was initially used as an argument for a separate short-term store that could be selectively damaged. Initially it was thought that such individuals suffered from a very fast decay rate of information in short-term memory. However, later research has indicated that the deficit is more likely to be due to massive proactive interference due to abnormal persistence of previously presented material (Hamilton & Martin, 2005, 2007).

Hamilton and Martin (2007) investigated proactive interference in patient ML who has a semantic short-term memory deficit. ML's memory span is less than three items although his one-word repetition is nearly normal. Hamilton and Martin (2007) used a probe recognition task in which a list of items is followed by a probe. The subject was asked to determine whether the probe had appeared on the list that was just presented. On some trials the probe was a letter that had appeared in the list prior to the current target list, the "recent negative" probe. These trials were compared to a condition in which the letter had appeared more than three lists before, the "nonrecent negative" condition. Control subjects showed significant interference effect of the recent compared to nonrecent negatives. However, patient ML showed a greatly exaggerated effect with many intrusions and extremely slow response times on the recent compared to the nonrecent probes. Experiment 2 replicated the finding with words that were either phonologically or semantically related to the probe item. Patient ML showed abnormal amounts of interference from both the semantic and the phonologically related lures. Importantly, if ML's deficit was due to rapid decay of representations in a short-term memory store he should actually show *less* interference from previous trials.

Finally, there have been some reports of brain-damaged individuals with impaired recall ability but with spared recognition performance (Mayes, Holdstock, Isaac, Hunkin, & Roberts, 2002; Holdstock, Mayes, Roberts, Cezayirli, Isaac, O'Reilly, & Norman, 2002). Holdstock et al. (2002) reported a case of an individual with brain damage due to the use of an opiate for relief of severe pain. The hippocampal patient, YR, and controls were shown nameable objects in a study phase. At test, YR performed substantially worse than controls on a free recall task but was unimpaired in a four-item forced-choice object recognition task. It is important to note that the tasks were equated for difficulty: the control subjects performed at the same level for all tests. Even more interesting for the present discussion is the finding that YR performed poorly on a yes/no object recognition task with targets and foils that were perceptually similar but normally on an identical task with dissimilar targets and foils (reported in Mayes, Holdstock, Isaac, Hunkin, & Roberts, 2002). Thus, YR is only impaired in the case of tasks that require recall of a specific item (or token) but not in cases that can be successfully carried out by recalling a generic object (or type). Note that all of the tasks described here have been identified as tapping episodic memory that is supposed to be what is damaged in these patients.

9.5 Proper Names

In a very clever experiment, McWeeny, Young, Hay, and Ellis (1987) experimentally demonstrated the intuitively obvious phenomenon that proper names are harder to recall than otherwise identical meaningful items. Subjects were asked to associate a face with both a name and a profession. The information was presented in two sentence frames: "This man is called Mr. X, and he is a Y" or "This man is a Y, and he is called Mr. X." At recall subjects were asked to state the profession and the name of each individual face. The critical test was between recall of an item when it was presented as a profession (e.g., "This man is a baker ...") compared to when it was presented as a name (e.g., "This man is called Mr. Baker ..."). McWeeny et al. found that the names were much more difficult to recall than an occupation even though the item information was controlled. Retrieval of proper names, then, is an example of our specificity principle applied to younger adults. We would thus predict that older adults, who experience difficulty retrieving specific information, should show particular deficits in retrieving proper names.

In support of this prediction Cohen and Faulkner (1986; see also Cohen & Burke, 1993) found that older adults are particularly susceptible to this face–name association: older adults reported many more retrieval blocks for proper names than younger adults, and recalled fewer names in a controlled experimental setting. Cohen and Faulkner (1986) suggested that the reason for this is that proper names lack semantic links and thus require more specific cues to access.

Rendell, Castel, and Craik (2005) replicated McWeeny et al.'s (1987) experiment with older adults and obtained the same result; names were recalled worse than professions even when the two stimulus sets were identical. However, they found no particular age-related decrement for names themselves; older adults recalled fewer names *and* fewer occupations than younger adults, with no interaction. A subsequent experiment, in contrast, did provide evidence for a special age-related difficulty for naming faces in comparison to naming uncommon objects. Further analyses revealed that this result hinged on the familiarity of the items: As familiarity increased, so did naming ability. This result emphasizes the continuous nature of memory; familiar representations are more likely to be interconnected and thus be more accessible compared to unfamiliar items, which are more likely to be unique.

9.6 Chapter Summary

Our final principle suggests that the more a task requires recall of specific features of the encoding event, a unique piece of information, or a specific instance of a category, the more fragile and susceptible to forgetting or interference it is. It may sound like Principle 7 violates the spirit of Principle 2, the encoding–retrieval principle, that items, processes, and cues do not have intrinsic mnemonic properties.[3] However, it should be clear from the examples above that it is precisely the relation between the encoding and retrieval conditions that is a critical factor in the decrement in performance that is the focus of the current chapter.

There are some suggestions in the literature that humans can strategically control the degree to which they rely on gist-based compared to specific information (e.g., Castel, Farb, & Craik, 2007; Koutstaal, 2006). It does seem that an adaptive response to changes in available resources is to concentrate on more "high value" gist-based information (Castel, 2007a,b). We demonstrated examples of this principle by showing that older adults and individuals with amnesia perform quite well on tasks that are supported by generic processing but less well (compared to younger adults) on those that require the recollection of a specific item or event. It is easy to see how this principle generalizes to memory as a whole: Even within a population of younger adults, performance is less fragile (less susceptible to changing context over time; less easily interfered with) in tasks requiring memory for specific events or in situations in which the cue uniquely specifies or narrows down the possible responses. Thus, we endorse Craik's (1983; 2002a) continuum of difficulty with remembering to remember on one end and procedural memory on the other, albeit for slightly different reasons.

---

[3] But keep in mind that we never claimed that tasks lack intrinsic mnemonic properties!

Evaluation, Limitations, and Implications

> The great tragedy of Science—the slaying of a beautiful hypothesis by an ugly fact.
>
> —**Thomas H. Huxley**

10.1 Principles of Memory

In all situations, the act of remembering begins with a cue which initiates the retrieval process (the *cue-driven principle*). Cues can become associated with more and more items at various encoding opportunities, thus reducing their effectiveness at the time of retrieval (the *cue overload principle*). In order to describe accurately how a cue works, it is necessary to take into account both the conditions at encoding and the conditions at retrieval (the *encoding–retrieval principle*). Accepting this principle entails accepting four consequences: (a) Items do not have intrinsic mnemonic properties; (b) processes do not have intrinsic mnemonic properties; and (c) cues do not have intrinsic mnemonic properties. The fourth consequence arises from the first three: if neither items nor processes nor cues have intrinsic mnemonic properties, forgetting cannot be due to an intrinsic mnemonic property. Therefore, (d) forgetting is due to extrinsic properties.

Memory, like other cognitive processes, is inherently constructive (the *reconstruction principle*). Information present at encoding, cues at retrieval, memories of previous recollections, indeed any possibly useful information are all exploited to construct a response to a cue. All memories, then, are false, as they are based, at least in part, on information that does not come directly from memory of the event itself. Memories are also inherently dynamic, continually changing: they will be reconstructed slightly differently each time, with each recollection added to the pool of possible sources of information for future recollection. One consequence of the reconstruction principle is the realization that on any task, people recruit and use a wide variety of information and processes. Therefore, tasks are not pure, and processes are not pure measures of memory (the *impurity principle*); inferences based on the assumption that a task taps a particular memory system or requires only one particular process are likely to be misguided.

Forgetting is due to extrinsic factors; in particular, items that have more close neighbors in the region of psychological space at the time of retrieval are less likely to be remembered than items with fewer close neighbors (the *relative distinctiveness principle*). In addition, tasks that require specific information about the context in which memories were formed seem to be more vulnerable to interference or forgetting at the time of the retrieval attempt than those that can rely on more general information (the *specificity principle*). Taken together, these principles suggest that the search for *the* forgetting function is not likely to be successful.

The above, we suggest, is an accurate overview of the major characteristics of how memory works. The principles reflect empirical regularities, offer explanations for a wide range of phenomenon, and describe not only how memory works but also offer suggestions for memory improvement. All do so without recourse to different underlying memory systems.

10.2 Relation to Other Sets of Principles

There have been relatively few attempts at a systematic delineation of the principles of memory. In this section, we compare our[1] principles to others that have been suggested.

10.2.1 Kihlstrom and Barnhardt's Principles

Kihlstrom and Barnhardt (1993) also proposed seven principles of memory, specifically noting that they relate to "memory function" (p. 89). Despite this shared emphasis on a functional approach, only one of their principles coincides exactly with one of ours. Their *reconstruction principle* states that "the memory of an event reflects a blend of information retrieved from a specific trace of that event with knowledge, expectations, and beliefs derived from other sources" (p. 92). One possible difference is

---

[1] We want to be clear that we use "our" simply to denote those principles sketched out here. We are not claiming that all of these principles are original to us.

that unlike Kihlstrom and Barnhardt, we explicitly extend our principle to apply to all types of memory, including memory stored in what structuralists might term *sensory memory* and *working memory*.

A second principle, the *encoding specificity principle*, is similar to what we have termed the *encoding–retrieval principle*: "The probability of remembering an event is a function of the extent to which cues processed at the time of encoding are also processed at the time of retrieval" (p. 91). We concur with the general spirit, but a subtle difference is that in our view, the cues at retrieval do not have to have been processed at encoding in order to help memory. Rather, what is important is the relation between the two sets of cues, not the similarity or the match or whether a particular cue has been processed before. Thus, providing different cues at test can enhance memory even though the cues were not processed at encoding (e.g., Bower & Mann, 1992). Kihlstrom and Barnhardt's principle seems to exclude this possibility.

Two more of Kihlstrom and Barnhardt's principles are, we argue, technically incorrect. The *time-dependency principle* states that "the probability of remembering an event is a negative function of the length of time between encoding and retrieval" (p. 90). (A slightly revised version of this, "the memorability of an event declines as the length of the storage interval (i.e., between encoding and retrieval) increases" [Kihlstrom, 1994, p. 338], makes it clear that the passage of absolute time is the key rather than what may happen at encoding and retrieval.) This principle runs into problems with the numerous empirical demonstrations of an increase in the probability of remembering an item occurs even when further study or rehearsal is not permitted (Neath & Knoedler, 1994; Wheeler, 1995; for reviews, see Bjork, 2001; Capaldi & Neath, 1995). As just one example, the time-dependency principle, is contradicted by the findings of Conway and Pleydell–Pearce (2000) that when older adults are asked to recall events from their own lives, they recall more from the period when they were approximately 15 to 25 years of age than they do from the period when they were approximately 30 to 40 years of age. The time-dependency principle is simply too often contradicted by the data to be a worthy candidate. As we noted in Chapter 4, "even if it were true in some cases, [it] is not the general law which it purports to be" (McGeoch, 1932, pp. 355–356).

Similarly, another proposed principle runs into empirical difficulties. The *cue-dependency principle* states that "the probability of remembering an event increases with the amount of information supplied by the retrieval cue" (p. 91). We showed, in Chapter 4, how a cue that has more information (Cue 2) and that is a better match to a target can actually result in a decreased probability of remembering an event (see also Nairne, 2001). The key factor that the principle, as stated, overlooks is that at retrieval, there are competitor items, and their presence or absence can modulate the effectiveness of a particular cue.

Two more principles violate our corollary that processes do not have intrinsic mnemonic properties. The *elaboration principle* states that "the probability of remembering an event is a function of the degree to which that event was related to preexisting knowledge during processing" (p. 89) and the *organization principle* states that "the probability of remembering an event is a function of the degree to which that event was related to other events during processing" (p. 89). These are reminiscent of the claim that memory is better the deeper the level of processing. Both of these fail to take into account the processing that will be performed at retrieval. Because of this, it is trivial to construct experiments in which the memorability of items will decrease even though the items were related to preexisting knowledge or other items at the time of encoding.

Finally, the *schematic processing principle* states that "the probability of remembering an event is a function of the degree to which that event is congruent with preexisting expectations and beliefs" (p. 91). (A revised formulation makes this more clear: "The memorability of an event increases when that event is relevant to expectations and beliefs about the event." [Kihlstrom, 1994, p. 440]). Our quibble here is one that in addition to ignoring the importance of the conditions at retrieval, recall of items inconsistent with expectations is also high (e.g., Brewer & Treyens, 1981). That is, the exact opposite of the principle is correct as well.

The problem with most of these principles, then, is that they lack sufficient precision in their formulation to really qualify as principles. Like the levels of processing theory, most do not take into account the fundamental importance of acknowledging both the conditions at encoding and those at retrieval.

10.2.2 Crowder's Four Principles

After acknowledging he wrote a book called *Principles of Learning and Memory* "without ever really coming out and saying what those principles were," Crowder (1993, p. 146) did propose four principles. However, he qualified these by stating that "the more I think about them, though, the more I realise that these four principles are closely related to one another."

The first is the principle of hyperspecificity, which occurs in relation to repetition priming. However, Crowder makes clear that "encoding specificity is the same principle of memory that has been called hyperspecificity in the case of priming" (p. 148). This point is also made by Willingham (1998), who argued that the encoding specificity result shows that declarative memories are as inflexible to changes in context as are procedural memory. The key point is whether a fundamental aspect of the representation is changed by the different contexts. This principle, then, is part of our encoding–retrieval principle. The second is transfer-appropriate processing. However, Crowder introduces this by noting (p. 149) that "transfer appropriate processing is the more global form" of hyperspecificity.

Crowder's third principle is processing-appropriate interference, and focuses on what events interfere with memory. This is "exactly complementary to transfer-appropriate processing," in that one can focus on an enhancement of performance when processing at retrieval is appropriate, given the processing performed at encoding, or one can focus on interference, given inappropriate processing.

His fourth principle concerned exemplar storage. Because "by definition every experience is at least slightly different from anything that has ever happened in the past, memories are accordingly for *exemplars* and not abstracted propositions" (p. 153; italics in original). In one sense, this is also part of hyperspecificity but again emphasizes a different aspect. In particular, it seems easier to adopt an exemplar view and then explain various aspects of memory that rely on more generalized or abstract knowledge (e.g., Hintzman, 1987) than to try to work out how a specific episode could be extracted from an abstracted form of representation.

We view, as we trust Crowder himself would, all of these as falling within the scope of the encoding retrieval principle.

10.2.3 Principles of Short-Term Memory

Not all proposed principles are designed to apply widely. For example, Jonides et al. (2008, p. 212–213) summarize "the principles of STM." (a) Long- and short-term memory representations differ in the amount of activation. (b) There is a focus of attention in which a chunk of information is immediately available for cognitive action. A "chunk" is "a set of items that are bound by a common functional context." (c) Entry into the focus of attention is either through perceptual encoding or by a cue-driven retrieval process from long-term memory. (d) Active maintenance of items in the focus of attention is required, and one such process is rehearsal. (e) Forgetting is when items leave the focus of attention, and can be due to interference (competition from other items for the limited capacity in the focus of attention) or decay (when the "fidelity of the representation declines over time" most likely due to a tendency for the firing neurons to get out of synchrony).

There are several incompatibilities between our principles and those described by Jonides et al. (2008). Most prominently, we do not acknowledge a difference between memory systems whereas Jonides et al. do. However, it is not clear that what Jonides et al. term STM is really memory. There is a large literature on the relation between attention and memory, and many times "memory" is used when a perhaps more accurate term is "attention" (see, for example, Baddeley, 1993; Cowan, 1995). Consistent with our claim that Jonides et al. are describing something closer to attention, they note the ever-decreasing capacity of the concept of STM over the years, from 7 ± 2 items to 2 s worth of information to just one chunk, and consequently, its diminished or even absent role in many memory situations. We think it an open question whether the focus of attention is memory, and further empirical work will either support our principles or confirm the status of an exception.

10.2.4 Seven Sins of Memory

Schacter (2001), in a book entitled *The Seven Sins of Memory*, describes the seven different categories of memory failures or "sins." These are not really principles in the sense that we use the term, although most are encompassed by one or more of our principles. Although the book was written for the nonexpert and includes many anecdotes and stories, the framework is solidly based on empirical research. The sins are divided into two main categories, those of omission (time-based transience, absent-mindedness, blocking, or interference), and those of commission (misattribution, suggestibility, bias, and persistence).

Three sins of commission—misattribution, suggestibility, and bias—are all related to our reconstruction principle. We describe misattribution in our section on reality monitoring, suggestibility in terms of the misinformation effect, and bias as being related to schemas, although there are many other examples of these "sins" at work when people construct and reconstruct memories. The fourth sin of commission, persistence, is not encompassed by any of our principles. This sin "entails repeated recall of disturbing information or events that we would prefer to banish from our minds altogether: remembering what we cannot forget" (Schacter, 2001 p. 5). In our view, this suggests the need for another principle, one concerning what Watkins (1989) termed "willful and nonwillful determinants of memory." Our current set of principles makes no mention of the extent to which an individual has control over memory.

Of the sins of omission, transience refers to a "weakening or loss of memory over time" (Schacter, 2001, p. 4). As such, it is similar to Kihlstrom and Barnhardt's (1993) time-dependency principle, therefore is subject to the same criticisms. Absent mindedness, in Schacter's account, is more a function of attention than memory: "The desired information isn't lost over time; it is either never registered in memory to begin with, or not sought after at the moment it is needed, because attention is focused elsewhere" (p. 4). As yet, we have no principles linking memory and attention. The final sin, blocking, "entails a thwarted search for information that we may be desperately trying to retrieve" (p. 5). This is encompassed in our view by most of our principles, as it fundamentally is about failing to remember.

10.2.5 Semon's Principles

Richard Semon (1923) proposed two principles of memory, although they are closely related: "*The first mnemic principle of engraphy: All simultaneous excitations (manifested in our case by sensations) within our organisms* form a connected simultaneous complex of excitations which, as such, acts engraphically, that is to say, leaves behind it a connected and, to that extent, unified engram-complex" (pp. 159–160; italics in original). The second mnemic principle "or the echphoric principle" is given as follows: "*The partial return of an energetic situation which has fixed itself engraphically acts in an echphoric sense upon a simultaneous engram-complex*" (p. 180; italics in original).

As usually translated, both principles can be difficult to understand. Essentially, however, the first proposes the existence of an engram, a memory trace. The second is quite similar to the idea of redintegration, discussed in Chapter 3, in that any one element can bring back the experience of the whole situation (see also Hollingsworth, 1924). A discussion of the engram is beyond the scope of the current work. The second principle, in a more general sense, follows nicely from viewing memory as cue driven.

10.2.6 Principles of Cognition

Chater and Brown (2008, p. 36) propose two "universal principles" of cognition. The simplicity principle states that "the cognitive system prefers patterns that provide simpler explanations of available data" and the scale-invariance principle states that "many cognitive phenomena are independent of the scale of relevant underlying physical variables, such as time, space, luminance, or sound pressure." They show how both of these are incorporated into SIMPLE (see Chapter 8), but argue these principles apply more widely than to just memory, and give examples of identification and categorization. Both of these principles are compatible with our set of principles, but we included neither among our seven. We consider scale invariance to be a likely principle of memory, but were not sure of its generality. Even Chater and Brown qualify their definition with "many" rather than "all," and at this point, we gave preference to principles that did not require such a qualification. The simplicity principle, although compatible, seems more appropriate for cognitive tasks other than memory, such as perception and categorization.

10.3 Relation to Laws of Memory

Relatively few memory researchers have listed principles of memory, and even fewer have been bold enough to propose laws of memory. Here, we compare these laws to our principles.

10.3.1 Cohen's Laws

Cohen (1985) proposed four laws, although his definition of a law is quite similar to our definition of a principle: A "memory law should be a statement about some empirical relationship in memory, which has transsituational generality and which looks like it will be around for some time to come" (Cohen, 1985, p. 252).

His first two laws deal with acquisition and forgetting, and both suffer from the same limitation: Neither acknowledges the interaction between encoding and retrieval. His first law stated that "the better something is learned, the greater the likelihood it will be remembered" (p. 253). Because it fails to acknowledge the interaction between encoding and retrieval, it fails to acknowledge that one can trivially change the conditions at retrieval (or encoding) such that something very well learned indeed is no longer recalled (e.g., Thomson & Tulving, 1970). The second law has the same problem: Originally formulated as "the longer something has to be retained in memory, the less the likelihood that it will be remembered" (p. 253), it was also suggested that it could be summarized as "recent is best" (p. 260). Recent memories are not always best, as the primacy effect or the reminiscence bump or any other number of studies show.

His third law dealt with retrieval: "The closer the match between encoding and retrieval conditions (the greater the overlap in episodic contexts) the better the memory performance)" (p. 264). This tackles much of the same ground as our encoding retrieval principle, but the specific wording renders it problematic. As we have shown, the match (or overlap) can be very high, but recall very low. While we fully agree with the spirit of the law, we cannot agree with the letter of the law.

After proposing these laws, Cohen (1985) also proposed a "zeroth" law of forgetting: "Individuals differ reliably in their memory capacities" (p. 270). We think this a good candidate for a principle, and discuss this further below.

10.3.2 Tulving–Wiseman Law

Nyberg (1995) proposed an additional law to those listed by Cohen (1985), namely the Tulving–Wiseman Law (Tulving & Wiseman, 1975). This term relates the probability of recognizing recallable items to the probability of recognizing all the items, regardless of whether they are recalled and, based on a large number of studies, there is a moderate correlation. As noted earlier, this was one of the few laws of memory that showed up in Teigen's (2002) search of the literature. Tulving himself is ambivalent, sometimes referring to this as a function (Tulving & Flexser, 1992) and sometimes a law (Nilsson, Law, & Tulving, 1988). In our view, it is closer to the ratio rule than to a principle in our sense of the term. First, like the ratio rule, there are some significant exceptions (e.g., Bryant, 1991; Lian, Glass, & Raanaas, 1998; Sikstrom & Gardiner, 1997), which makes us unwilling to confer law status. Second, also like the ratio rule, there is a question of generality: although there have been many variations of the basic procedure, it still essentially compares only free recall and recognition; it does not apply to other tasks, and has not been sufficiently tested in tasks thought to tap other memory systems. Like the ratio rule, it is an empirical regularity, but in our view, more needs to be done before its status is elevated.

10.3.3 Roediger's Laws

Roediger's (2008, p. 227) definition of a law is similar to our definition of a principle: "an empirical regularity, an established functional relation, one that holds widely (ideally, universally) across manipulation of other variables" (p. 227). We suggest that the major difference between his conclusion that "laws of memory do not seem to exist" (p. 247), and ours is that our principles were defined as taking into account variability in encoding conditions, retrieval conditions, events (materials and tasks), and (albeit to a limited extent) subject variables. That is, we acknowledge from the outset that the interaction between encoding and retrieval is critical, and this combined with (primarily) the purity and the relative distinctiveness principles is why many of his candidate laws often fail to hold (e.g., the spacing effect, the generation effect, the mirror effect, the picture superiority effect, the various forgetting functions, etc.). As such, our principles operate at a higher or more abstract level and are less likely to be influenced by minor changes in experimental procedure.

10.3.4 Ribot's Law

Ribot's law (e.g., Ribot, 1881) states that older memories are more likely to be preserved following trauma than newer memories; it is now usually expressed as "temporally graded retrograde amnesia" in which after a trauma, a person is most likely to have difficulty recalling events closer to the time of the trauma than older events. There is substantial evidence for such gradients (e.g., Squire, Clark, & Knowlton, 2001), but again, we are not convinced that this empirical regularity should have at this time principle status, let alone law status.

One problematic aspect is its generality. It is clear that people can have trouble remembering events from prior to a trauma, but typically such gradients are established using either recall or recognition tests of auto-biographical information. It is not usually possible to assess the information in other ways. However, with experimentally induced amnesia, such studies are possible. The results (which may be limited, due to the use of electrical shock to induce amnesia) show that alternate ways of testing reveal the information to be present (see chapter 6 of Neath & Surprenant, 2003). Thus, Ribot's "law" is again more like an effect than a principle.

10.3.5 Jost's Laws

Jost (1897) advanced two ideas that are now referred to as Jost's laws. As formulated by Wixted (2004b, p. 864), these laws "hold that that if two associations (i.e., two memory traces) are of equal strength but different ages, the older one will (a) benefit more from an additional learning trial and (b) decay less rapidly in a given period of time than the younger one." From our perspective, the difficulty in evaluating these laws is in ascrib-ing an intrinsic property (i.e., strength, decay) to an association or an item. The encoding–retrieval principle prohibits these forms of statement. If one qualifies the laws such that the encoding and retrieval conditions are held constant, then one is still ascribing an intrinsic property (viz., decay) to an item and asserting that the passage of time causes forgetting. To our knowledge, this has not been tested empirically when holding relative distinctiveness constant at the two testing times.

Beyond that, there are published studies that counter the predictions of Jost's laws. As Roediger (2008) noted, Jost's first law is often not observed (e.g., Underwood, 1961) and sometimes reverses (e.g., Balota, Duchek, & Paullin, 1989). Similarly, there are numerous studies in which Jost's second law does not hold, including studies that show an improvement in performance over time when rehearsal and further opportunity to study the material is pre-cluded (e.g., Dudai, 2004; McGaugh, 2000; see also Chapter 4).

10.3.6 Aristotle's Laws of Association

Philosophers and psychologists have identified three laws of association within the works of Aristotle (e.g., Buckingham & Finger, 1997; Warren, 1916):

Events will tend to be associated when they occur close together in time or space (the law of contiguity), when they are similar (the law of similarity), and when they contrast with each other (the law of contrast). Although influential, and although items do tend to be associated under these conditions, these are not really laws in the strict sense of the word.

10.4 Possible Principles

We began this monograph asserting that the seven principles listed are not an exhaustive list and that more principles can and will be identified. Moreover, it is likely that the seven principles listed are not necessarily the most important. When we first formulated some principles (Neath & Surprenant, 2005), there were 10. Of these, four have now been "demoted" to corollary status as we now feel they are better thought of as implications of the more general encoding retrieval principle than principles in their own right. We have added two principles since then: The relative distinctiveness principle and the specificity principle. We have also deleted the invariance principle, as we now view it as being inherent in a principle as we define it.

There are other candidates for principles. Here, we consider a few that have been suggested.

An individual difference principle. In addition to the four laws noted above, Cohen (1985) proposed a "zeroth" law that held that individuals differ reliably in their memory abilities. We address some of this with our specificity principle, but it may be appropriate to have this as a separate principle. Back in 1985, Cohen noted (p. 270) that "the existence of individual differences in memory [is] a fact of life ignored by most memory theorists." Since then, the situation has changed: There is a growing awareness, for example, that there are reliable individual differences in the major benchmark effects that define Baddeley's (1986) working memory such as the acoustic confusion effect and the word length effect (e.g., Logie, Della Sala, Laiacona, Chalmers, & Wynn, 1996). At least one formal model of memory, the feature model, has been applied to this very issue (Beaman, Neath, & Surpenant, 2008). However, most formal models of memory continue to ignore this issue.

An organization principle. Hunt and McDaniel (1993, p. 421) posed the question, "How can both similarity and difference be beneficial to memory?" Our relative distinctiveness principle emphasizes difference, but does not really tackle organization in any fundamental way. There is a long history of the study of organization (see, for example, the volume edited by Tulving & Donaldson, 1972), but our principles do not really incorporate any of these ideas.

An association principle. Although we dismiss Aristotle's "laws" of association above, it seems as though there should be a fundamental principle about how two ideas (or a cue and a response) become associated. We have two principles specifically about cues, and several others in which cues play a leading role, but no real statement about the original associating of the cue with the response.

A vacuum principle. A common criticism has been that many theorists treat each trial in an experiment as an isolated event, the so-called trial-unit model (Estes, 1991). As Estes noted, there is "no support for the idea that short-term memory is reset at the start of each experimental trial" (p. 168). The vacuum principle, then, would state simply that memory does not work in a vacuum; one particular trial is not independent of what has happened before. We hesitated to include this, as it overlaps substantially with the impurity principle as well as with the reconstruction principle.

A forgetting principle. We do not think there will be a forgetting principle. The reason is that a failure to remember can be due to multiple different causes, much like the failure of a car to move can be due to multiple different causes.

10.5 Evaluation

We defined a principle as being a generalization about memory that must be valid (empirically true) and must be universal. That is, the principles should apply to "all kinds of rememberers, to-be-remembered events, encoding operations, and retrieval information, in appropriately controlled and sufficiently sensitive experiments" (Tulving, 1983, p. 265). We also required that each principle have at least one (and hopefully more than one) of the following three properties: (a) they should state an important empirical regularity, (b) they should be able to serve as an intermediate explanation, and (c) they should offer useful information on how memory works.

10.5.1 Possible Weaknesses

Our principles are, in one sense, empirically untestable. That is, one could never test all possible experiments involving different tasks, different hypothetical underlying memory systems, different stimuli, different modalities, and so on. As Tulving (1983) pointed out with regard to his encoding specificity principle, this is unrelated to whether the principles have empirical support. We have presented only a fraction of the studies that support the seven principles.

The most common kind of data that appears to contradict our principles concern null results, that is, failing to find proactive interference in certain short-term memory tasks, failing to find effects of distinctiveness in implicit memory tasks, and so on. We have attempted to show why these studies did not obtain the predicted result, but ultimately, this is an empirical issue: further research will show whether our interpretation of the data is correct.

A related issue is the problem of finding studies that test each hypothetical memory system in order to demonstrate the generality of the principles. In particular, we had difficulty finding studies thought to tap procedural memory that were relevant to our principles. Our view is that we make a strong prediction that if such experiments were conducted, the results would support the principles we propose, although it is possible that such tests might place limits on a principle, or contradict it entirely.

Another possible weakness is that we have not had time to consider whether the principles apply not only in laboratory settings, but also in the so-called "real world." We have no reason to believe that they will not apply,[2] but the debate over whether laboratory-based studies inform us about memory in general keeps resurfacing (see, for example, the article by Banaji & Crower, 1989, and the ensuing comments). Again, this is ultimately an empirical issue: in principle, one can run appropriate experiments that explicitly test whether the principles apply both to laboratory-based research as well as to memory outside of the laboratory.

Finally, we have not had time to consider the extent to which the seven principles are compatible with one another. That is, do any of the principles contradict any of the others? Are they all sufficiently different to warrant inclusion? We do not believe these to be problems, but we could be wrong.

10.5.2 Conclusions

Where does this enumeration of principles get us? What can be gained by discussing memory in terms of these few principles? What does it predict and how does it move the field forward?

The most obvious way in which the current contribution may move the field forward is in terms of more empirical testing of the principles. In a narrow sense, the principles make numerous new predictions that need to be tested: particular findings from one domain should be observable in quite different domains. For example, we have recently been testing the detrimental effects of irrelevant speech in paradigms other than immediate

---

[2] As McGeoch and Irion (1952, p. 8) put it, "life in the laboratory is just as 'real' as life may be anywhere else."

serial recall. Most of the original work focused on this paradigm, as irrelevant speech is thought, by the most popular theoretical accounts, to disrupt short-term or working memory. Why, then, look for disruptions of other types of memory? We have shown that irrelevant speech has a similar disruptive effect on "implicit memory" (Farley, Neath, Allbritton, & Surprenant, 2007) as well as "statistical learning" (Neath, Guérard, Jalbert, Bireta, & Surprenant, in press). Similarly, we are exploring the extent to which the relative distinctiveness principle explains age-related differences in memory (Surprenant, Neath, & Brown, 2006). In a similar vein, we are exploring whether proactive interference can be widely observed in tasks thought to tap working memory and the focus of attention, as well as examining the roles of cues in working memory.

Should the principles turn out to apply as widely as claimed, then it may cause multiple systems theorists to reconsider their current taxonomy. An extreme reaction might be to argue that there is only one memory system or rather, as Toth and Hunt (1999) put it, zero memory systems. That is, memory per se does not exist; rather, it is better thought of as complex, coordinated processing.

What if the principles turn out, like the laws considered by Roediger (2008), not to apply widely? What if Tulving (1985a, p. 385) is correct in that "no profound generalizations can be made about memory as a whole"? In that case, we have still succeeded, for as Greene (2007, p. 54) notes, "some of the most important contributions made by general principles have been those times when they spurred investigations into how they fail." And if Tulving is right, we have failed spectacularly.

REFERENCES

Albert, M. S., Heller, H. S., & Milberg, W. (1988). Changing in naming ability with age. *Psychology and Aging, 3,* 173–178.

Anderson, J. R. (1974). Retrieval of propositional information from long-term memory. *Cognitive Psychology, 6,* 451–474.

Anderson, R. E., (1984). Did I do it or did I only imagine doing it? *Journal of Experimental Psychology: General, 113,* 594–613.

Angell, J. R. (1906). *Psychology: An introductory study of the structure and function of human consciousness, 3rd edition, revised.* New York: Henry Holt.

Atkins, A. S., & Reuter-Lorenz, P. A. (2008). False working memories? Semantic distortion in a mere 4 seconds. *Memory & Cognition, 36,* 74–81.

Atkinson, R. C., Herrmann, D. J., & Wescourt, K. T. (1974). Search processes in recognition memory. In R. L. Solso (Ed.), *Theories in cognitive psychology: The Loyola Symposium* (pp. 101–146). Potomac, MD: Erlbaum.

Baddeley, A. (1993). Working memory or working attention? In A. Baddeley & L. Weiskrantz (Eds.), *Attention: Selection awareness & control: A tribute to Donald Broadbent* (152–170). Oxford: Oxford University Press.

Baddeley, A. D. (1976). *The psychology of memory.* New York: Basic Books.

Baddeley, A. D. (1978). The trouble with levels: A reexamination of Craik and Lockhart's framework for memory research. *Psychological Review, 85,* 3, 139–152.

Baddeley, A. D. (1986). *Working memory.* New York: Oxford University Press.

Baddeley, A. D. (1990). *Human memory.* Boston: Allyn & Bacon.

Baddeley, A. D. (1994). Working memory: The interface between memory and cognition. In D. L. Schacter & E. Tulving (Eds.), *Memory systems 1994* (pp. 351–367). Cambridge, MA: MIT Press.

Baddeley, A. D. (2000). The episodic buffer: A new component of working memory? *Trends in Cognitive Sciences, 4,* 417–423.

Baddeley, A. D., & Scott, D. (1971). Short-term forgetting in the absence of proactive interference. *Quarterly Journal of Experimental Psychology, 23,* 275–283.

Baddeley, A. D., Lewis, V., & Vallar, G. (1984). Exploring the articulatory loop. *Quarterly Journal of Experimental Psychology, 36A,* 233–252.

Baddeley, A. D., Thomson, N., & Buchanan, M. (1975). Word length and the structure of short-term memory. *Journal of Verbal Learning and Verbal Behavior, 14,* 575–589.

Bain, A. (1855). *The senses and the intellect.* London: John W. Parker & Son.

Balota, D. A., & Chumbley, J. I. (1984). Are lexical decisions a good measure of lexical access: The role of word frequency in the neglected decision stage. *Journal of Experimental Psychology: Human Perception and Performance, 10,* 340–357.

Balota, D. A., & Neely, J. H. (1980). Test-expectancy and word-frequency effects in recall and recognition. *Journal of Experimental Psychology: Human Learning and Memory, 6,* 576–587.

Balota, D. A., Cortese, M. J., Duchek, J. M., Adams, D., Roediger, H. L. III., McDermott, K. B., & Yerys, B. E. (1999). Veridical and false memories in healthy older adults and in dementia of the Alzheimer's type. *Cognitive Neuropsychology, 16,* 361–384.

Balota, D. A., Duchek, J. M., & Paullin, R. (1989). Age-related differences in the impact of spacing, lag, and retention interval. *Psychology and Aging, 4*, 3–95.

Banaji, M. R., & Crowder, R. G. (1989). The bankruptcy of everyday memory. *American Psychologist, 44*, 1185–1193.

Bartlett, F. C. (1932). *Remembering: A study in experimental and social psychology.* Cambridge: Cambridge University Press.

Beaman, C. P. (2006). The relationship between absolute and proportion scores of serial order memory: Simulation predictions and empirical data. *Psychonomic Bulletin & Review, 13*, 92–98.

Beaman, C. P., Neath, I., & Surprenant, A. M. (2008). Modeling distributions of immediate memory effects: No strategies needed? *Journal of Experimental Psychology: Learning, Memory, and Cognition, 34*, 219–229

Begg, I., Upfold, D., & Wilton, T. (1978). Imagery in verbal communication. *Journal of Mental Imagery, 2*, 165–186.

Bellezza, F. S., & Cheney, T. L. (1973). Isolation effect in immediate and delayed recall. *Journal of Experimental Psychology, 99*, 55–60.

Bergman, E. T., & Roediger, H. L. III (1999). Can Bartlett's repeated reproduction experiments be replicated? *Memory & Cognition, 27*, 937–947.

Bireta, T. J., Surprenant, A. M., & Neath, I. (2008). Age-related differences in the Von Restorff isolation effect. *Quarterly Journal of Experimental Psychology, 61*, 345–352.

Bjork, R. A. (2001). Recency and recovery in human memory. In H. L. Roediger III, J. S. Nairne, I. Neath, & A. M. Surprenant (Eds.), *The nature of remembering: Essays in honor of Robert G. Crowder* (pp. 211–232). Washington, DC: APA.

Bjork, R. A., & Whitten, W. B. II. (1974). Recency sensitive retrieval processes in long-term free recall. *Cognitive Psychology, 6*, 173–189.

Blankenship, A. B. (1938). Memory span: A review of the literature. *Psychological Bulletin, 35*, 1–25.

Blaxton, T. A. (1989). Investigating dissociations among memory measures: Support for a transfer-appropriate processing framework. *Journal of Experimental Psychology: Learning, Memory, and Cognition, 15*, 657–668.

Bolton, T. L. (1892). The growth of memory in school children. *American Journal of Psychology, 4*, 362–380.

Bone, R. N., & Goulet, L. R. (1968). Serial position and the Von Restorff isolation effect. *Journal of Experimental Psychology, 76*, 494–496.

Borg, I., & Groenen, P. J. F. (2005). *Modern multidimensional scaling: Theory and applications,* 2nd edition. New York: Springer.

Botvinick, M., & Bylsma, L. M. (2005). Regularization in short-term memory for serial order. *Journal of Experimental Psychology: Learning, Memory, and Cognition, 31*, 351–358.

Bourassa, D. C., & Besner, D. (1994). Beyond the articulatory loop: A semantic contribution to serial order recall of subspan lists. *Psychonomic Bulletin & Review, 1*, 122–125.

Bowen, R., Pola, J., & Matin, L. (1974). Visual persistence: Effects of flash luminance, duration and energy. *Vision Research, 14*, 295–303.

Bower, G. H. (1970). Mental imagery and associative learning. In L. Gregg (Ed.), *Cognition in learning and memory* (pp. 51–58). New York: Wiley.

Bower, G. H., & Mann, T. (1992). Improving recall by recoding interfering material at the time of retrieval. *Journal of Experimental Psychology: Learning, Memory, and Cognition, 18*, 1310–1320.

Bower, G. H., Black, J. B., & Turner, T. J. (1979). Scripts in memory of text. *Cognitive Psychology, 11,* 177–220.

Bowers, J. S., & Schacter, D. L. (1990). Implicit memory and test awareness. *Journal of Experimental Psychology: Learning, Memory, and Cognition, 16,* 404–416.

Bowles, N. L., & Poon, L. W. (1985). Aging and retrieval of words in semantic memory. *Journal of Gerontology, 40,* 71–77.

Bransford, J. D., Franks, J. J., Morris, C. D., & Stein, B. S. (1979). Some general constraints on learning and memory research. In L. S. Cermak and F. I. M. Craik (Eds.), *Levels of processing in human memory* (pp. 331–354). Hillsdale, NJ: Lawrence Erlbaum Associates.

Bressler, S. L., & Kelso, J. A. S. (2001). Cortical coordination dynamics and cognition. *Trends in Cognitive Sciences, 5,* 26–36.

Brewer, W. F., & Treyens, J. C. (1981). Role of schemata in memory for places. *Cognitive Psychology, 13,* 207–230.

Brooks, L. R. (1968). Spatial and verbal components of the act of recall. *Canadian Journal of Psychology, 22,* 349–368.

Brown, G. D. A., & Lamberts, K. (2003). Double dissociations, models, and serial position curves. *Cortex, 39,* 148–152.

Brown, G. D. A., Morin, C., & Lewandowsky, S. (2006). Evidence for time-based models of free recall. *Psychonomic Bulletin & Review, 13,* 717–723.

Brown, G. D. A., Neath, I., & Chater, N. (2007). A temporal ratio model of memory. *Psychological Review, 114,* 539–576.

Brown, G. D. A., Preece, T., & Hulme, C. (2000). Oscillator-based memory for serial order. *Psychological Review, 107,* 127–181.

Brown, J. (1958). Some tests of the decay theory of immediate memory. *Quarterly Journal of Experimental Psychology, 10,* 12–21.

Bryant, D. J. (1991). Exceptions to recognition failure as a function of the encoded association between cue and target. *Memory & Cognition, 19,* 210–219.

Buckingham, H. W., & Finger, S. (1997). David Hartley's psychobiological associationism and the legacy of Aristotle. *Journal of the History of the Neurosciences, 6,* 21–37.

Burgess, N., & Hitch, G. (1999). Memory for serial order: A network model of the phonological loop and its timing. *Psychological Review, 106,* 551–581.

Burke, D. M., MacKay, D G., Worthley, J. S., & Wade, E. (1991). On the tip of the tongue: What causes word finding failures in young and older adults? *Journal of Memory and Language, 30,* 542–579.

Burnham, W. H. (1888). Memory, historically and experimentally considered. I. An historical sketch of the older conceptions of memory. *American Journal of Psychology, 2,* 39–90.

Cabeza, R., Dolcos, F., Graham, R., & Nyberg, L. (2002). Similarities and differences in the neural correlates of episodic memory retrieval and working memory. *NeuroImage, 16,* 317–330.

Cabeza, R., Dolcos, F., Prince, S. E., Rice, H. J., Weissman, D. H., & Nyberg, L. (2003). Attention-related activity during episodic memory retrieval: A cross-function fMRI study. *Neuropsychologia, 41,* 390–399.

Cabeza, R., Kapur, S., Craik, F. I. M., McIntosh, A. R., Houle, S., & Tulving, E. (1997). Functional neuroanatomy of recall and recognition: A PET study of episodic memory. *Journal of Cognitive Neuroscience, 9,* 277–288.

Calkins, M. W. (1894). Association. *Psychological Review, 1,* 476–483.

Calkins, M. W. (1906). A reconciliation between structural and functional psychology. *Psychological Review, 13*, 61–81.

Campell, J. I., & Fugelsang, J. A. (2002). Effects of lexicality and distinctiveness on repetition blindness. *Journal of Experimental Psychology: Human Perception and Performance, 28*, 948–962.

Capaldi, E. J., & Neath, I. (1995). Remembering and forgetting as context discrimination. *Learning & Memory, 2*, 107–132.

Carmichael, L., Hogan, H. P., & Walter, A. A. (1932). An experimental study of the effect of language on the reproductions of visually perceived forms. *Journal of Experimental Psychology, 15*, 73–86.

Castel, A. D. (2007a). Aging and memory for numerical information: The role of specificity and expertise in associative memory. *Journal of Gerontology: Psychological Sciences, 62*, 194–196.

Castel, A. D. (2007b). The adaptive and strategic use of memory by older adults: Evaluative processing and value-directed remembering. In A. S. Benjamin & B. H. Ross (Eds.), *The psychology of learning and motivation* (Vol. 48). San Diego, CA: Academic Press.

Castel, A. D., Farb, N., & Craik, F. I. M. (2007). Memory for general and specific value information in younger and older adults: Measuring the limits of strategic control. *Memory & Cognition, 35*, 689–700.

Ceci, S. J. (1995). False beliefs: Some developmental and clinical considerations. In D. L. Schacter (Ed.), *Memory distortions* (pp. 91–125). Cambridge, MA: Harvard University Press.

Chao, L. L., & Knight, R. T. (1995). Human prefrontal lesions increase distractibility to irrelevant sensory inputs. *Neuroreport, 6*, 1605–1610.

Chater, N., & Brown, G. D. A. (2008). From universal laws of cognition to specific cognitive models. *Cognitive Science, 32*, 36–67.

Chater, N., & Vitányi, P. M. B. (2003). The generalized universal law of generalization. *Journal of Mathematical Psychology, 47*, 346–369.

Chun, M. M., & Phelps, E. A. (1999). Memory deficits for implicit contextual information in amnesic patients with hippocampal damage. *Nature Neuroscience, 2*, 844–847.

Cleary, A. M., & Greene, R. L. (2000). Recognition without identification. *Journal of Experimental Psychology: Learning, Memory, and Cognition, 26*, 1063–1069.

Cleary, A. M., & Greene, R. L. (2004). True and false memory in the absence of perceptual identification. *Memory, 12*, 231–236.

Cleary, A. M., & Greene, R. L. (2005). True and false memory in the absence of perceptual identification. *Quarterly Journal of Experimental Psychology, 58A*, 1143–1152.

Coane, J. H., McBride, D. M., Raulerson, B. A. III, & Jordon, J. S. (2007). False memory in a short-term memory task. *Experimental Psychology, 54*, 62–70.

Cohen, G., & Burke, D. M. (1993). Memory for proper names: A review. *Memory 1*, 249–263.

Cohen, G., & Faulkner, D. (1986). Memory for proper names: Age differences in retrieval. *British Journal of Developmental Psychology, 4*, 187–197.

Cohen, G., & Faulkner, D. (1989). Age differences in source forgetting: Effects on reality monitoring and eyewitness testimony. *Psychology and Aging, 4*, 10–17.

Cohen, R. L. (1985). On the generality of the laws of memory. In L.-G. Nilsson & T. Archer (Eds.), *Perspectives on learning and memory* (pp. 247–277). Hillsdale, NJ: Erlbaum.

Coltheart, M. (1980). Iconic memory and visible persistence. *Perception & Psychophysics, 27*, 183–228.

Conrad, R. (1964). Acoustic confusions in immediate memory. *British Journal of Psychology, 55*, 75–84.

Conway, M. A. (Ed.) (1997). *Recovered memories and false memories*. New York: Oxford University Press.

Conway, M. A., & Pleydell-Pearce, C. W. (2000). The construction of autobiographical memories in the self-memory system. *Psychological Review, 107*, 261–288.

Cowan, N. (1988). Evolving conceptions of memory storage, selective attention, and their mutual constraints within the human information processing system. *Psychological Bulletin, 104*, 163–191.

Cowan, N. (1995). *Attention and memory: An integrative framework*. New York: Cambridge University Press.

Cowan, N. (1999). An embedded-processes model of working memory. In A. Miyake & P. Shah (Eds.), *Models of working memory: Mechanisms of active maintenance and executive control* (pp. 62–101). New York: Cambridge University Press.

Cowan, N. (2000). The magical number 4 in short-term memory: A reconsideration of mental storage capacity. *Behavioral and Brain Sciences, 24*, 87–114.

Cowan, N., Beschin, N., & Della Sala, S. (2004). Verbal recall of amnesics under conditions of diminished retroactive interference. *Brain, 127*, 825–834.

Cowan, N., Johnson, T. D., & Saults, J. S. (2005). Capacity limits in list item recognition: Evidence from proactive interference. *Memory, 13*, 293–299.

Cowan, N., Saults, J. S., & Nugent, L. D. (1997). The role of absolute and relative amounts of time in forgetting within immediate memory: The case of tone pitch comparisons. *Psychonomic Bulletin & Review, 4*, 393–397.

Cowan, N., Saults, J. S., & Nugent, L. D. (2001). The ravages of absolute and relative amounts of time on memory. In H. L. Roediger III, J. S. Nairne, I. Neath, & A. M. Surprenant (Eds.), *The nature of remembering: Essays in honor of Robert G. Crowder* (pp. 315–330). Washington, DC: APA.

Craik, F. I. M. (1979). Levels of processing: Overview and closing comments. In L. S. Cermak & F. I. M. Craik (Eds.), *Levels of processing in human memory* (pp. 447–462). Hillsdale, NJ: Erlbaum.

Craik, F. I. M. (1983). On the transfer of information from temporary to permanent memory. *Philosophical Transactions of the Royal Society of London B, 302*, 341–359.

Craik, F. I. M. (1985). Paradigms in human memory research. In L.-G. Nilsson & T. Archer (Eds.), *Perspectives on learning and memory* (pp. 197–221). Hillsdale, NJ: Erlbaum.

Craik, F. I. M. (1994). Memory changes in normal aging. *Current Directions in Psychological Science, 3*, 155–158.

Craik, F. I. M. (2002a). Levels of processing: Past, present, … and future? *Memory, 10*, 305–318.

Craik, F. I. M. (2002b). Human memory and aging. In L. Backman and C. von Hofsten (Eds.), *Psychology at the turn of the millennium* (pp. 261–280), Hove, UK: Psychology Press.

Craik, F. I. M., & Lockhart, R. S. (1972). Levels of processing: A framework for memory research. *Journal of Verbal Learning and Verbal Behavior, 11*, 671–684.

Craik, F. I. M., & McDowd, J. M. (1987). Age differences in recall and recognition. *Journal of Experimental Psychology: Learning, Memory, and Cognition, 13,* 474–479.

Craik, F. I. M., & Tulving, E. (1975). Depth of processing and the retention of words in episodic memory. *Journal of Experimental Psychology: General, 104,* 268–294.

Craik, F. I. M., & Watkins, M. J. (1973). The role of rehearsal in short-term memory. *Journal of Verbal Learning and Verbal Behavior, 12,* 599–607.

Craik, F. I. M., Byrd, M., & Swanson, J. M. (1987). Patterns of memory loss in three elderly samples. *Psychology and Aging, 2,* 79–86.

Crowder, R. G. (1967). Prefix effects in immediate memory. *Canadian Journal of Psychology, 21,* 450–461.

Crowder, R. G. (1976). *Principles of learning and memory.* Hillsdale, NJ: Erlbaum.

Crowder, R. G. (1982). The demise of short-term memory. *Acta Psychologica, 5,* 291–323.

Crowder, R. G. (1983). The purity of auditory memory. *Philosophical Transactions of the Royal Society of London, B. 302,* 251– 265.

Crowder, R. G. (1993). Systems and principles in memory theory: Another critique of pure memory. In A. F. Collins, S. E. Gathercole, M. A. Conway, & P. E. Morris (Eds.), *Theories of memory* (pp. 139–161). Hove, UK: Erlbaum.

Crowder, R. G., & Neath, I. (1991). The microscope metaphor in memory. In W. E. Hockley & S. Lewandowsky (Eds.), *Relating theory and data: Essays on human memory in honour of Bennet B. Murdock Jr.* (pp. 111–125). Hillsdale, NJ: Erlbaum.

Crowder, R. G., & Surprenant, A. M. (2000). Sensory memory. In A. E. Kazdin (Ed.), *Encyclopedia of psychology* (pp. 227–229). New York: Oxford University Press and American Psychological Association.

Cunningham, T. F., Marmie, W. R., & Healy, A. F. (1998). The role of item distinctiveness in short-term recall of order information. *Memory & Cognition, 26,* 463–476.

Dallett, K. (1965). "Primary memory": The effects of redundancy upon digit repetition. *Psychonomic Science, 3,* 237–238.

Deese, J. (1959a). Influence of inter-item associative strength upon immediate free recall. *Psychological Reports, 5,* 305–312.

Deese, J. (1959b). On the prediction of occurrence of particular verbal intrusions in immediate recall. *Journal of Experimental Psychology, 58,* 17–22.

Dehaene, S. (1997). *The number sense: How the mind creates mathematics.* Oxford: Oxford University Press.

Dell, G. S., Reed, K. D., Adams, D. R., & Meyer, A. S. (2000). Speech errors, phonotactic constraints, and implicit learning: A study of the role of experience in language production. *Journal of Experimental Psychology: Learning, Memory, and Cognition, 26,* 1355–1367.

Della Sala, S., Cowan, N., Beschin, N., & Perini, M. (2005). Just lying there, remembering: Improving recall of prose in amnesic patients with mild cognitive impairment by minimizing interference. *Memory, 14,* 435–440.

Dick, A. O. (1974). Iconic memory and its relation to perceptual processing and other memory mechanisms. *Perception & Psychophysics, 16,* 575–596.

Dienes, Z., & McLeod, P. (1993). How to catch a cricket ball. *Perception, 22,* 1427–1439.

Donders, F. C. (1969). On the speed of mental processes (W. G. Koster, Trans.). In W. G. Koster (Ed.), *Attention and performance II, Acta Psychologica, 30,* 412–431. (Original work published 1868).

Dudai, Y. (2004). The neurobiology of consolidation, or, how stable is the engram? *Annual Review of Psychology, 55*, 51–86.

Durso, F. T., & O'Sullivan, C. S. (1983). Naming and remembering proper and common nouns and pictures. *Journal of Experimental Psychology: Learning, Memory, and Cognition, 9*, 497–510.

Dywan, J., & Jacoby, L. L. (1990). Effect of aging and source monitoring: Differences in susceptibility to false fame. *Psychology and Aging, 3*, 379–387.

Earhard, M. (1967). Cued recall and free recall as a function of the number of items per cue. *Journal of Verbal Learning and Verbal Behavior, 6*, 257–263.

Earhard, M. (1977). Retrieval failure in the presence of retrieval cues: A comparison of three age groups. *Canadian Journal of Psychology, 31*, 139–150.

Ebbinghaus, H. (1885). *Über das Gedächtnis: Untersuchungen zur experimentellen Psychologie*. Leipzig: Duncker and Humboldt. Reprinted as H. E. Ebbinghaus (1964). *Memory: A contribution to experimental psychology*. H. A. Ruger (Trans.). New York: Dover.

Einstein, G. O., McDaniel, M. A., Richardson, S. L., Guynn, M. J., & Cunfer, A. R. (1995). Aging and prospective memory: Examining the influences of self-initiated retrieval processes. *Journal of Experimental Psychology: Learning, Memory, and Cognition, 21*, 996–1007.

Erdfelder, A., & Buchner, A. (1998). *Journal of Experimental Psychology: General, 127*, 83–97.

Ericsson, K. A., & Kintsch, W. (1995). Long-term working memory. *Psychological Review, 102*, 211–245.

Ericsson, K. A., & Staszewski, J. (1989). Skilled memory and expertise: Mechanisms of exceptional performance. In D. Klahr & K. Kotovsky (Eds.), *Complex information processing: The impact of Herbert A. Simon* (pp. 235–267). Hillsdale, NJ: Erlbaum.

Estes, W. K. (1991). On types of item coding and source of recall in short-term memory. In W. E. Hockley & S. Lewandowsky (Eds.), *Relating theory and data: Essays on human memory in honor of Bennet B. Murdock* (pp. 155–174). Hillsdale, NJ: Erlbaum.

Estes, W. K. (1997). Processes of memory loss, recovery, and distortion. *Psychological Review, 104*, 148–169.

Farley, L. A., Neath, I., Allbritton, D. W., & Surprenant, A. M. (2007). Irrelevant speech effects and sequence learning. *Memory & Cognition, 35*, 156–165.

Fisher, R. P. (1981). Interactions between encoding distinctiveness and test conditions. *Journal of Experimental Psychology: Human Learning and Memory, 7*, 306–310.

Fisher, R. P., & Craik, F. I. M. (1977). Interaction between encoding and retrieval operations in cued recall. *Journal of Experimental Psychology: Human Learning and Memory, 3*, 701–711.

Foster, J. K., & Jelicic, M. (Eds.) (1999). *Memory: Systems, process, or function?* New York: Oxford University Press.

Friston, K. J., Price, S. J., Fletcher, P., Moore, C., Frackowiak, R. S. J., & Dolan, R. J. (1996). The trouble with cognitive subtraction. *NeuroImage, 4*, 97–104.

Gabrieli, J. D. E. (1999). The architecture of human memory. In J. K. Foster & M. Jelicic (Eds.), *Memory: Systems, process, or function?* (pp. 205–231). New York: Oxford University Press.

Gabrieli, J. D., Poldrack, R. A., & Desmond, J. E. (1998). The role of left prefrontal cortex in language and memory. *Proceedings of the National Academy of Sciences, USA, 3*, 95, 906–913.

Gallistel, C. R., & Gelman, R. (1992). Preverbal and verbal counting and computation. *Cognition, 44,* 43–74.

Gallo, D. A. (2006). *Associative illusions of memory.* New York: Psychology Press.

Gallo, D. A., Cotel, S. C., Moore, C. D., & Schacter, D. L. (2007). Aging can spare recollection-based retrieval monitoring: The importance of event distinctiveness. *Psychology and Aging, 22,* 209–213.

Garavan, H. (1998). Serial attention within working memory. *Memory & Cognition, 26,* 263–276.

Gardiner, J. M. (1988). Functional aspects of recollective experience. *Memory & Cognition, 16,* 309–313.

Gardiner, J. M., & Java, R. I. (1990). Recollective experience in word and nonword recognition. *Memory & Cognition, 18,* 23–30.

Gardiner, J. M., & Parkin, A. J. (1990). Attention and recollective experience in recognition memory. *Memory & Cognition, 18,* 579–583.

Gardiner, J. M., Craik, F. I. M., & Birtwistle, J. (1972). Retrieval cues and release from proactive inhibition. *Journal of Verbal Learning and Verbal Behavior, 11,* 778–783.

Garner, W. R., Hake, H. W., & Ericksen, C. W. (1956). Operationism and the concept of perception. *Psychological Review, 63,* 149–159.

Gathercole, S. E., Pickering, S. J., Hall, M., & Peaker, S. M. (2001). Dissociable lexical and phonological influences on serial recognition and serial recall. *Quarterly Journal of Experimental Psychology, 54A,* 1–30.

Geraci, L., & Rajaram, S. (2004). The distinctiveness effect in the absence of conscious recollection: Evidence from conceptual priming. *Journal of Memory and Language, 51,* 217–230.

Gillund, G., & Shiffrin, R. M. (1984). A retrieval model for both recognition and recall. *Psychological Review, 91,* 1–65.

Giovanni, F. d'A. (1994). Order of strokes writing as a cue for retrieval in reading Chinese characters. *European Journal of Cognitive Psychology, 6,* 337–355.

Glenberg, A. M., Bradley, M. M., Kraus, T. A., & Renzaglia, G. J. (1983). Studies of the long-term recency effect: Support for the contextually guided retrieval hypothesis. *Journal of Experimental Psychology: Learning, Memory, and Cognition, 9,* 231–255.

Goddard, L., Pring, L., & Felmingham, N. (2005). The effects of cue modality on the quality of personal memories retrieved. *Memory, 13,* 79–86.

Graf, P., & Schacter, D. L. (1987). Selective effects of interference on implicit and explicit memory for new associations. *Journal of Experimental Psychology: Learning, Memory, and Cognition, 13,* 45–53.

Greene, R. L. (2004). Recognition memory of counterfeit lists. Paper presented at the 76th Annual Meeting of the Midwestern Psychological Association. Chicago, IL.

Greene, R. L. (2007). Foxes, hedgehogs, and mirror effects: The role of general principles in memory research. In J. S. Nairne (Ed.), *The foundations of remembering: Essays in honor of Henry L. Roediger III* (pp. 53–66). New York: Psychology Press.

Gregg, V. H. (1976). Word frequency, recognition, and recall. In J. Brown (Ed.), *Recall and recognition* (pp. 183–216). New York: Wiley.

Groninger, L. D., & Murray, K. N. (2004). Reminiscence, forgetting, and hypermnesia using face-name learning: Isolating the effects using recall and recognition memory measures. *Memory, 12,* 351–365.

Guérard, K., Hughes, R. W., & Tremblay, S. (2008). An isolation effect in serial memory for spatial information. *Quarterly Journal of Experimental Psychology, 61,* 752–762.

Halford, G. S., Maybery, M. T., & Bain, J. D. (1988). Set-size effects in primary memory: An age-related capacity limitation? *Memory & Cognition, 16,* 480–487.

Hamilton, A. C., & Martin, R. C. (2005). Dissociations among tasks involving inhibition: A single-case study. *Cognitive, Affective and Behavioral Neuroscience, 5,* 1–13.

Hamilton, A. C., & Martin, R. C. (2007). Proactive interference in a semantic short-term memory deficit: Role of semantic and phonological relatedness. *Cortex, 43,* 112–123.

Hamilton, M., & Rajaram, S. (2003). States of awareness across multiple memory tasks: Obtaining a "pure" measure of conscious recollection. *Acta Psychologica, 112,* 43–69.

Hanley, M. J., & Scheirer, C. J. (1975). Proactive inhibition in memory scanning. *Journal of Experimental Psychology: Human Learning and Memory, 1,* 81–83.

Hashtroudi, S., Johnson, M. K., & Chrosniak, L. D. (1990). Aging and qualitative characteristics of memories for perceived and imagined complex events. *Psychology and Aging, 5,* 119–126.

Healy, A. F. (1974). Separating item from order information in short-term memory. *Journal of Verbal Learning and Verbal Behavior, 13,* 644–655.

Hintzman, D. L. (1984). Episodic versus semantic memory: A distinction whose time has come—and gone? *Behavioral and Brain Sciences, 7,* 240–241.

Hintzman, D. L. (1987). Recognition and recall in MINERVA 2: Analysis of the "recognition-failure" paradigm. In P. E. Morris (Ed.), *Modeling cognition* (pp. 215–229). Chichester, UK: Wiley.

Hintzman, D. L. (1990). Human learning and memory: Connections and dissociations. *Annual Review of Psychology, 41,* 109–139.

Hintzman, D. L. (1991). Why are formal models useful in psychology? In W. E. Hockley & S. Lewandowsky (Eds.), *Relating theory and data: Essays on human memory in honour of Bennet B. Murdock Jr* (pp. 39–56). Hillsdale, NJ: Erlbaum.

Hirst, W., Johnson, M. K., Phelps, E. A., & Volpe, B. T. (1988). More on recognition and recall in amnesics. *Journal of Experimental Psychology: Learning, Memory, and Cognition, 14,* 758–763.

Holdstock, J. S., Mayes, A. R., Roberts, N., Cezayirli, E., Isaac, C. L., O'Reilly, R., & Norman, K. (2002). Under what conditions is recognition spared relative to recall after selective hippocampal damage in humans? *Hippocampus, 12,* 341–351.

Hollingworth, H. L. (1924). Particular features of meaning. *Psychological Review, 31,* 79–90.

Howe, M. L., Courage, M. L., Vernescu, R., & Hunt, M. (2000). Distinctiveness effects in children's long-term retention. *Developmental Psychology, 36,* 778–792.

Huang, I.-N., & Wille, C. (1979). The von Restorff isolation effect in free recall. *The Journal of General Psychology, 101,* 27–34.

Hulme, C., Maughan, S., & Brown, G. D. A. (1991). Memory for familiar and unfamiliar words: Evidence for a long-term memory contribution to short-term memory span. *Journal of Memory and Language, 30,* 685–701.

Hulme, C., Neath, I., Stuart, G., Shostak, L., Surprenant, A. M., & Brown, G. D. A. (2006). The distinctiveness of the word-length effect. *Journal of Experimental Psychology: Learning, Memory, and Cognition, 32,* 586–594.

Hulme, C., Roodenrys, S., Brown, G. D. A., & Mercer, R. (1995). The role of long-term memory mechanisms in memory span. *British Journal of Psychology, 86,* 527–536.

Hulme, C., Stuart, G., Brown, G. D. A., & Morin, C. (2003). High- and low-frequency words are recalled equally well in alternating lists: Evidence for associative effects in serial recall. *Journal of Memory and Language, 49,* 500–518.

Humphreys, M. S., & Tehan, G. (1999). Cues and codes in working memory tasks. In C. Izawa (Ed.), *On human memory: Evolution, progress, and reflections on the 30th anniversary of the Atkinson–Shiffrin model* (pp. 127–149). Mahwah, NJ: Erlbaum.

Humphreys, M. S., Bain, J. D., & Pike, R. (1989). Different ways to cue a coherent memory system: A theory for episodic, semantic, and procedural tasks. *Psychological Review, 96,* 208–244.

Hunt, R. R., & McDaniel, M. A. (1993). The enigma of organization and distinctiveness. *Journal of Memory and Language, 32,* 421–445.

Hyde, T. S., & Jenkins, J. J. (1973). Recall of words as a function of semantic, graphic, and syntactic orienting tasks. *Journal of Verbal Learning and Verbal Behavior, 12,* 471–480.

Hyman, I. E., & Pentland, J. (1996). The role of mental imagery in the creation of false childhood memories. *Journal of Memory and Language, 35,* 101–117.

Hyman, I. E. Jr., & Rubin, D. C. (1990). Memorabeatlia: A naturalistic study of long-term memory. *Memory & Cognition, 18,* 205–214.

Jacoby, L. L. (1983). Remembering the data: Analyzing interactive processes in reading. *Journal of Verbal Learning and Verbal Behavior, 22,* 485–508.

Jacoby, L. L. (1991). A process dissociation framework: Separating automatic from intentional uses of memory. *Journal of Memory and Language, 30,* 513–541.

Jacoby, L. L., Toth, J. P., & Yonelinas, A. P. (1993). Separating conscious and unconscious influences of memory: Measuring recollection. *Journal of Experimental Psychology: General, 122,* 139–154.

James, W. (1890). *The principles of psychology.* New York: Henry Holt. [Reprinted as W. James (1983). *The principles of psychology.* Cambridge, MA: Harvard University Press.]

Jenkins, J. G., & Dallenbach, K. M. (1924). Oblivescence during sleep and waking. *American Journal of Psychology, 35,* 605–612.

Jenkins, J. J. (1979). Four points to remember: A tetrahedral model of memory experiments. In L. S. Cermack & F. I. M. Craik (Eds.), *Levels of processing in human memory* (pp. 429–446). Hillsdale, NJ: Erlbaum.

Jennings, J. M., McIntosh, A. R., Kapur, S., Tulving, E., & Houle, S. (1997). Cognitive subtractions may not add up: The interaction between semantic processing and response mode. *NeuroImage, 5,* 229–239.

Jersild, A. (1929). Primacy, recency, frequency, and vividness. *Journal of Experimental Psychology, 12,* 58–70.

Johnson, M. K., & Raye, C. L. (1981). Reality monitoring. *Psychological Review, 88,* 67–85.

Jones, G. V. (1979). Analyzing memory by cuing: Intrinsic and extrinsic knowledge. In N. S. Sutherland (Ed.), *Tutorial essays in psychology: A guide to recent advances,* Volume 2 (pp. 119–147). Hillsdale, NJ: Erlbaum.

Jonides, J., Lewis, R. L., Nee, D. E., Lustig, C. A., Berman, M. G., & Moore, K. S. (2008). The mind and brain of short-term memory. *Annual Review of Psychology, 59,* 193–224.

Jordan, M. I. (1995). The organization of action sequences: Evidence from a relearning task. *Journal of Motor Behavior, 27*, 179–192.

Jost, A. (1897). Die Assoziationsfestigkeit in ihrer Abhängigkeit von der Verteilung der Wiederholungen [The strength of associations in their dependence on the distribution of repetitions]. *Zeitschrift fur Psychologie und Physiologie der Sinnesorgane, 16*, 436–472.

Just, M. A. & Carpenter, P. A. (1987). *The psychology of reading and language comprehension.* Boston, MA: Allyn & Bacon.

Kanwisher, N. G. (1987). Repetition blindness: Type recognition without token individuation. *Cognition, 27*, 117–143.

Kelley, M. R., & Nairne, J. S. (2001). von Restorff revisited: Isolation, generation, and memory for order. *Journal of Experimental Psychology: Learning, Memory, and Cognition, 27*, 54–66.

Keppel, G., & Underwood, B. J. (1962). Proactive inhibition in short-term retention of single items. *Journal of Verbal Learning and Verbal Behavior, 1*, 153–161.

Kihlstrom, J. F. (1994). Hypnosis, delayed recall, and the principles of memory. *International Journal of Clinical and Experimental Hypnosis, 42*, 337–345.

Kihlstrom, J. F., & Barnhardt, T. M. (1993). The self-regulation of memory. In D. M. Wegner & J. W. Pennebaker (Eds.), *Handbook of mental control* (pp. 88–125). Englewood Cliffs, NJ: Prentice-Hall.

Kime, S. K., Lamb, D. G., & Wilson, B. A. (1996). Use of a comprehensive programme of external cueing to enhance procedural memory in a patient with dense amnesia. *Brain Injury, 10*, 17–25.

Kinder, A. & Shanks, D. R. (2003). Neuropsychological dissociations between priming and recognition: A single-system connectionist account. *Psychological Review, 110*, 728–744.

Kintsch, W., Healy, A. F., Hegarty, M., Pennington, B. F., & Salthouse, T. A. (1999). Models of working memory: Eight questions and some general issues. In A. Miyake & P. Shah (Eds.), *Models of working memory: Mechanisms of active maintenance and executive control* (pp. 412–441). Cambridge: Cambridge University Press.

Knoedler, A. J., Hellwig, K. A., & Neath, I. (1999). The shift from recency to primacy with increasing delay. *Journal of Experimental Psychology: Learning, Memory, and Cognition, 25*, 474–487.

Koffka, K. (1935). *Principles of Gestalt psychology.* London: Routledge & Kegan-Paul.

Kolers, P. A., & Roediger, H. L. III. (1984). Procedures of mind. *Journal of Verbal Learning and Verbal Behavior, 23*, 425–449.

Koutstaal, W. (2006). Flexible remembering. *Psychonomic Bulletin & Review, 13*, 84–91.

Laming, D. (1985). Some principles of sensory analysis. *Psychological Review, 92*, 462–485.

Lefton, L. A. & Spragins, A. B. (1974). Orthographic structure and reading experience affect the transfer from iconic to short-term memory. *Journal of Experimental Psychology, 103*, 775–781.

Lewandowsky, S., & Murdock, B. B., Jr. (1989). Memory for serial order. *Psychological Review, 96*, 25–57.

Lewandowsky, S., Brown, G. D. A., Wright, T., & Nimmo, L. M. (2006). Timeless memory: Evidence against temporal distinctiveness models of short term memory for serial order. *Journal of Memory and Language, 54*, 20–38.

Lewandowsky, S., Duncan, M., & Brown, G. D. A. (2004). Time does not cause forgetting in short-term serial recall. *Psychonomic Bulletin & Review, 11,* 771–790.

Lian, A., Glass, A. L., & Raanaas, R. K. (1998). Item-specific effects in recognition failure: Reasons for rejection of the Tulving–Wiseman function. *Memory & Cognition, 26,* 692–707.

Light, L. L., Prull, M. W., La Voie, D. J., & Healy, M. R. (2000). Dual-process theories of memory in old age. In T. J. Perfect and E. A. Maylor (Eds.), *Models of cognitive aging* (pp. 238–300). New York: Oxford University Press.

Loftus, E. F. (1993). The reality of repressed memories. *American Psychologist, 48,* 518–537.

Loftus, E. F., & Palmer, J. C. (1974). Reconstruction of automobile destruction: An example of the interaction between language and memory. *Journal of Verbal Learning and Verbal Behavior, 13,* 585–589.

Loftus, E. F., & Zanni, G. (1975). Eyewitness testimony: The influence of the wording of a question. *Bulletin of the Psychonomic Society, 5,* 86–88.

Loftus, G. R., & Irwin, D. E. (1998). On the relations among different measures of visible and informational persistence. *Cognitive Psychology, 35,* 135–199.

Logie, R. H., Della Sala, S., Laiacona, M., Chalmers, P., & Wynn, V. (1996). Group aggregates and individual reliability: The case of verbal short-term memory. *Memory & Cognition, 24,* 305–321.

Lovatt, P., Avons, S. E., & Masterson, J. (2000). The word-length effect and disyllabic words. *Quarterly Journal of Experimental Psychology. Human Experimental Psychology, 53,* 1–22.

Luce, R. D. (1959). *Individual choice behavior.* New York: Wiley.

Luce, R. D. (1963). Detection and recognition. In R. D. Luce, R. R. Bush, & E. Galanter (Eds.), *Handbook of mathematical psychology* (pp. 103–189). New York: Wiley.

Luce, R. D. (1977). The choice axiom after twenty years. *Journal of Mathematical Psychology, 15,* 215–233.

Lustig, C., & Hasher, L. (2001a). Implicit memory is not immune to interference. *Psychological Bulletin, 127,* 618–628.

Lustig, C., & Hasher, L. (2001b). Implicit memory is vulnerable to proactive interference. *Psychological Science, 12,* 408–412.

Marken, R. S., (2005). Optical trajectories and the informational basis of fly ball catching. *Journal of Experimental Psychology: Human Perception and Performance, 31,* 630–634.

Martin, P. R., & Fernberger, S. W. (1929). Improvement in memory span. *American Journal of Psychology, 41,* 91–94.

Masson, M. E. J., & MacLeod, C. M. (1997). Episodic enhancement of processing fluency. In D. L. Medin (Ed.), *The psychology of learning and motivation: Advances in research and theory* (Volume 37) (pp. 155–210). San Diego, CA: Academic Press.

Masson, M. E. J., Caldwell, J. I., & Whittlesea, B. W. A. (2000). When lust is lost: Orthographic similarity effects in the encoding and reconstruction of rapidly presented word lists. *Journal of Experimental Psychology: Learning, Memory, and Cognition, 26,* 1005–1022.

Mathews, R. (1954). Recall as a function of number of classificatory categories. *Journal of Experimental Psychology, 47,* 241–347.

Mayes, A. R., Holdstock, J. S., Isaac, C. L., Hunkin, N. M., & Roberts, N. (2002). Relative sparing of item recognition memory in a patient with damage limited to the hippocampus. *Hippocampus, 12,* 525–540.

Maylor, E. A. (2002). Serial position effects in semantic memory: Reconstructing the order of verses of hymns. *Psychonomic Bulletin & Review, 9,* 816–820.

Mayzner, M. S., & Schoenberg, K. M. (1964). Single-letter and diagram frequency effects in immediate serial recall. *Journal of Verbal Learning and Verbal Behavior, 3,* 397–400.

McBride, D. M., & Dosher, B. A. (2002). A comparison of conscious and automatic memory processes for picture and word stimuli: A process dissociation analysis. *Consciousness and Cognition: An International Journal, 11,* 423–460.

McElree, B. (2001). Working memory and focal attention. *Journal of Experimental Psychology: Learning, Memory, and Cognition, 27,* 817–835.

McElree, B., & Dosher, B. A. (1989). Serial position and set size in short-term memory: The time course of recognition. *Journal of Experimental Psychology: General, 118,* 346–373.

McGaugh, J. L. (2000). Memory: a century of consolidation. *Science, 287,* 248–251.

McGeoch, J. A. (1932). Forgetting and the law of disuse. *Psychological Review, 39,* 352–370.

McGeoch, J. A., & Irion, A. L. (1952). *The psychology of human learning.* New York: Longmans, Green.

McIntyre, J. S., & Craik, F. I. M. (1987). Age differences in memory for item and source information. *Canadian Journal of Experimental Psychology, 41,* 175–192.

McKoon, G., Ratcliff, R., & Dell, G. S. (1986). A critical evaluation of the semantic/episodic distinction. *Journal of Experimental Psychology: Learning, Memory, and Cognition, 12,* 295–306.

McWeeny, K. H., Young, A. W., Hay, D. C., & Ellis, A. W. (1987). Putting names to faces. *British Journal of Psychology, 78,* 143–149.

Mead, K. M. L., & Ball, L. J. (2007). Music tonality and context-dependent recall: The influence of key change and mood mediation. *European Journal of Cognitive Psychology, 19,* 59–79.

Meegan, D. V., Purc-Stephenson, R., Honsberger, M. J. M., & Topan, M. (2004). Task analysis complements neuroimaging: An example from working memory research. *NeuroImage, 21,* 1026–1036.

Melton, A. W. (1963). Implications of short-term memory for a general theory of memory. *Journal of Verbal Learning and Verbal Behavior, 2,* 1–21.

Mewhort, D. J. K. (1972). Scanning, chunking and the familiarity effect in tachistoscopic recognition. *Journal of Experimental Psychology, 93,* 69–71.

Mewhort, D. J. K., & Leppman, K. P. (1985). Information persistence: Testing spatial and identity information with a voice probe. *Psychological Research, 47,* 51–58.

Mewhort, D. J. K., Campbell, A. J., Marchetti, F. M., & Campbell, J. I. D. (1981). Identification, localization, and "iconic" memory: An evaluation of the bar-probe task. *Memory & Cognition, 9,* 50–67.

Mewhort, D. J., Merikle, P. M., & Bryden, M. P. (1969). On the transfer from iconic to short-term memory. *Journal of Experimental Psychology. 81,* 89–94.

Micco, A., & Masson, M. J. (1992). Age-related differences in the specificity of verbal encoding. *Memory & Cognition, 20,* 244–253.

Miller, G. A. (1956). The magical number seven plus or minus two: Some limits on our capacity for processing information. *Psychological Review, 63,* 81–97.

Miller, M. B., & Van Horn, J. D. (2007). Individual variability in brain activations associated with episodic retrieval: A role for large-scale databases. *International Journal of Psychophysiology, 63,* 205–213.

Miyake, A., & Shah, P. (Eds.) (1999). *Models of working memory: Mechanisms of active maintenance and executive control.* New York: Cambridge University Press.

Monsell, S. (1978). Recency, immediate recognition memory, and reaction time. *Cognitive Psychology, 10,* 465–501.

Moore, T. V. (1910). The process of abstraction: An experimental study. *California University Publications in Psychology, 1,* 73–197.

Morris, C. D., Bransford, J. D., & Franks, J. J. (1977). Levels of processing versus transfer appropriate processing. *Journal of Verbal Learning and Verbal Behavior, 16,* 519–533.

Moscovitch, M. (1994). Memory and working with memory: Evaluation of a component process model and comparisons with other models. In D. L. Schacter & E. Tulving (Eds.), *Memory systems 1994* (pp. 269–308). Cambridge, MA: MIT Press.

Moscovitch, M., Vriezen, E., & Goshen-Gottstein, Y. (1993). Implicit tests of memory in patients with focal lesions or degenerative brain disorders. In F. Boller and J. Grafman (Eds.), *Handbook of neuropsychology,* Vol. 8 (pp. 133–173). Amsterdam: Elsevier.

Müller, S., Abernethy, B., & Farrow, D. (2006). How do world-class cricket batsmen anticipate a bowler's intention? *Quarterly Journal of Experimental Psychology, 59,* 2162–2186.

Mulligan, N. W. (1996). The effects of perceptual interference at encoding on implicit memory, explicit memory, and memory for source. *Journal of Experimental Psychology: Learning, Memory, and Cognition, 22,* 1067–1087.

Murdock, B. B. Jr. (1960). The distinctiveness of stimuli. *Psychological Review, 67,* 16–31.

Murdock, B. B. Jr. (1967). Recent developments in short-term memory. *British Journal of Psychology, 58,* 421–433.

Murdock, B. B. Jr. (1977). [Review of the book *Principles of learning and memory* by R. G. Crowder.] *American Journal of Psychology, 90,* 329–333.

Murphy, G. (1929). *An historical introduction to modern psychology.* New York: Harcourt, Brace.

Naghavi, H. R., & Nyberg, L. (2005). Common fronto-parietal activity in attention, memory, and consciousness: Shared demands on integration? *Consciousness and Cognition: An International Journal, 1,* 390–425.

Nairne, J. S. (1990). A feature model of immediate memory. *Memory & Cognition, 18,* 251–269.

Nairne, J. S. (1992). The loss of positional certainty in long-term memory. *Psychological Science, 3,* 199–202.

Nairne, J. S. (1996). Short-term/Working Memory. In E. L. Bjork & R. A. Bjork (Eds.), *Handbook of perception and cognition, Volume 10: Memory.* (pp. 101–126) New York: Academic Press.

Nairne, J. S. (2001). A functional analysis of memory. In H. L. Roediger III, J. S. Nairne, I. Neath, & A. M. Surprenant (Eds.), *The nature of remembering: Essays in honor of Robert G. Crowder* (pp. 283–296). Washington, DC: APA.

Nairne, J. S. (2002a). The myth of the encoding-retrieval match. *Memory, 10,* 389–395.

Nairne, J. S. (2002b). Remembering over the short-term: The case against the standard model. *Annual Review of Psychology, 53,* 53–81.

Nairne, J. S. (2003). Sensory and working memory. In A. H. Healy & R. W. Proctor (Eds.), *Comprehensive handbook of psychology: Volume 4: Experimental psychology* (pp. 423–446). New York: Wiley.

Nairne, J. S. (2005). The functionalist agenda in memory research. In A. F. Healy (Ed.), *Experimental cognitive psychology and its applications: Festschrift in honor of Lyle Bourne, Walter Kintsch, and Thomas Landauer* (pp. 115–126). Washington, DC: APA.

Nairne, J. S., & Neath, I. (2000). Long-term memory span. *Behavioral and Brain Sciences, 24,* 134–135.

Nairne, J. S., Neath, I., Serra, M., & Byun, E. (1997). Positional distinctiveness and the ratio rule in free recall. *Journal of Memory and Language, 37,* 155–166.

Neath, I. (1993). Distinctiveness and serial position effects in recognition. *Memory & Cognition, 21,* 689–698.

Neath, I. (1997). Modality, concreteness, and set-size effects in a free reconstruction of order task. *Memory & Cognition, 25,* 256–263.

Neath, I. (2000). Modeling the effects of irrelevant speech on memory. *Psychonomic Bulletin & Review, 7,* 403–423.

Neath, I. (2005). Serial position effects and position error gradients in "iconic" memory. *Memory Lab Technical Report 2005-02,* Purdue University. http://memory.psych.mun.ca/pubs/reprints/tr2005-02.pdf.

Neath, I. (2006). A SIMPLE account of Baddeley & Scott (1971). *Memory Lab Technical Report 2006-01,* Memorial University of Newfoundland. http://memory.psych.mun.ca/pubs/reprints/tr2006-01.pdf.

Neath, I., & Brown, G. D. A. (2006). SIMPLE: Further applications of a local distinctiveness model of memory. In B. H. Ross (Ed.), *The psychology of learning and motivation* (pp. 201–243). San Diego, CA: Academic Press.

Neath, I., & Brown, G. D. A. (2007). Making distinctiveness models of memory distinct. In J. S. Nairne (Ed.), *The foundations of remembering: Essays in honor of Henry L. Roediger III* (pp. 125–140). New York: Psychology Press.

Neath, I., & Crowder, R. G. (1990). Schedules of presentation and temporal distinctiveness in human memory. *Journal of Experimental Psychology: Learning, Memory, and Cognition, 16,* 316–327.

Neath, I., & Crowder, R. G. (1996). Distinctiveness and very short-term serial position effects. *Memory, 4,* 225–242.

Neath, I., & Knoedler, A. J. (1994). Distinctiveness and serial position effects in recognition and sentence processing. *Journal of Memory and Language, 33,* 776–795.

Neath, I., & Nairne, J. S. (1995). Word-length effects in immediate memory: Overwriting trace-decay theory. *Psychonomic Bulletin & Review, 2,* 429–441.

Neath, I., & Surprenant, A. M. (2003). *Human memory: An introduction to research, data, and theory* (2nd edition). Belmont, CA: Wadsworth.

Neath, I., & Surprenant, A. M. (2005). Mechanisms of memory. In K. Lamberts & R. L. Goldstone (Eds.), *Handbook of cognition* (pp. 221–238). London: Sage.

Neath, I., & Surprenant, A. M. (2008). Short- vs. long-term memory. In A. S. Benjamin, J. S. de Belle, B. Etnyre, & T. Polk (Eds.), *Human learning: Biology, brain, and neuroscience* (pp. 21–31). Amsterdam, Elsevier.

Neath, I., Bireta, T. J., & Surprenant, A. M. (2003). The time-based word length effect and stimulus set specificity. *Psychonomic Bulletin & Review, 10,* 430–434.

Neath, I., Brown, G. D. A., McCormack, T., Chater, N., & Freeman, R. (2006). Distinctiveness models of memory and absolute identification: Evidence for local, not global, effects. *Quarterly Journal of Experimental Psychology, 59,* 121–135.

Neath, I., Guérard, K., Jalbert, A., Bireta, T. J., & Surprenant, A. M. (in press). Irrelevant speech and statistical learning. *Quarterly Journal of Experimental Psychology.*

Neisser, U. (1967). *Cognitive Psychology.* New York: Appleton-Century-Crofts.

Nelson, D. L., & Brooks, D. H. (1974). Relative effectiveness of rhymes and synonyms as retrieval cues. *Journal of Experimental Psychology, 102,* 503–507.

Nelson, D. L., Wheeler, J. W., Borden, R. C, Brooks, D. H. (1974). Levels of processing and cuing: Sensory versus meaning features. *Journal of Experimental Psychology, 103,* 971–977.

Newell, A. (1973). You can't play 20 questions with nature and win: Projective comments on the papers of this symposium. In W. G. Chase (Ed.), *Visual information processing* (pp. 283–308). New York: Academic Press.

Nilsson, L.-G., & Gardiner, J. (1993). Identifying exceptions in a database of recognition failure studies from 1973 to 1992. *Memory & Cognition, 21,* 397–410.

Nilsson, L.-G., Law, J., & Tulving, E. (1988). Recognition failure of recallable unique names: Evidence for an empirical law of memory and learning. *Journal of Experimental Psychology: Learning, Memory, and Cognition, 14,* 266–277.

Norman, K. A., & Schacter, D. L. (1997). False recognition in younger and older adults: Exploring the characteristics of illusory memories. *Memory & Cognition, 25,* 838–848.

Nosofsky, R. M. (1992). Similarity scaling and cognitive process models. *Annual Review of Psychology, 43,* 25–53.

Nosofsky, R. M., & Zaki, S. R. (1998). Dissociations between categorization and recognition in amnesic and normal individuals: An exemplar-based interpretation. *Psychological Science, 9,* 247–255.

Nyberg, L. (1995). Memory for enacted and non-enacted events: Is there a need for separate laws? *European Journal of Cognitive Psychology, 7,* 55–64.

Nyberg, L., Cabeza, R., & Tulving, E. (1996). PET studies of encoding and retrieval: The HERA model. *Psychonomic Bulletin & Review, 3,* 135–148.

Oberauer, K. (2002). Access to information in working memory: Exploring the focus of attention. *Journal of Experimental Psychology: Learning, Memory, and Cognition, 28,* 411–212.

Paivio, A., Rogers, T. B., & Smythe, P. C. (1968). Why are pictures easier to recall than words? *Psychonomic Science, 11,* 137–138.

Park, D. C., Smith, A. D., & Cavanaugh, J. C. (1990). Metamemories of memory researchers. *Memory & Cognition, 18,* 321–327.

Parkin, A. J. (1980). Levels of processing and the cue overload principle. *Quarterly Journal of Psychology, 32,* 427–434.

Parkin, A. J. (1998). The central executive does not exist. *Journal of the International Neuropsychological Society, 4,* 518–522.

Parkin, A. J. (1999). Component processes versus systems: Is there really an important difference? In J. K. Foster & M. Jelicic (Eds.), *Memory: Systems, process, or function* (pp. 273–287). New York: Oxford University Press.

Parkman, J. M. (1971). Temporal aspects of digit and letter inequality judgments. *Journal of Experimental Psychology, 91*, 191–205.

Payne, D. G. (1987). Hypermnesia and reminiscence in recall: A historical and empirical review. *Psychological Bulletin, 101*, 5–27.

Peterson, L. R., & Peterson, M. J. (1959). Short-term retention of individual items. *Journal of Experimental Psychology, 61*, 12–21.

Peynircioğlu, Z. F. (1990). A feeling-of-recognition without identification. *Journal of Memory and Language, 29*, 493–500.

Pillsbury, W. B., & Rausch, H. L. (1943). An extension of the Kohler–Restorff inhibition phenomenon. *American Journal of Psychology, 56*, 293–298.

Posner, M. I. (1978). *Chronometric explorations of the mind.* Hillsdale, NJ: Erlbaum.

Procter, R. W., & Dutta, A. (1995). *Skill acquisition and human performance.* Thousand Oaks, CA: Sage.

Proctor, R. W., & Van Zandt, T. (1994). *Human factors in simple and complex systems.* Boston, MA: Allyn & Bacon.

Raaijmakers, J. G. W., & Shiffrin, R. M. (1981). Search of associative memory. *Psychological Review, 88*, 93–134.

Rabinowitz, F. M., & Andrews, S. R. (1973). Intentional and incidental learning in children and the von Restorff effect. *Journal of Experimental Psychology, 100*, 315–318.

Rabinowitz, J. C., Craik, F. I. M., & Ackerman, B. P. (1982). A processing resource account of age differences in recall. *Canadian Journal of Psychology, 36*, 325–344.

Rajaram, S. (1998). Perceptual effects on remembering: recollective processes in picture recognition memory. *Journal of Experimental Psychology: Learning, Memory, and Cognition, 22*, 365–377.

Ratcliff, R. (1992). Models of memory. In L. R. Squire (Ed.), *Encyclopedia of learning and memory* (pp. 428–431). New York: Macmillan.

Raymond, B. (1969). Short-term storage and long-term storage in free recall. *Journal of Verbal Learning and Verbal Behavior, 8*, 567–574.

Reder, L. M., Oates, J. M., Dickison, D., Anderson, J. R., Gyulai, F., Quinlan, J. J., Ferris, J. L., Dulik, M., & Jefferson, B. F. (2007). Retrograde facilitation under midazolam: The role of general and specific interference. *Psychonomic Bulletin & Review, 14*, 261–269.

Rendell, P. G., Castel, A. D., & Craik, F. I. M. (2005). Memory for proper names in old age: A disproportionate impairment? *The Quarterly Journal of Experimental Psychology, 58A*, 54–71.

Restle, F. (1974). Critique of pure memory. In R. L. Solso (Ed.), *Theories of cognitive psychology: The Loyola symposium* (pp. 203–217). Potomac, Maryland: Erlbaum.

Ribot, T. (1881). *Les maladies de la memoire* [Diseases of memory]. New York: Appleton-Century-Crofts.

Roediger, H. L. III (2008). Relativity of remembering: Why the laws of memory vanished. *Annual Review of Psychology, 59*, 225–254.

Roediger, H. L. III, & Blaxton, T. A. (1987). Effects of varying modality, surface features, and retention interval on priming in word-fragment completion. *Memory & Cognition, 15*, 379–388.

Roediger, H. L. III, & McDermott, K. B. (1993). Implicit memory in normal human subjects. In F. Boller & J. Grafman (Eds.), *Handbook of neuropsychology*, Vol. 8 (pp. 63–131). Amsterdam: Elsevier.

Roediger, H. L. III, & McDermott, K. B. (1995). Creating false memories: Remembering words not presented in lists. *Journal of Experimental Psychology: Learning, Memory, and Cognition, 21,* 803–814.

Roediger, H. L. III, & Weldon, M. S. (1987). Reversing the picture superiority effect. In M. A. McDaniel & M. Presley (Eds.), *Imagery and related mnemonic processes: Theories, individual differences, and applications* (pp. 151–174). New York: Springer-Verlag.

Roediger, H. L. III, Buckner, R. L., & McDermott, K. B. (1999). Components of processing. In J. K. Foster & M. Jelicic (Eds.), *Memory: Systems, process, or function?* (pp. 32–65). New York: Oxford University Press.

Roediger, H. L. III, Weldon, M. S., & Challis, B. H. (1989). Explaining dissociations between implicit and explicit measures of retention: A processing account. In H. L. Roediger III and F. I. M. Craik (Eds.), *Varieties of memory and consciousness: Essays in honour of Endel Tulving* (pp. 3–39). Hillsdale, NJ: Erlbaum.

Roediger, H. L. III, Rajaram, S., & Srinivas, K. (1990). Specifying criteria for distinguishing memory systems. In A. Diamond (Ed.), *The development and neural bases of higher cognitive functions* (pp. 572–595). New York: New York Academy of Sciences Press.

Roodenrys, S., & Hinton, M. (2002). Sublexical or lexical effects on serial recall of nonwords? *Journal of Experimental Psychology: Learning, Memory, and Cognition, 28,* 29–33.

Roodenrys, S., & Miller, L. M. (2008). A constrained Rasch model of trace redintegration in serial recall. *Memory & Cognition, 36,* 578–587.

Roodenrys, S., & Quinlan, P. T. (2000). The effects of stimulus set size and word frequency on verbal serial recall. *Memory, 8,* 71–78.

Roodenrys, S., Hulme, C., Lethbridge, A., Hinton, M., & Nimmo, L. M. (2002). Word-frequency and phonological-neighborhood effects on verbal short-term memory. *Journal of Experimental Psychology: Learning, Memory, and Cognition, 28,* 1019–1034.

Rovee-Collier, C. (1997). Dissociations in infant memory: Rethinking the development of implicit and explicit memory. *Psychological Review, 104,* 467–498.

Rovee-Collier, C. (1999). The development of infant memory. *Current Directions in Psychological Science, 8,* 80–85.

Rumelhart, D. E., Smolensky, P., McClelland, J. L., & Hinton, G. E. (1986). Schemata and sequential thought processes in PDP models. In J. L. McClelland & D. E. Rumelhart (Eds.), *Parallel distributed processing: Explorations in the microstructure of cognition, Vol. 2* (pp. 7–57). Cambridge, MA: MIT Press.

Russell, B. (1931). *The scientific outlook.* London: Allen and Unwin.

Rutherford, A. (2004). Environmental context-dependent recognition memory effects: An examination of ICE model and cue-overload hypotheses. *The Quarterly Journal of Experimental Psychology, 57A,* 107–127.

Ryan, J. D., & Cohen, N. J. (2003). Evaluating the neuropsychological dissociation evidence for multiple memory systems. *Cognitive, Affective, & Behavioral Neuroscience, 3,* 168–185.

Ryan L., Ostergaard A., Norton L., & Johnson J. (2001). Search and selection processes in implicit and explicit word-stem completion performance in young, middle-aged, and older adults. *Memory & Cognition, 29,* 678–690.

Schab, F. R., & Crowder, R. G. (1995). Odor recognition memory. In F. R. Schab & R. G. Crowder (Eds.), *Memory for odors* (pp. 9–20). Hillsdale, NJ: Erlbaum.

Schab, F. R., & Crowder, R. G. (Eds.) (1995). *Memory for odors*. Hillsdale, NJ: Erlbaum.

Schacter, D. L. (1990). Perceptual representation systems and implicit memory: Toward a resolution of the multiple memory systems debate. *Annals of the New York Academy of Sciences, 608,* 543–571.

Schacter, D. L. (2001). *The seven sins of memory: How the mind forgets and remembers.* New York: Houghton Mifflin.

Schacter, D. L. & Tulving, E. (1994). What are the memory systems of 1994? In D. L. Schacter & E. Tulving (Eds.), *Memory systems 1994* (pp. 1–38). Cambridge, MA: MIT Press.

Schacter, D. L., Israel, L., & Racine, C. (1999). Suppressing false recognition in younger and older adults: The distinctiveness heuristic. *Journal of Memory and Language, 40,* 1–24.

Schacter, D. L., Koutstaal, W., & Norman, A. (1997). False memories and aging. *Trends in Cognitive Sciences, 1,* 229–236.

Schacter, D. L., Wagner, A. D., & Buckner, R. L. (2000). Memory systems of 1999. In E. Tulving and F. I. M. Craik (Eds.), *The Oxford handbook of memory* (pp. 627–643). New York: Oxford University Press.

Schweickert, R. (1993). A multinomial processing tree model for degradation and redintegration in immediate recall. *Memory & Cognition, 21,* 168–175.

Scoville, W. B., & Milner, B. (1957). Loss of recent memory after bilateral hippocampal lesions. *Journal of Neurological and Neurosurgical Psychiatry, 20,* 11–21.

Semon, R. (1923). *Mnemic psychology* (B. Duffy, Trans.). New York: Macmillan.

Shepard, R. N. (1987). Toward a universal law of generalization for psychological science. *Science, 237,* 1317–1323.

Shepard, R. N. (2004). How a cognitive psychologist came to seek universal laws. *Psychonomic Bulletin & Review, 11,* 1–23.

Sherry, D. F., & Schacter, D. L. (1987). The evolution of multiple memory systems. *Psychological Review, 94,* 439–454.

Shiffrin, R. M. (1999). 30 years of memory. In C. Izawa (Ed.), *On human memory: Evolution, progress, and reflections of the 30th anniversary of the Atkinson–Shiffrin model* (pp. 17–33). Mahwah, NJ: Erlbaum.

Sikstrom, S. P., & Gardiner, J. M. (1997). Remembering, knowing, and the Tulving–Wiseman Law. *European Journal of Cognitive Psychology, 9,* 167–185.

Simon, H. A. (1990). Invariants of human behavior. *Annual Review of Psychology, 41,* 1–19.

Sloman, S. A., Hayman, C. A. G., Ohta, N., Law, J., & Tulving, E. (1988). Forgetting in primed fragment completion. *Journal of Experimental Psychology: Learning, Memory, and Cognition, 14,* 223–239.

Slotnik, S. D. (2004). Visual memory and visual perception recruit common neural substrates. *Behavioral and Cognitive Neuroscience Reviews, 3,* 207–221.

Smith, R. E., & Hunt, R. R. (2000). The effects of distinctiveness require reinstatement of organization: The importance of intentional memory instructions. *Journal of Memory and Language, 43,* 431–446.

Sohn, M.-H., Anderson, J. R., Reder, L. M., & Goode, A. (2004). Differential fan effect and attentional focus. *Psychonomic Bulletin & Review, 11,* 729–734.

Sommers, M. S. & Lewis, B. R. (1999). Who really lives next door: Creating false memories with phonological neighbors. *Journal of Memory and Language, 40,* 83–108.

Spencer, W. D., & Raz, N. (1995). Differential effects of aging on memory for context and content: A meta-analysis. *Psychology and Aging, 10,* 527–539.

Sperling, G. (1960). The information available in brief visual presentations. *Psychological Monographs, 74* (Whole No. 11).

Sperling, G. (1967). Successive approximations to a model for short-term memory. *Acta Psychologica, 27,* 285–292.

Squire, L. R. (1994). Declarative and nondeclarative memory: Multiple brain systems supporting learning and memory. In D. L. Schacter & E. Tulving (Eds.), *Memory systems 1994* (pp. 203–231). Cambridge: MIT Press.

Squire, L. R., Clark, R. E., & Knowlton, B. J. (2001). Retrograde amnesia. *Hippocampus, 11,* 50–55.

Sternberg, S. (1966). High speed scanning in human memory. *Science, 153,* 652–654.

Stuart, G. P., Patel, J., & Bhagrath, N. (2006). Ageing affects conceptual but not perceptual memory processes. *Memory, 14,* 345–358.

Surprenant, A. M., & Neath, I. (2008). The 9 lives of short-term memory. In A. Thorn & M. Page (Eds.), *Interactions between short-term and long-term memory in the verbal domain* (pp. 16–43). Hove, UK: Psychology Press.

Surprenant, A. M., Neath, I., & Brown, G. D. A. (2006). Modeling age-related differences in immediate memory using SIMPLE. *Journal of Memory and Language, 55,* 572–586.

Tehan, G., & Humphreys, M. S. (1995). Transient phonemic codes and immunity to proactive interference. *Memory & Cognition, 23,* 181–191.

Tehan, G., & Humphreys, M. S. (1996). Cueing effects in short-term recall. *Memory & Cognition, 24,* 719–732.

Tehan, G., & Humphreys, M. S. (1998). Creating proactive interference in immediate recall: Building a DOG from a DART, a MOP, and a FIG. *Memory & Cognition, 26,* 477–489.

Teigen, K. H. (2002). One hundred years of laws in psychology. *American Journal of Psychology, 115,* 103–118.

Thomas, A. K., & Sommers, M. S. (2005). Attention to item-specific processing eliminates age effects in false memories. *Journal of Memory and Language, 52,* 71–86.

Thomson, D. M., & Tulving, E. (1970). Associative encoding and retrieval: Weak and strong cues. *Journal of Experimental Psychology, 86,* 255–262.

Thorn, A. S. C., & Page, M. (Eds.) (2008*). Interactions between short-term and long-term memory in the verbal domain.* Hove, UK: Psychology Press.

Thorn, A. S. C., Gathercole, S. E., & Frankish, C. R. (2005). Redintegration and the benefits of long-term knowledge in verbal short-term memory: An evaluation of Schweickert's (1993) multinomial processing tree model. *Cognitive Psychology, 50,* 133–158.

Titchener, E. B. (1898). The postulates of a structural psychology. *Philosophical Review, 7,* 449–465.

Tolan, G. A., & Tehan, G. (1999). Determinants of short-term forgetting: Decay, retroactive interference, or proactive interference? *International Journal of Psychology, 34,* 285–292.

Toth, J. P., & Hunt, R. R. (1999). Not one versus many, but zero versus any: Structure and function in the context of the multiple memory systems debate. In J. K. Foster and M. Jelicic (Eds.), *Memory: Systems, process, or function?* (pp. 232–272). New York: Oxford University Press.

Tulving, E. (1974). Cue-dependent forgetting. *American Scientist, 62,* 74–82.

Tulving, E. (1983). *Elements of episodic memory.* New York: Oxford University Press.

Tulving, E. (1985a). How many memory systems are there? *American Psychologist, 40,* 385–398.

Tulving, E. (1985b). Memory and consciousness. *Canadian Psychology 26,* 1–12.

Tulving, E. (1998). Neurocognitive processes of human memory. In C. von Euler, I. Lundberg, & R. Llinas (Eds.), *Basic mechanisms in cognition and language* (pp. 261–281). Amsterdam: Elsevier.

Tulving, E. (2002). Episodic memory: From mind to brain. *Annual Review of Psychology. 53,* 1–25.

Tulving, E., & Colatla, V. (1970). Free recall of trilingual lists. *Cognitive Psychology, 1,* 86–98.

Tulving, E., & Craik, F. I. M. (Eds.), (2000). *The Oxford handbook of memory.* New York: Oxford University Press.

Tulving, E., & Donaldson, W. (Eds.) (1972). *Organization of memory.* New York: Academic Press.

Tulving, E., & Flexser, A. J. (1992). On the nature of the Tulving–Wiseman function. *Psychological Review, 99,* 543–546.

Tulving, E., & Pearlstone, Z. (1966). Availability versus accessibility of information in memory for words. *Journal of Verbal Learning and Verbal Behavior, 5,* 381–391.

Tulving, E., & Thomson, D. M. (1973). Encoding specificity and retrieval processes in episodic memory. *Psychological Review, 80,* 352–373.

Tulving, E., & Wiseman, S. (1975). Relation between recognition and recognition failure of recallable words. *Bulletin of the Psychonomic Society, 6,* 79–82.

Tulving, E., Hayman, C. A., & Macdonald, C. A. (1991). Long-lasting perceptual priming and semantic learning in amnesia: A case experiment. *Journal of Experimental Psychology: Learning, Memory, and Cognition, 17,* 595–617.

Tulving, E., Kapur, S., Craik, F. I. M., Moscovich, M., & Houle, S. (1994). Hemispheric encoding/retrieval asymmetry in episodic memory: Positron emission tomography findings. *Proceedings of the National Academy of Sciences, USA, 91,* 2016–2020.

Tulving, E., Schacter, D. L., & Stark, H. (1982). Priming effects in word-fragment completion are independent of recognition memory. *Journal of Experimental Psychology: Human Learning and Memory, 8,* 336–342.

Tun, P. A., Wingfield, A., Rosen, M. J., & Blanchard, L. (1998). Response latencies for false memories: Gist-based processes in normal aging. *Psychology and Aging, 13,* 230–241.

Turvey, M. T., Brick, P., & Osborn, J. (1970). Proactive interference in short-term memory as a function of prior-item retention interval. *Quarterly Journal of Experimental Psychology, 22,* 142–147.

Underwood, B. J. (1961). Ten years of massed practice on distributed practice. *Psychological Review, 68,* 229–247.

Underwood, B. J., & Schultz, R. W. (1960). *Meaningfulness and verbal learning.* Philadelphia: Lippincott.

Unsworth, N., Heitz, R. P., Parks, N. (2008). The importance of temporal distinctiveness on forgetting from working memory. Manuscript submitted for publication.

Uttl, B., Ohta, N., & Siegenthaler, A. L. (Eds.) (2006). *Memory and emotion: Interdisciplinary perspectives*. Malden, MA: Blackwell.

Van Buskirk, W. L. (1932). An experimental study of vividness in learning and retention. *Journal of Experimental Psychology, 15*, 563–573.

Van Dyke, J. A., & McElree, B. (2006). Retrieval interference in sentence comprehension. *Journal of Memory and Language, 55*, 157–166.

Van Orden, C. G., Pennington, B. F., & Stone, G. O. (2001). What do double dissociations prove? *Cognitive Science, 25*, 111–172.

Van Zandt, T., & Ratcliff, R. (1995). Statistical mimicking of reaction time data: single process models, parameter variability, and mixtures. *Psychonomic Bulletin & Review, 2*, 20–54.

Verhaeghen, P., & Basak, C. (2005). Ageing and switching of the focus of attention in working memory: Results from a modified N-Back task. *Quarterly Journal of Experimental Psychology, 58A*, 134–154.

Verhaeghen, P., Cerella, J., & Basak, C. (2004). A working memory workout: How to expand the focus of serial attention from one to four items in 10 hours or less. *Journal of Experimental Psychology: Learning, Memory, and Cognition, 30*, 1322–1337.

von Restorff, H. (1933). Analyse von Vorgangen in Spurenfeld. I. Über die Wirkung von Bereichsbildungen im Spurenfeld [Analysis of processes in the memory trace. I. On the effect of group formations on the memory trace]. *Psychologische Forschung, 18*, 299–342.

Wallace, W. P. (1965). Review of the historical, empirical, and theoretical status of the von Restorff phenomenon. *Psychological Bulletin, 63*, 410–424.

Wallace, W. P. (1978). Recognition failure of recallable words and recognizable words. *Journal of Experimental Psychology: Human Learning and Memory, 4*, 441–452.

Warren, H. C. (1916). Mental association from Plato to Hume. *Psychological Review, 23*, 208–230.

Warrington, E, K., & Shallice, T. (1984). Category specific semantic impairments. *Brain, 107*, 829–854.

Warrington, E. K., & Weiskrantz, L. (1970). Amnesic syndrome: Consolidation or retrieval? *Nature, 228*, 628–630.

Warrington, E. K., & Weiskrantz, L. (1974). The effect of prior learning on subsequent retention in amnesia patients. *Neuropsychologia, 16*, 169–176.

Watkins, M. J. (1977). The intricacy of memory span. *Memory & Cognition, 5*, 529–534.

Watkins, M. J. (1979). Engrams as cuegrams and forgetting as cue overload: A cueing approach to the structure of memory. In C. R. Puff (Ed.), *Memory organization and structure* (pp. 347–372). New York: Academic Press.

Watkins, M. J. (1989). Willful and nonwillful determinants of memory. In H. L. Roediger III & F. I. M. Craik (Eds.), *Varieties of memory and consciousness: Essays in honour of Endel Tulving* (pp. 59–72). Hillsdale, NJ: Erlbaum.

Watkins, M. J. (2001). The modality effect and the gentle law of speech ascendancy. In H. L. Roediger III, J. S. Nairne, I. Neath, & A. M. Surprenant (Eds.), *The nature of remembering: Essays in honor of Robert G. Crowder* (pp. 189–209). Washington, DC: APA.

Watkins, M. J., & Peynircioğlu, Z. F. (1990). The revelation effect: When disguising test items induces recognition. *Journal of Experimental Psychology: Learning, Memory, and Cognition, 16*, 1012–1020.

Watkins, M. J., & Tulving, E. (1975). Episodic memory: When recognition fails. *Journal of Experimental Psychology: General, 104*, 5–29.

Watkins, O. C., & Watkins, M. J. (1975). Buildup of proactive inhibition as a cue-overload effect. *Journal of Experimental Psychology: Human Learning and Memory, 1*, 442–452.

Watkins, S. H. (1915). Immediate memory and its evaluation. *British Journal of Psychology, 7*, 319–348.

Waugh, N. C., & Norman, D. A. (1965). Primary memory. *Psychological Review, 72*, 89–104.

Wechsler, D. B. (1963). Engrams, memory storage, and mnemonic coding. *American Psychologist, 18*, 149–153.

Weldon, M. S. (1999). The memory chop shop: Issues in the search for memory systems. In J. K. Foster and M. Jelicic (Eds.), *Memory: Systems, process, or function?* (pp. 162–204). New York: Oxford University Press.

Weldon, M. S., & Coyote, K. C. (1996). Failure to find the picture superiority effect in implicit conceptual memory tests. *Journal of Experimental Psychology: Learning, Memory, and Cognition, 22*, 670–686.

Weldon, M. S., & Roediger, H. L. III. (1988). Altering retrieval demands reverses the picture superiority effect. *Memory & Cognition, 15*, 269–280.

Weldon, M. S., Roediger, H. L., & Challis, B. H. (1989). The properties of retrieval cues constrain the picture superiority effect. *Memory & Cognition, 17*, 95–105.

Wheeler, M. A. (1995). Improvement in recall over time without repeated testing: spontaneous recovery revisited. *Journal of Experimental Psychology: Learning, Memory, and Cognition, 21*, 173–184.

Wheeler, M. A., & Roediger, H. L., III. (1992). Disparate effects of repeated testing: Reconciling Ballard's (1913) and Bartelett's (1932) results. *Psychological Science, 3*, 240–245.

Whittlesea, B. A. (1997). Production, evaluation, and preservation of experiences: Constructive processing in remembering and performance tasks. In D. L. Medin (Ed.), *The psychology of learning and motivation: Advances in research and theory (Volume 37)* (pp. 211–264). San Diego: Academic Press.

Whittlesea, B. W. A. & Dorkin, M. D. (1993). Incidentally, things in general are particularly determined: An episodic-processing account of implicit learning. *Journal of Experimental Psychology: General, 122*, 227–248.

Wickens, D. D. (1970). Encoding categories of words: An empirical approach to meaning. *Psychological Review, 77*, 1–15.

Wickens, D. D., Born, D. G., & Allen, C. K. (1963). Proactive inhibition and item similarity in short-term memory. *Journal of Verbal Learning and Verbal Behavior, 2*, 440–445.

Wickens, D. D., Moody, M. J., & Dow, R. (1981). The nature of timing of the retrieval process and of interference effects. *Journal of Experimental Psychology: General, 110*, 1–20.

Willingham, D. B. (1998). What differentiates declarative and procedural memories: Reply to Cohen, Poldrack, and Eichenbaum (1997). *Memory, 6*, 689–699.

Willingham, D. B., & Goedert, K. (2001). The role of taxonomies in the study of human memory. *Cognitive, Affective, & Behavioral Neuroscience, 1*, 250–265.

Willingham, D. B., & Preuss, L. (1995). The death of implicit memory. *PSYCHE*, 2, http://psyche.cs.monash.edu.au/v2/psyche-2-15-willingham.html.

Wixted, J. T. (2004a). The psychology and neuroscience of forgetting. *Annual Review of Psychology, 55*, 235–269.

Wixted, J. T. (2004b). On common ground: Jost's (1897) Law of Forgetting and Ribot's (1881) Law of Retrograde Amnesia. *Psychological Review*, 113, 864–879.

Wixted, J. T. (2005). A theory about why we forget what we once knew. *Current Directions in Psychological Science, 14*, 6–9.

Wixted, J. T., & McDowell, J. J. (1989). Contributions to the functional analysis of single-trial free recall. *Journal of Experimental Psychology: Learning, Memory, and Cognition, 15*, 685–697.

Wolters, G., & Verduin, C. J. (1982). Retention performance as a function of the distinctiveness of memory traces and retention task. *Psychological Research, 44*, 257–267.

Yonelinas, A. P. (2002). The nature of recollection and familiarity: A review of 30 years of research. *Journal of Memory and Language, 46*, 441–517.

Zaki, S. R., Nosofsky, R. M., Jessup, N. M., & Unverzagt, F. W. (2003). Categorization and recognition performance in a memory-impaired group: Evidence for single-system models. *Journal of the International Neuropsychological Society, 9*, 394–406.

AUTHOR INDEX

179

SUBJECT INDEX